AF213254

Theory of Political Representation

STUDIES IN POLITICS, SECURITY AND SOCIETY

Edited by Stanisław Sulowski
Institute of Political Science of the University of Warsaw

VOLUME 2

PETER LANG
EDITION

Jarosław Szymanek

Theory of Political Representation

PETER LANG
EDITION

Bibliographic Information published by the Deutsche Nationalbibliothek
The Deutsche Nationalbibliothek lists this publication in the Deutsche Nationalbibliografie; detailed bibliographic data is available in the internet at http://dnb.d-nb.de.

This publication was financially supported
by the Institute of Political Science of the University of Warsaw.

Library of Congress Cataloging-in-Publication Data
Szymanek, Jarosław
Theory of political representation / Jarosław Szymanek. – Peter Lang edition.
pages cm
Includes bibliographical references.
ISBN 978-3-631-65714-0
1. Representative government and representation. 2. Democracy. I. Title.
JF1051.S98 2015
321.8–dc23
2015019655

ISSN 2199-028X
ISBN 978-3-631-65714-0 (Print)
E-ISBN 978-3-653-05005-9 (E-Book)
DOI 10.3726/ 978-3-653-05005-9

© Peter Lang GmbH
Internationaler Verlag der Wissenschaften
Frankfurt am Main 2015
All rights reserved.
Peter Lang Edition is an Imprint of Peter Lang GmbH.

Peter Lang – Frankfurt am Main · Bern · Bruxelles · New York · Oxford · Warszawa · Wien

All parts of this publication are protected by copyright. Any utilisation outside the strict limits of the copyright law, without the permission of the publisher, is forbidden and liable to prosecution. This applies in particular to reproductions, translations, microfilming, and storage and processing in electronic retrieval systems.

This publication has been peer reviewed.

www.peterlang.com

Contents

Introduction

Political representation that in a nutshell means speaking for a sovereign of some smaller group (the representatives) whose will is then regarded as the will of all (the sovereign), hence in a dual system of representation – as the will of the so-called 'represented', is a solution widely applied across all democratic systems nowadays. It cannot be otherwise, anyway, as it is hardly possible to imagine mechanisms of direct democracy, in spite of their appeal, being used on a wide scale.[1] Notwithstanding its highly positive recognition, direct democracy can only be an accessory and, by definition, a complementary form of exercising the sovereign's power. Hence, the *normal*, *regular* or *everyday* form of democracy is indirect and will probably remain so for a long time to come (should it ever be able to revert back to its ancient origins), whereby a few speak on behalf of all, but an opinion of a few is regarded as the opinion of all.

Typicality, familiarity with and – even more – in a sense a certain absence of an alternative and the resulting obviousness of prevalence of direct or representative democracy does not, however, eliminate major questions that may be put à propos this form of democracy.[2] The first question that arises at once is: Who represents whom? Is the status of a representative vested in an individual (a deputy, a member of parliament), or perhaps the body for which the deputy is only a personal substratum? If we were to accept the latter, i.e. the 'institutional' version of representation, another question would then come to light, namely whether it is only the traditional parliament (which is, after all, popularly known as the representative body[3]) that is endowed with the power to represent, or whether

1 All the more so, since direct democracy is also not free from defects and other deficiencies that generally surface when mechanisms of direct democracy, particularly the referendum, are deployed in practice. More on this topic: *Leréférendum expression directe de la souveraineté du peuple. Essai critique sur la rationalisation de l'expression référendaire en droit comparé*, Paris 2012.

2 Cf.: J. Boulad-Ayoub, P.-M. Vernes, *Aux fondements théoriques de la représentation politique*, Paris 2007.

3 On the margin it is perhaps worth mentioning that, for instance, in French literature, the notions of the 'representative system' and the 'parliamentary system' were regarded as synonymous, at least by some authors. Therefore, a mark of equality was often put between *régime représentatif* and *régime parlementaire*. Naturally, it was practiced mainly by those theoreticians who had an apologetic approach to the system of a strong (absolute) power of the parliament, such as, for instance, Adhémar Esmein.

such powers also are (or at least might be) vested in other bodies or, more generally, in other entities; and if so, in which specific entities and why? If we were to adopt the option of the so-called 'pluralist representation' that assumes a multitude of bodies and structures to express someone's interests,[4] then it quite naturally invokes questions concerning mutual relationships between these entities and whether they form a hierarchy of sorts or, perhaps, despite all, they are (or should be) equal to each other. Furthermore, another question should be posed, namely what is nowadays the relationship between political representation and other forms of representation (for instance social, professional or territorial)? Are these individual types or forms of representation competitive with or complementary to each other? Or, perchance, they all blend into some communal and homogenous whole which only then incarnates a full, genuine and in a way complete representation? Questions that arise in connection with a representative also pertain to the scope of the potential, admissible, or – for instance – optimal representation, as well as extremely crucial questions regarding the consequences of representation, whereby it is not only the strictly juridical, but also sociological or for instance political, particularly practical, competences that come into play. Certain, actually purely fundamental, questions with regard to the representative are unavoidable, such as whether in line with the etymological roots of the word 'representation', the representative merely presents the views, the will and the opinions of others, or perhaps he is, at least in a certain sense, the creator of this will? Accordingly, does a representative, regardless of whether such representative is an individual person or a body, merely aggregate the will voiced by others or perhaps express it himself in a certain way and, if so, how and to what extent? Further along this path, at a certain point in time an inevitable question comes up whether representation is not by chance only an abstract idea, which finds its embodiment in the will of the representative rather than in the will of the represented, since being the 'last link in the chain' of a complex process of representation, the latter merely acknowledges a project that in fact fulfills the primary function of a democratic legitimization of the entire system, yet its substance remains in fact void, since, if truth be told, the represented 'cannot do anything' without the representative.[5] And the list of questions does not end here at all.

4 Cf. T. Debard, *Dictionnaire de droit constitutionnel*, Paris 2002, p. 270.

5 It is not by chance, after all, that we constantly hear of the crisis of political representation, and of it being fictional, deceptive and superficial, and therefore of the need to seek alternative solutions. Cf. for instance D. Mineur, *Archéologie de la représentation politique*, Paris 2010, p. 20 *et seq.*

Other equally important questions appear, this time pertaining to the represented, including the most rudimentary question of all – namely who or what the represented really is? Is it a more or less unidentified collective body (the people, the nation, the sovereign, the citizens, the electorate[6]), or is it perhaps an individual, a certain group or else a conceptualized community (such as the electoral district, ethnic group, professional, social, economic or regional group, and – in the era of the increasingly rapid and ever closer integration processes – also a state, national or, for a change, supra-state or supranational group)? And if, as viewed by the traditional doctrine, representation is to be an interpersonal relation between the representative and the represented, then perhaps the represented is a specifically named person who made a personal choice of his representative? And perhaps, looking at it from another angle, a specific and personal choice does not carry the slightest significance here, since representation stands for a general idea of representing everyone regardless of whether and how these persons have voted and – even more – regardless of whether these persons have at all been endowed with voting rights (which in a way corresponds to virtual representation as we know it)? Vital questions should also be asked in connection with the relationship (ties) between the representative and the represented, including fundamental questions such as whether and to what extent the representative is bound by the will of the represented, and to what extent, if at all, he does have a free margin for action. Another non-trivial question in this regard touches upon, plausibly, the nature of sanctions imposed in the event the wills of both these entities diverge and whether such sanctions are at all admissible, and – if so – should they have a predominantly political or legal status?

The nature of relationship between the representative and the represented should also be determined. Is this relationship of strictly legal or political nature, or perhaps one and the other at the same time? Conceivably, and this cannot be *a priori* ruled out, this relationship is construed based on other scales of judgment such as morality, ethics, or simple integrity and decency. A particularly vital question pertaining to the mutual relation between the representative and the represented concerns also (if not above anything else) the essence of representation, that is whether the will voiced via the representative body is formed only by aggregating the wills of the individual represented persons or whether – a view promoted by some – it is an outcome of a deliberate search for some other, newfangled will which cannot be trimmed down to a simple summation of wills

6 The dispersion of ideas was particularly high here, for example: *corps électoral*, *corps des citoyens*, *nation*, *peuple*, *tous les citoyens*, *toutes les personnes*.

of individual members of the represented group.[7] It should be highlighted without further ado that this question is a constant and perhaps the most important motive of all political, philosophical and, ultimately, legal discourses on representation and generates a wide range of views and opinions. Therefore, it is not surprising that the problem of representation till this very day constitutes one of the major issues of a widely understood political thought.[8]

Last but not least, more general, if not even sketchy, questions come to mind. For instance, what exactly is representation? What is the general will or the will of the general public or, simply the will of the nation or the people? What is general good or what does it mean to act *pro publico bono*, which – after all – almost always lies at the heart of political representation (at least in its theoretical perspective)? Amongst the most far-reaching questions it is also considerate to ask whether it is not so that the idea (the principle) of political representation at present constitutes merely a flaunting form of legitimizing contemporary political systems, yet one devoid of any real, down-to-earth substance. Or, in other words, whether such capacious and ambiguous concepts as 'general will' or the 'will of the general public', the 'will of the people', 'general welfare' or 'common welfare', being material components of representation, in fact find their designate in the political system or whether they are nothing more than a graceful rhetoric figure, a legal fiction aimed at dressing the system into the clothes of democracy, where for obvious reasons not everyone may make decisions. Another question, which is as much general as elementary, touches upon the effectiveness of political representation. Apart from obviously being a spectacular model of contemporary democracy, is it an effective formula as well? Or perhaps the attractive form of political representation does not go hand in hand with the appeal and, importantly, the practicality of its substance? Questions that trouble those pondering upon the complex issue of representation also focus on whether it is a certain constant condition, a *constans*, or perhaps an ongoing and steadily progressing process, and hence one which undergoes changes? Or whether – and it does not in any way exhaust the list of questions or doubts – representation is more of a political idea, a constitutional principle or a tangible political being, though built on strong constitutional foundations. Along these lines, as it is easy to guess, important questions come to mind one after the other, this time relating to axiological and teleological functions of representation, and amongst them,

7 More on this topic: M.B. Brown, *Science in Democracy. Expertise, Institutions and Representation*, Cambridge 2009, p. 65 *et seq.*

8 Cf. B. Manin, *On Legitimacy and Political Deliberation*, "Political Theory" 1987, no. 15, p. 338 *et seq.*

the most fundamental question of all: What is the essence of representation today and what are its functions in the political system of the state?[9]

Hence, observably, political representation is an extremely fertile and, above anything else, still enormously important and up-to-date field for analysis carried out on the grounds of the constitutional law as well as methodologically based on political science. A set of tools based on political science and constitutional legal grounds seems indispensable for analyzing political representation as well as the majority of institutions falling within the scope of a widely understood constitutional law.[10] It is so, since state (constitutional) institutions most often cannot be viewed from a purely dogmatic angle of the constitutional law. True enough, political representation as a systemic principle dressed in a bodice of the constitution does have its own specific, juridical, viz. constitutional sense, which must be subjected to a proverbial first step towards the genuine and full cognizance and understanding of political representation. It so happens particularly when we acknowledge that political representation is not only a constitutional idea or principle (otherwise worth pondering upon from a scientific angle), but above all a process of the so-called correlation, i.e. reconciliation or else assimilation (homogenization) of the political wills of the representative and the represented. Once this viewpoint is adopted, it becomes clear that without an arsenal of methodology a political scientist is equipped with, political representation cannot be simply digested or comprehended.

This book aims to offer answers to these and many other questions. Nonetheless, it should be pointed out right at the outset that readers will by no means find satisfying answers to all the questions raised in this book, while some of the answers to be found will be heavily nuanced, perplexing, multi-threaded and not leading towards a single solution only. What's more, other questions and problems which arise in the process of probing the phenomenon of political

9 It is worth noting that these questions were being answered in quite a different way in different places and at different times. More on this topic: P. Fournier, *Institutions et représentations du politique: Espagne, France, Italie, XVIIe-XXe siècles*, Paris 2006; P. Rosanvallon, *Le Peuple introuvable: Histoire de la représentation démocratique en France*, Paris 2002; A.-M. Le Pourhiet, B. Mathieu, F. Mélin-Soucramanien, D. Rousseau, *Représentation et représentativité*, Paris 2008.

10 Cf. for instance J. Meynaud, *Introduction à la science politique*, Paris 1959, p. 11 *et seq.*; M. Duverger, *Méthodes de la science politique*, Paris 1959, p. 33 *et seq.*; S. Bouiffror, D.K. Nanopoulos, *Droit constitutionnel. Méthodologie*, Paris 2006; F. Dieu, *Introduction à la méthode de la science politique*, Paris 2008; Y. Schemeil, *Introduction à la science politique. Objets, méthodes, résultats*, Paris 2012.

representation will come to light in this book. All these newly raised questions and issues, even if they remain unanswered in an ultimate or satisfactory manner, underscore that it is worth brooding over political representation despite it being – or perhaps just because it is – a permanent theme of all discussions and discourses on the political system of a state. It is unfeasible to imagine any major political project over the past two hundred years that would fail to touch upon the issue of representation (regardless of whether representation was in its foreground or somewhere in the background). As much as political representation remains the most vital and rudimentary theme, it is also infinite. Hence, understandably, this theme does not end with this book, which should be regarded as just a 'voice in a discussion' and a certain, definitely modest, attempt at sketching a discourse summary. Time will show how the future of political representation will play out and where the discussion on representation will head towards.

Apart from answering the raised questions, this book aspires to achieve at least a few objectives. First and foremost, it is to present and to set clarity in the findings from research on political representation that has been continued for no less than two hundred years and has still not lost its intensity as well as acuteness of debates, discussions and formulated views. Secondly, it is to prove that representation cannot be demoted to a single meaning or political idea. Depending on the angle of view, it can be perceived in many different ways and, as a result, it can be diversely arranged and accommodated as a specific institution of the system of government. Thirdly, this book is to illustrate that classical structures in the form of an imperative mandate and a free mandate are already in a certain sense *passé* and, therefore, different and new formulas of political and juridical relationship between the representative and the represented should be sought. Fourthly, this book aims to demonstrate that political parties, not long ago dragged through the muck and mire, are a necessary component of political representation under the circumstances of contemporary democracy, on the one hand having the greatest modifying impact upon it, yet on the other hand being a structure – even if originally unplanned – that is currently durable, stable and in fact devoid of an alternative. Fifthly, this study purports to reveal the crisis plaguing contemporary representation and the various methods of overcoming it. One of the signs is no doubt proliferation of entities claiming to be endowed with the right to be represented and to be a representative. As it is being rightly noted, it is the multiplication of claims to representation[11] that is one of the most vivid symptoms of the crisis that troubles political representation

11 I.M. Young, *Inclusion and Democracy*, Oxford 2002, p. 53.

nowadays. Paradoxically, this multiplication alone constitutes, as it seems, a sagacious riposte to the malfunction of the classical (parliamentary) mechanisms of representation. The second way out of the crisis of representation is an ambitious project of supra-national representation which may in a way reinstate the genuine or original idea of representation, which has over the years been prone to various deformations and distortions. Regardless of its form, each and every project of political representation in fact has the same objective, namely to be able to echo the will of the represented subject in the best possible way (that is most precisely) through the representative body. Last but not least, sixthly, this book aims at expanding our knowledge of representation. One should always bear in mind that while engaging in research on various institutions of the political system, such as representation, we *malgré tout* do so first and foremost to expand our expertise, so that once we become familiar with the findings, we are more knowledgeable than beforehand.

Chapter I: Axiological and Teleological Assumptions of Representation

1. Representative Versus Direct Democracy

The functioning of modern political systems without political representation is indeed inconceivable. An ideal whereby all citizens participate in public affairs by taking ultimate and binding decisions is presently a bygone historical scheme, albeit attractive and alluring, yet impossible to implement in practice on a large scale[1] (and, what is at times forgotten, fraught with remarkably many dangers that in extreme circumstances may turn democracy into a caricature[2]). A number of reasons predetermined the irrevocable, as it seems, passing into history of the concept of direct democracy, also known as pure democracy (and regarded as the one and only embodiment of supreme power). One of those reasons was, paradoxically, a quantitative increase in the number of those who had a say in the matters of the *polis*. The sheer size of the political staff at some point made the ideal of the involvement of all in the matters of all virtually impossible to pursue. After all, it must be kept in mind that although the slogan of direct democracy was highly catchy, yet it was not so that *all* were in fact participating in democracy.[3] *Demos* who was being implemented thanks to the concept of *kratos* was indeed quite narrow, greatly limited and definitely exclusive rather than inclusive. Direct democracy only seemingly had an egalitarian dimension.[4] In reality, it remained a sublime and elite form of political participation, in which a class of citizens (understood as those who held the decision-making privilege)

---

1 Cf.: V.N. Lenoir, *La démocratie et son histoire*, Paris 2006; L. Canfora, *La démocratie: histoire d'une idéologie*, Paris 2006.

2 Thus, not by coincidence, the procedures of direct involvement of citizens are often deployed by non-democratic states, which turn the sense of direct democracy 'upside down', in consequence putting in place or consolidating authoritarian systems (the French Second Republic and, more contemporarily, Belarus, may serve as an excellent example). On the other hand, in democratic systems the forms of direct democracy might be instrumentally abused to attain certain preconceived objectives. More on this topic: L.J. Samons, *What's Wrong with Democracy? From Athenian Practice to American Worship*, London 2004, p. 41 *et seq*.

3 F. Jockey, *La Grèce antique*, Paris 2005, p. 13.

4 Cf. P. Vidal-Naquet, *Les Grecs. Les historiens la démocratie*, Paris 2000, p. 5 *et seq*.

was limited.[5] It was achieved via complex, highly exorbitant selection mechanisms, which made it possible to single out, from the overall population of the state, the most virtuous, most worthy, most righteous and noblest by various standards. All of them were granted a special status, i.e., the status of a citizen, which entailed the right to political participation, albeit it was assumed that this right depended on social and political status and at the same time incarnated an extremely important commitment, honour, privilege as well as an immense responsibility for a flawless course of public affairs. Being deeply exclusive and 'contained', direct democracy was indeed axiologically sturdy and rooted in principles and values that might be called a democratic ethos.[6] A citizen carried a heavy responsibility of not only making certain decisions in the area of *res publica,* but also of taking into consideration the welfare of all, of which he was a custodian of sorts.[7] It is noteworthy that this concept of the *ethos* of democracy (direct democracy) embraced, at least to a certain degree, also some idea of representation.[8] A citizen who, by virtue of his qualities, received the noble right of political participation worked, after all, not only in his own name and with effect for himself, but in some sense for no less than the entire organism of the *polis.* This brings to mind a much later concept of virtual representation, concluded in the thesis that the representative works not only on behalf of the voters (and thus the constituents in a strict sense of the term), but on behalf of all the others, who in juridical sense are placed beyond the boundaries of the process of political representation, as well.[9]

Needless to say, it was not, however, a contemporary version of representation nor any of its varieties that today we might be inclined to consider a mutation or one of the versions of political representation.[10] If we were to use the expression 'representation' here at all (which may be controversial), it would only be in the sense of an object, not a subject. 'Non-citizens' were not represented in any event

5 Cf. R.K. Sinclair, *Democracy and Participation in Athens*, Cambridge 1993, p. 24 *et seq.*
6 Cf. R. Osborne, *Athens and Athenian Democracy*, Cambridge 2010, p. 25 *et seq.*
7 More on this topic: C. Mossé, *Histoire d'une démocratie: Athènes*, Paris 1971.
8 Cf. F. Jockey, *La Grèce antique…*, p. 45 *et seq.*
9 This theory reached its splendor in England during the nineteenth century, however, it was also known on the American continent. Cf. J.P. Reid, *The Concept of Representation in the Age of the American Revolution*, London 1989, p. 50 *et seq.*
10 More on this topic: O. Törnquist, *Introduction: The Problem is Representation! Towards an Analytical Framework*, [in:] *Rethinking Popular Representation*, O. Törnquist, N. Webster, K. Stokke (eds.), New York 2010, p. 1 *et seq.*

or manner.[11] Like an English lord, a proud citizen of Athens represented himself only. Representation, on the other hand (assuming that it is actually representation we are dealing with here) referred to the object, i.e., to the fact that decisions made by citizens impacted those citizens as well as all others (a greater majority of others), who had no rights whatsoever and embodied a passive and grey mass in the structure of the political organism. Therefore, we are free to claim that although by definition a citizen of the ancient world partaking in forms of direct political involvement did constitute a minority, yet he always acted perhaps not in the name of *all*, but certainly for all, thus putting into practice, firstly, the ideal of democracy, and, secondly, the ideal of representation[12] (even though, clearly, it was of secondary importance, in a way latent, at least in terms of its legal structure[13]). On the margin, it is worthy of note that the mere expression 'direct' correlated with a democratic form of government suggested not only the sheer technical mechanism of political action (as could be presumed at the outset), but its effect, i.e., that decisions made on the *agora* had a direct bearing upon all, although they were not in fact taken by all[14] (and in this sense, the ancient ideal of democracy finds a common ground with contemporary democracy[15]).

Democracy in its ancient form was therefore narrow in principle, in the sense that few actually participated in it, although all were encompassed by the effects of decisions made through democratic processes.[16] Such shape of democracy was dismantled when, as the class of citizens was gradually expanding, those who were not only the addressees of decisions, but decision-makers themselves, began to grow in numbers.[17] Departure from exclusivity of those who participated in the public life thus had to, by necessity, imply an abandonment of this in fact very narrow form of political participation.[18] To a certain degree it is hence a paradox by itself that expansion, or perhaps more precisely a deepening of democracy understood as a quantitative growth in the number of persons endowed with political rights, made this democracy (then understood as involvement of all those possessed of political rights) simply non-functional at a certain point

11 Cf. L.J. Samons, *What's Wrong with Democracy*..., p. 187.
12 R.K. Sinclair, *Democracy and Participation*..., p. 77.
13 Cf. P. Woodruff, *First Democracy. The Challenge of an Ancient Idea*, Oxford 2005, p. 145 *et seq*.
14 Cf. R. Osborne, *Athens and Athenian Democracy*..., p. 244 *et seq*.
15 Cf. F. Jockey, *La Grèce antique*..., p. 14.
16 Cf. R. Osborne, *Athens and Athenian Democracy*..., p. 39 *et seq*.
17 More on this topic: H. Aird, *The Rise and Fall of Athenian Democracy*, London 2003.
18 Cf. M.I. Finley, *Polityka w świecie starożytnym*, Kraków 2000, p. 87 *et seq*.

in time. The more participants, the more difficult it became to maintain the pure form of democracy which is, after all, elitist by definition and where actual participation takes place on a very limited scale.[19] Hence, the more democratic direct democracy grew, the less direct it became (certainly in the most rudimentary sense, which of course does not imply in the one and only sense, meaning that decisions were made by citizens only and the citizens were their addressees only).

The second factor which eventually contributed towards abandonment of the concept of participatory democracy in its ancient form was a geographic expansion of states. Not by coincidence, it is being claimed that pure democracy may be maintained in relatively small, if not undersized political organisms.[20] As they grow steadily, the proverbial critical mass is exceeded at some point and continued involvement of people at large in the affairs of their community becomes simply impossible. Thus, it is acknowledged that direct democracy is essentially genetically embedded in the logic of the functioning of a city-state (only), which means that departure from this system must automatically trigger a transition to other, more complex systems of political participation.[21] Hence, only a relatively small political organization such as the city-state was able to uphold direct democracy as a fitting (basic) form of citizens' participation without the need to engage, in various ways and to various degrees, institutionalized, permanent and developed intermediary structures. Even a more encompassing and ambitious, yet, despite everything, still quite small structure of the state such as the medieval democratic city-republic in the Middle Ages[22] was unable to function based only on the archaic structure of direct democracy, which is more apt for micro-scale organisms. Expansion of the state in geographic terms (and, what follows, in terms of population) from a traditional *polis* through a city-republic to a contemporary national state made deployment of the mechanisms of political participation devoid of relevance. The answer to question why a large political organism extending beyond the traditional boundaries of a citystate was incapable of cultivating direct democracy seems obvious. Nonetheless, apart from the first and self-imposing answer, namely its plain size that actually prevented all from decision-making on the affairs of all, it is worth pointing out to one more aspect, which, paradoxically, remains to this day one of the fundamental

19 Cf. R. Osborne, *Athens and Athenian Democracy…*, p. 40 *et seq.*

20 Cf. R.K. Sinclair, *Democracy and Participation…*, p. 202 *et seq.*

21 More on this topic: M.H. Hansen, *Polis et cité-état. Un concept antique et son* équivalent *moderne*, Paris 2001.

22 Cf. D. Waley, *The Italian City-Republics*, London 1989, p. 32 *et seq.*

issues across the representation theory and to all minor and major problems associated with it. It is, as one might easily guess, the relationship between the decision maker (later between the representative and the represented) and the socio-political structure of the territory on which the democratic procedures (indirect or direct) are applied. The city-state bestowed, after all, not only a sense of participation, but also clearly, almost tangibly, defined the scope of matters that were subject to the democratic debate and, consequently, subject to the decision in line with the slogan that a citizen always rightly decided about himself and his affairs.[23] This extremely strongly reflected the 'ties' between a citizen and his decision (and its consequences). Also in this sense the democracy was direct, since it was the citizen who decided about himself and everything associated with himself in a direct way.[24] The subsequent growth of the state, which had in consequence halted the possibility of further deployment of democracy in its pure form had, besides many other effects, above all nullified these 'ties'. Their unearthing and then re-establishment (even artificial) will constitute one of the primary problems of the modern debate on representation.[25] A discussion on who exactly is the re-presentative and what is the content of his mandate, but also on who is in fact represented at the source, has at its roots the most vital element, namely the structure (territorial, social, economic, political and legal) of the constituency.[26]

Last but not least, the factor that caused the abandonment of the ideal of direct participation, and thus triggered transition to other mechanisms of political decision-making was a rapid increase and complexity of issues that needed to be resolved. Democracy involving all could have been maintained under conditions in which the total of the decisions and the degree of their complexity, in particular attention to detail and need of professional approach, were relatively minor. However, when public decision-making space expanded while the issues that needed to be solved rapidly multiplied and, what's equally relevant, when the degree of their complexity and professionalism increased, then transition to other, less obvious, and – as it was deemed – less democratic ways of making

23 Cf. R.K. Sinclair, *Democracy and Participation...*, p. 20 *et seq*.

24 Cf. M.H. Hansen, *Polis et cité-état...*, p. 220 *et seq*.

25 Cf. N. Chandhoke, *What is Relationship Between Participation and Representation?*, [in:] *Rethinking Popular Representation...*, p. 25 *et seq*.

26 More on this topic: M.A. Smith, *Bringing Representation Home: State Legislators among their Constituencies*, University of Missouri 2003; J.E. Jackson, *Constituencies and Leaders in Congress. Their Effects on Senate Voting Behavior*, Harvard 1974; K.C. Miler, *Constituency Representation in Congress*, Cambridge 2010.

decisions became only a matter of time. Substantive intricacies of decisions which democratic gatherings faced as well as their momentous, but above all substantial, growth in numbers toppled the former ideal of direct participation.[27] All in all, it confirms the old truth that the effectiveness of state organization (in any of its forms) always embarks on a conflict with its democratism. Political structures may thus either be democratic, yet time-consuming and often ineffective, or effective, but usually at the expense of departing from real, authentic democracy.

The arsenal of ideas as to how the formula of direct democracy, in which politically everyone makes decisions (which does not mean everyone in the sociological sense at all), should be replaced and what to replace it with was nonetheless limited. What was well-known and remained in a certain way without an alternative was markedly the direction this solution might take. It was known that decisions were no doubt to be taken by a smaller rather than a greater number of those whom the ultimate effect of these decisions would concern. Democracy which involved truly all (particularly, if the group of the said *all* was systematically growing) was regarded as a phantasmagoria right from the outset, as a project which, though highly interesting, was nonetheless practically impossible and not viable. Thus, an indirect form was embraced as an alternative to the ancient way of thinking about democracy. Though affecting all, decisions had to be taken by a group of citizens that was narrow and, by assumption, limited.[28] In order, however, to prevent this group from developing some kind of deformity, pathology or other deviant form, it had to maintain a minimum of democratic features. The latter explicitly suggested that the group had to be elected or otherwise chosen, but always in such a way that it could be, at least formally, regarded as an emanation of all, that is – once again referring to the ancient sources of direct democracy – of those who for some reason had ceased exercising their right to make final political decisions in a direct and instant manner.

Consequently, direct democracy could only be replaced, of course on the condition that the democratic form of the political regime was maintained, with indirect democracy where, as the designation itself suggests, someone's acting as an intermediary and legitimization of his actions by way of an electoral selection mechanism are fundamental (meaning both component as well as vital)

27 Cf. P. Pasquino, *Emmanuel Sieyes, Benjamin Constant et le «gouvernment des modernes»*. Contribution à *l'histoire du concept de représentation politique*, „Revue Française de Science Politique" 1987, number 2, p. 221 *et seq.*

28 Cf. L.J. Samons, *What's Wrong with Democracy…*, p. 68 *et seq.*

elements.[29] It is the selection mechanism that allows to endow a representative with a fully democratic character, but also – by far more importantly – it is to attest in its own way that he is the representative not only because he is so called and so treated, but because he has been appointed as such by way of an appropriate procedure.[30] The procedural mechanism for the establishment of representation that is comprised in the process of determining who is the representative and to what extent, is not only a component of the very definition of representation, but also makes it more than just a nominal value or a certain idea, but a formal institution as well.[31] At the same time, this mechanism has made representation utterly democratic,[32] thus correlating the general, if not generally vague, idea with its actual realization.[33] It is so, since the concept of representation invariably comprises some unspecified mechanism of validation or establishment of representation, or, if we were to approach the problem from another angle, a mechanism via which an 'input' is being converted into an 'output'. The former is nothing but individual views or decisions of 'members of the group' which ultimately is to be represented, while the latter is a view or a decision of the representative regarded, through a specific feedback, as a view or decision of the represented.[34] The 'input'/'output' conversion mechanism is an

29 Cf. D. Turpin, *Démocratie représentative et démocratie participative*, [in:] *Constitutions et pouvoirs. Mélanges en l'honneur de Jean Gicguel*, Paris 2008, p. 565 *et seq.*

30 Cf. H. Pitkin, *Representation*, [in:] *Political Innovation and Conceptual Change*, T. Ball, J. Farr, R.L. Hanson (eds.), Cambridge 1989, p. 132 *et seq.*

31 Cf. G. Brennan, A. Hamlin, *On Political Representation*, „British Journal of Political Science" 1999, vol. XXIX, p. 109 *et seq.*

32 On the other hand, it opened up a very interesting and, as it seems, still ongoing discussion on the mutual relation between representation and democracy. In a nutshell, the main question focuses on whether representation is an indispensable component and at the same time an essential outcome of democracy, or whether perhaps democracy forms a component and at the same time a mandatory element of representation. In other words, putting it in a somewhat simplified way, the question is whether representation is democratic or whether democracy is representative. The dispute thus evolves, above all, around what really makes up the 'founding idea of modern politics', i.e., whether it is democracy, for which representation is 'only' a tool, or whether it is representation, which depending on the institutionalization model can follow a democratic or undemocratic direction. More on this topic: D. Runciman, M. Brito Vieira, *Representation*, Cambridge 2008, p. 3 *et seq.*; N. Urbinati, *Representative Democracy. Principles and Genealogy*, Chicago 2008, p. 18 *et seq.*

33 Cf. L.J. Samons, *What's Wrong with Democracy…*, p. 68.

34 Cf. D. Runciman, *The Paradox of Political Representation*, „Journal of Political Philosophy" 2007, number 1, p. 93 *et seq.*

imperative element of representation; what's more, provided it is laced up in a bodice of elections, it gives representation an utterly democratic, and hence acceptable, dimension. It is thus the origin of the distinctive archetype of indirect democracy which identifies it with elections (moreover, today invariably associated with parliamentary elections).[35]

2. Accountability: Necessary Prerequisite of Representation

Thus, holding any election to a collective body which makes political decisions in the name, and on the account, of voters is usually seen as an application of the idea of indirect (representative) democracy. Indirect democracy as such (and by extension of that logic, also political representation) is consequently seen as an equivalent of elections and for this reason often referred to as electoral democracy.[36] It is so not only because elections are an obligatory element of any democracy, hence also of indirect democracy, but also because they are just as obligatory an element of representation.[37] One cannot imagine the latter without some sort of mechanism for selecting or establishing a representative, which mechanism *per se* comprises many components of the concept of representation. These components include, firstly, defining the represented subject (hence answering the essentially fundamental question who is to be represented); secondly, establishing the representative, which in turn requires creating adequate technical and procedural tools; thirdly, the representative's acting in the name, and on the behalf, of the subject who appointed (delegated, elected) the representative, which, as we know, is what representation is all about; and fourthly, a relationship of responsibility resulting initially from being elected by, and subsequently from acting on behalf of, the elector.[38] The last of the presented elements, which is sometimes completely forgotten,[39] is at the same time a defining component of representation[40] (but also of democracy[41]). One

35 Cf. F. Borella, *Élements de droit constitutionnel*, Paris 2008, p. 220 *et seq.*

36 Cf. M.-A. Cohendet, *Droit constitutionnel*, Paris 2008, p. 436.

37 Cf. J. Gastil, *By Popular Demand: Revitalizing Representative Democracy Through Deliberative Elections*, London 2000, p. 10 *et seq.*

38 More on this topic zob J. Stimson, M. Mackuen, R. Erikson, *Dynamic Representation*, „American Political Science Review" 1995, number 3, p. 543 *et seq.*

39 Although historically it was probably the most accentuated one.

40 Cf. B. Manin, A. Przeworski, S.C. Stokes, *Elections and Representation*, [in:] *Democracy, Accountability and Representation*, B. Manin, A. Przeworski, S.C. Stokes (eds.), Cambridge 1999, p. 29 *et seq.*

41 Cf. R.K. Sinclair, *Democracy and Participation...*, p. 77 *et seq.*

can hardly speak of representation when there exist none, even the least, forms of responsibility (or, more accurately, accountability).[42] Absence of mechanisms guaranteeing proper accountability causes representation to be in a way 'suspended in a vacuum', making it an idea without an equivalent in reality.[43] It is only accountability that makes the representative a real one, truly acting on behalf of his principal, but also – and this is a necessary prerequisite of representation – remaining under the latter's supervision.[44] As it is being pointed out in this respect, responsibility, or rather accountability, when applied to the representative–represented relationship, does not necessarily mean the right to revoke the representative (known, for example, from the so-called imperative mandate model), but has to comprise a specific right to veto, i.e. the represented subject's right to formulate a different opinion when the existing one does not express the standpoint of the represented (thus failing to represent him). Of course, the prerequisite of accountability is a minimum and this can, and indeed should, go further, which nowadays is expressed mainly in the so-called electoral accountability, the most noticeable sign of which is the so-called reprobation, i.e. the possibility to transfer trust to another person and establish a new representative.[45]

What was yet another tool of accountability was the rule that decisions which did not gain electoral acclamation were politically void, which rule was applicable in the mandate theory. It boiled down to the view, typical of the accountability approach, that fundamental political decisions could not fail to be consulted with the represented subject. As a consequence, changing them or adopting completely new projects and proposals, not presented to the voters beforehand, made them actually pointless as long as they were not subjected to public judgment taking place through general election. Thus in this convention elections

---

42 Which applies with increasing frequency. Cf. P. Aguilar, I. Sánchez-Cuenca, *Performance or Representation? The Determinants of Voting in Complex Political Contexts*, [in:] *Controlling Governments. Voters, Institutions and Accountability*, J.M. Maravall, I. Sánchez-Cuenca (eds.), Cambridge 2008, p. 105 *et seq*.

43 Cf. J. Dunn, *Situating Democratic Political Accountability*, [in:] *Democracy, Accountability and Representation…*, p. 329 *et seq*.

44 More on this topic: N. Urbinati, *Representative Democracy and its Critics*, [in:] *The Future of Representative Democracy*, S. Alonso, J. Keane, W. Merkel (eds.), Cambridge 2011, p. 23 *et seq*.; R. Mulgan, *Holding Power to Account: Accountability in Modern Democracies*, London 2003, p. 36 *et seq*.

45 More on this topic: C.T. Borowiak, *Accountability and Democracy. The Pitfalls and Promise of Popular Control*, Oxford 2011, p. 150 *et seq*.

were not just a technical method of selecting representatives, but also a method of determining the content of the mandate (understood as the scope of matters in which representatives are authorized to act in the name, and on the account, of the represented subjects). Looking at the mandate identified this way from the other perspective, elections were also a tool of true accountability, which guaranteed that representatives' decisions corresponded to expectations of the represented subjects.[46] Because representatives could not go further than the mandate's substance permitted and if they wanted to, they had to apply for a new mandate.

An imperative mandate, with the consequence of the holder losing it in case of transgressing the authorizations or disrespecting them in any other way, on the one hand, while on the other hand, the theory of mandate, which required recourse to elections if the representative's actions went beyond the content of the mandate granted earlier, are two different legal forms in which the idea of accountability is applied.[47] While the former unquestionably has an individualist dimension, referring to a single mandate holder and carrying the sanction of losing the mandate, the latter definitively has a collectivist dimension, referring not to *a* representative, but to *all* representatives, making renewal of mandate conditional upon the legal and political efficiency of their actions. In both versions of accountability the aim is the same, i.e. subjecting the representatives to detailed control (including its negative sanction), which will generate and adequately secure authentic respect for the will of the represented subject. Another difference between these two approaches to accountability, apart from the above one, was the time of reaching for accountability mechanisms. The imperative mandate was applied an a repressive manner, because it was – in the true sense of the word – a penalty for a behaviour the represented subject did not accept. But the theory of mandate, especially in its most mature version, the English one, had a preventive effect. It did not allow certain decisions to be made as long as they were not approved by voters. Nevertheless, we should remember that the idea of accountability is not an end in itself or for itself. Accountability, regardless of how it is finally arranged, aims to result in a correlation between the views

---

46 Cf. P. Aguilar, I. Sánchez-Cuenca, *Performance or Representation? The Determinants of Voting…*, p. 105 *et seq.*

47 More on this topic: K. Strøm, *Parliamentary Democracy and Delegation*, [in:] *Delegation and Accountability in Parliamentary Democracies*, K. Strøm, W.C. Müller, T. Bergman (eds.), Oxford 2003, p. 55 *et seq.*

of the representative and the represented subject, because this correlation is what defines the proper relationship of representation.[48]

However, it is worth pointing out that the essence of accountability in both cases of its legal institutionalization (i.e. imperative mandate and theory of mandate) is not limited to just the simple character of the representative (an individual or a group), but its effects reach much further and deeper. At least to some extent it characterizes representatives in general, seeing them as the voters' 'men of confidence' or the proverbial 'constituency ambassadors' or as 'good party men'[49]. The dispute about who the representative actually is has not been resolved definitively till this day. In this area, we are dealing with at least several different ways to view the representative's political (but also legal) role. In the simplest scenario, the representative represents his electors, which was amply emphasised by the construction of imperative mandate. In a slightly more nuanced scenario, the represented subject is no longer a voter or a group of voters, but a constituency or, in other words, the place of origin of the mandate.[50] In yet another scenario, nowadays commonly institutionalized in constitutional solutions, a principle is adopted that the representative represents the nation (people), which in turn means, according to critics, that in reality they represent nobody but themselves.[51] Finally, it is assumed that representative in fact represents political parties, because in the present day they are the fundamental electoral machine, by the way very often legitimized by the law, which is not far from making them the proper representative. It is worth pointing out that the underlying issue in the discussion about who is actually represented and whose interests the mandate holder should represent is actually a fundamental problem, namely the need for accountability, the more so that it is a mechanism for selecting representatives (which general elections nowadays are) that is seen as the key moment of the whole conception of accountability. Indeed, the search for the proper representative and the represented subject should lead to making the idea of accountability efficient.[52]

---

48 More on this topic: P.F. Nardulli, *Popular Efficacy in the Democratic Era. An Reexamination of Electoral Accountability in the United States*, Princeton 2005, p. 180 *et seq.*

49 I. Jennings, *The British Constitution*, Cambridge 1966, p. 82.

50 Cf. W.E. Miller, D.E. Stokes, *Constituency Influence in Congress*, [in:] *Legislatures and Legislators*, P. Norton (ed.), Sydney 1998, p. 377 *et seq.*

51 Cf. N. Urbinati, *Representative Democracy and its Critics*..., p. 23 *et seq.*

52 Cf. K. Strøm, W.C. Müller, T. Bergman, B. Nyblade, *Dimensions of Citizens Control*, [in:] *Delegation and Accountability*..., p. 651 *et seq.*

A completely different kind of accountability, apart from the aforementioned imperative mandate and theory of mandate, which is currently gaining growing recognition, is the introduction of the mechanism of direct democracy, which is seen as nothing else but a form of control and indeed accountability of representatives to represented subjects.[53] Today it is a fairly widespread belief that precisely reaching for the ideal of direct democracy is perhaps the best mechanism for ensuring adequate accountability; not only because it is, by any account, democratic, but mainly because it allows avoiding the troublesome answers to the questions about who is represented and what the actual role of the represented subject is.[54] It is so because direct democracy is installed, so to speak, next to representative democracy. Consequently it is not, or at least should not be, treated as a sanction of the latter or even competition for it, but as a kind of adjustment or supplement.[55] Direct democracy with its different forms (referendum, popular veto or civic legislative initiative) is also convenient in that it very well corresponds to the constitutional principle that representatives express the will of the nation. Thanks to it, it simply 'fits in' with today's model of political representation, whereby the representative expresses the will of a collectively understood people or nation, which – in addition to having the right to designate its representatives sitting on the parliament – can also use tools which are by definition competitive, which tools it can apply to substitute its representatives, often expressing this way its disapproval for their activities. Thanks to it, we get a fairly coherent picture of the system of representation, whose core is the general election in which representatives are delegated to representative bodies, with the supplementing element of procedures of pure democracy, the use of which procedures can be perceived as a form of control of those who govern by those who are governed, as well as a certain manifestation of their accountability.[56]

Regardless of the final scale of application of various mechanisms of accountability, it is unquestionable that some forms of accountability are necessary in

---

53 Cf. S. Odugbemi, T. Lee, *Taking Direct Accountability Seriously*, [in:] *Accountability through Public Opinion. From Inertia to Public Action*, S. Odugbemi, T. Lee (eds.), Washington 2010, p. 3 *et seq*.

54 More on this topic: W. Marxer, Z.T. Pállinger, *Stabilizing or Destabilizing? Direct-democratic Instruments in Different Political Systems*, [in:] *Referendums and Representative Democracy. Responsiveness, Accountability and Deliberation*, M. Satälä, T. Schiller (eds.), New York 2009, p. 34 *et seq*.

55 Or, as A. Esmein used to call it, 'counterweight' (*contrepoids*).

56 Cf. B. Wessels, *Performance and Deficits of Present-day Representation*, [in:] *The Future of Representative Democracy…*, p. 96 *et seq*.

order for the representation project to be maintained at all. More and more often it is recognized, while accepting the irrevocability of political representatives,[57] that possibly what is the best form of accountability is the adapting of various forms of direct democracy, which may be applied in order to 'veto', which is treated as part and parcel of the relationship of representation.[58] Consequently, while some time ago direct representation was still seen as an antonym of democracy with the features of indirect (representative) democracy and the relationship between them was defined by the 'either-or' principle, today they are rather spoken of as 'both one and the other'. At the same time it is assumed that indirect form of exercising authority is the main and basic one, while simple democracy has a complementary or supplementary nature, but also, in a way, a securing (controlling, restraining) one. It may be a kind of sanction, triggered by defective operation of the mechanisms of representative government, but with undisputed recognition that this form of government is, for the time being, the basic form of exercising power. Nevertheless direct democracy is seen, at most, as competitive for, or supplementary to, representative democracy, or – in line with the slogan of accountability – as a procedure of adequate securing of the latter through creation of a specific mechanism of responsibility via which representatives' decisions can be challenged or modified, or corrected, or via which representatives may even be forced (legally or politically) to step down.

3. Crisis of Representative Democracy

Deployment of indirect (complex) democracy is a response to only one basic question, that is, what the immediate (pure, direct) democracy, regarded at a certain point in time as excellent (though not perfect by any means), should be replaced with? It also opens up a whole range of other, no less important questions.[59] These questions concern issues such as how to choose the representatives, without which, after all, a representative democracy could not exist in any way, as well as specific, sometimes very detailed mechanisms of systemic arrangement of their status. In the background there remain other vital questions, such as whether indirect democracy, nowadays regarded as a fundamental form of citizens' political participation, is the one and only acceptable form of democracy,

57 In accordance with free mandate, nowadays commonly recognized. Cf. M. van der Hulst, *The Parliamentary Mandate. A Global Comparative Study*, Geneva 2000, p. 8.

58 Cf. G. Tsebelis, *Veto Players. How Political Institutions Work*, Princeton 2002, p. 67 *et seq*.

59 Cf. D. Mineur, *Archéologie de la représentation politique*, Paris 2010, p. 245 *et seq*.

or whether it may in some way be reconciled with elements of direct democracy. If the response to the last question is positive and it might be acknowledged that a complex form of democracy, namely the representative system, does not at all preclude deployment of the direct form, then there arises a question as to the arrangement or proportions in which direct mechanisms for civic participation might be reverted to at present and which of these mechanisms could or should be applied, given that it is not possible to completely rule out the representative system or even minimize it considerably.

From the perspective of political science, further questions appear against this background about the nature and extent of political participation and all the consequent, more or less far-reaching issues, particularly the problem of civic involvement. For if indeed we were to believe that the degree of civic participation is the most appropriate (and perhaps the sole) indicator of democracy in a system, then there appears an essential question of how to construct a mechanism of mixed democracy (involving both direct and indirect forms) to ensure the best possible form of citizens' effective participation in the conduct of the affairs of the *polis*[60] and their, after all, subjective belief that they are the real subjects, and not just objects, of politics? These days it is quite commonly acknowledged that democracy in its representative form, as long as it is not offset by some even minimal procedures of direct articulation of the sovereign's will, is burdened with substantial drawbacks, generally contributing towards civic apathy and lowering the degree of political involvement of citizens as well as creating an extremely high risk of a gap between the will of the *demos* and the will of the representatives at the decision-making level, which is all the more possible if the rules of accountability are frail.

In extreme circumstances, absence of direct democracy institutions coupled with defective functioning of representative democracy can even lead to undermining the grounds that legitimize the entire political system. Electoral democracy, as the representative democracy is sometimes called, is burdened with both genetic and acquired defects. The former are associated with the obvious exclusivity of the idea of representation itself (which is perceptible especially, though not only, on the part of the elected), the latter in turn are the result of changes taking place in political representation as well as all the mechanisms which have changed it and, at least in some sense, distorted it (*vide* political parties, organized

60 It is quite commonly acknowledged that the best solution is to combine representative democracy with at least one form of direct participation of citizens, such as the referendum. Cf. M. Duverger, *Demain la République*, Paris 1958, p. 21, 22.

pressure groups, the media, etc.). Therefore, in the event of cumulation of undesirable or even defective features significantly deforming the system of indirect democracy, the entire regime of representative democracy might be contested. Concurrence with other events and consequences (of political, cultural, social and economic nature) may activate a phenomenon of counter-democracy, that is setting up alternative forms of civic participation, competing at the same time with existing representative institutions.[61] Even if counter-democracy does not emerge in an open or merely explicit shape, the slogan of a crisis of representation is still present[62] and indicates a fundamental problem, that is, the lack of correlation between the will of the representative and that of the represented and a general sense of weakness of accountability procedures.

It is not by coincidence that today we observe relatively many forms of the most bottom-up, spontaneous, unorganized or, even more, non-institutionalized participation. They most often materialize on an *ad hoc* basis, like an array of social and civic movements that originate most often as a result of opposition against political decisions taken at various levels of the representative system.[63] They are accompanied by episodic and occasional protests, most often arising at the spur of a moment and unfolding in various ways, usually through strikes, protests, pickets, demonstrations and lock-outs aimed at expressing a veto and, given the failure of accountability mechanisms, they are usually taken to the streets.[64] What's more, the Internet is of course an increasingly important tool of political participation. The appearance of the web was viewed by a significant number of political scientists and futurists as almost going back to the basics, reverting to direct democracy, and thus to a situation where everyone would actually (at least potentially) participate in the political community.[65] In any case, some time ago at least, the Internet was very often perceived as a true restoration

---

61 More on this topic: P. Rosanvallon, *La contre-démocratie. La politique à l'âgne de la défiance*, Paris 2006.

62 Cf.: D. Mineur, *Archéologie de la représentation…*, p. 199 *et seq.*

63 Interestingly enough, these movements are usually adversative (they are the so-called protest groups), movements with qualities of positive groups advocating for something rather than against something are a rare incident. It is correlated with a much wider phenomenon of negative politics, including negative elections that always imply voting against someone or something rather than for someone or something.

64 Cf.: B. Wessels, *Performance and Deficits of Present-day Representation…*, p. 100 *et seq.*; N. Urbinati, *Representative Democracy. Principles and Genealogy…*, p. 35 *et seq.*

65 Cf.: I. Budge, *The New Challenge of Direct Democracy*, Cambridge 1996; L.K. Grossman, *The Electronic Republic: Reshaping Democracy in the Information Age*, New York 1995; G. Meikle, *Future Active. Media Activism and the Internet*, London 2002;

of ancient direct democracy in its purest form unaffected by the sin of exclusion. It was also, quite understandably, regarded to be a viable alternative for the often inefficient indirect democracy which is plagued by a number of drawbacks, in which the authentic and uncontaminated or untwisted will of the citizens is distorted or otherwise mutated. At present, this overly optimistic perspective of a proverbial return to the source and restoring mechanisms of a true democracy seems a bit remote. True enough, the Internet is still considered an extremely relevant tool of practicing, in the fullest sense of the word, the civic politics, however, by definition it is a complementary tool that offers an opportunity of a real participation, though rather episodic and incidental, and therefore in no way substituting for the well-established institutions of the representative system. Furthermore, it is being pointed out that the Internet today remains rather in the service of counter-democracy, facilitating organization of protests and civic movements, where the *telos* is set by the prospect of voicing opposition against decisions taken by representatives. Hence, it is not a genuine form of direct democracy in reconstruction.[66] Nevertheless, it should be brought to light that the forecast whereby the Internet were to become a kind of surrogate of mechanisms for direct participation in the affairs of the *polis* was by far too optimistic, not to say detached from reality, particularly in its most far-reaching version which proclaimed an end to the existing forms of representative democracy and their redundancy in the face of universal access to the Internet. Actual abandonment of representative democracy today is indeed unimaginable. The Internet does involve citizens in political affairs, sometimes on a mass scale, yet the logic of its operation seems nevertheless limited. It is so, first and foremost, because still, despite everything, the Internet is not a tool of governance, but rather a tool for disseminating and seeking information; secondly, the circle of its users is still narrow; and thirdly and finally, in the field of (broadly understood) politics, the Internet has so far revealed a greater capacity for *contra*, rather than *pro*, pose. That is why, it has grown to be a great forum for counter-democracy, yet still an insufficient forum for democracy as such, that is democracy understood as a positive action, not just a civic protest.[67]

H. Rhetngold, *The Virtual Community. Homesteading on Electronic Frontier*, London 1993.

66 Cf. A.G. Wilhelm, *Democracy in the Digital Age. Challenges to Political Life in Cyberspace*, New York 2000, p. 105 *et seq.*

67 More on this topic: D. Saco, *Cybering Democracy: Public Space and the Internet*, University of Minnesota 2002, p. 35 *et seq.*

The same is anyway true for the 'classical' forms of direct democracy. Their quite frequent and keen exercise is by no means a threat to the monopoly of indirect democracy. Institutions such as the referendum or people's legislative initiative from their very foundation may, after all, be adhered to only incidentally and episodically and may under no circumstances become a tool of the common or everyday politics. Developed and more frequent and welcome forms of direct democracy cannot thus replace the indirect (representative) democracy, which still remains the most typical and the most established form of political participation of citizens in contemporary political systems. Therefore, although the political relevance of the direct form of embodiment of democracy is evident and indisputable, nonetheless, the political practice has unambiguously revealed that indirect democracy is the steady and regular mechanism, while pure democracy is, in the full sense of the word, an occasional method of making decisions by the sovereign. Constitutional mechanisms of the 'political game' can admittedly make use of the forms of direct democracy, however, there can be no mention of their dominant position (in practice). At most we may speak of the two forms of democracy combined, or of a subsidiary or ancillary application of the mechanisms of direct democracy, and, even more, of two parallel paths of embodiment of democracy (as, for example, the French doctrine sees it[68]), but these paths, if we were to continue this comparison, are not the same. The path that delineates the route of representative (indirect) democracy is far wider, and more frequently and strongly trodden.

On the one hand, typicality and, on the other, the universality of indirect democracy does not, however, eliminate the symptoms of its crisis or otherwise the general feeling of dissatisfaction with the functioning of the traditional mechanisms of political participation, which is still based on the choice of the representatives by the represented.[69] In connection with the foregoing, the need for reconstruction, or perhaps restoration (depending on the diagnosis of the phenomenon) of representative democracy is more and more often and loudly

68 This term was coined in the context of the amendment procedure of the constitution of the French Fifth Republic, which includes, as alternative mechanisms, procedures envisaging a national referendum and procedures closing the process of amending the constitution 'in the parliament'. This was the origin of the idea to name the mechanism of amending the constitution as the procedure of 'two parallel paths' (*deux voies parallèles*). Therefore, the French doctrine is of the opinion that 'democracy in general' today has two major shapes or forms, i.e., direct and indirect. J. Chapsal, *La vie politique sous la Ve République*, Paris 1984, p. 396.

69 Cf. N. Urbinati, *Representative Democracy. Principles and Genealogy…*, p. 52 *et seq.*

voiced. It is acknowledged that today's image of political representation is deformed, and that at least as regards a few elements. The first is an insufficient, as it is being claimed, definition of the represented subject which, after all, undergoes significant changes. The second is imprecise definition of the representative and his legal and political role, which today is quite widely regarded as a kind of fiction. The third is a mechanism of correlation and, more specifically, an insufficient mechanism of correlation which widens the gap between the will of the representative and the will of the represented. The last but not least element, which by no means ends the list of shortcomings, that highlights the key aspects only,[70] comprises the defective forms of accountability, which in fact, acting on the principle of some sort of feedback, are conducive to maintaining and exacerbating the absence of a proper correlation. Therefore, in general, the crisis of representation is rooted in the sense of political powerlessness of citizens who, besides the general elections, do not in fact have a sense of being truly represented.[71] In a very many cases, representation boils down to a simple act of voting and it ends there. Apart from elections, representation does not actually exist.[72] Everywhere else, after all, there exist mechanisms or malfunctions that either renounce representation or otherwise oppose it. An excellent example thereof are political parties that replaced the represented, or absence of procedures for maintaining an actual correlation between the will of both the parties and reducing representation to the mere act of voting, or, finally, the ineffectiveness of accountability, which is today further legitimized by the constitutional principle of representative's mandate, creating in many cases the room for completely arbitrary conduct of the mandate holder. The latter is too often perceived not only as correlated with representation of general public (which for some means almost nobody), but also creating legal grounds for the absence of accountability, which actually openly contests the principle of representation.

The present crisis of representation, if indeed we were to recognize the legitimacy of its existence, [73] is generally the sum total of two circumstances of

---

70 Cf. D. Mineur, *Archéologie de la représentation…*, p. 202 *et seq.*

71 More on this topic: N. Chandhoke, *What is Relationship Between Participation and Representation…*, p. 25 *et seq.*

72 Cf. F. Goguel, *Quelques remarques sur le problème des institutions politique de la France*, „Revue Française de Science Politique" 1964 number 2, p. 17.

73 One can, after all, assume that representation has not so much fallen into a deep and irrevocable crisis, but has merely undergone a change simply because it is not and cannot remain a constant structure. As a result, in some of its regions, it must by definition be variable and unstable, while in others it is (and should be) surprisingly

key importance for the entire system of representation, namely the absence of dialogue between the governing and the governed (*dialogue entre gouvernents et gouvernés*), as such a dialogue maintains the status of correlation, and the absence of sufficient confidence on the part of citizens (*confiance des citoyens*), which in turn is maintained through correlation and guaranteed through procedures of accountability.[74] As it is easy to guess, both these issues, i.e., the dialogue between the representatives and the represented as well as the trust between them are the elements that define representation and determine its most elementary meaning. Should they be missing, flawed or wrong, the representation itself can eventually be challenged. On the other hand, in order to properly identify and then institutionalize them, a fundamental question must be answered first and foremost, namely how representation should be understood. In the search for ways out of the crisis, the starting point is thus to redefine what political representation should actually be and what purpose it serves. Here, as it turns out, there are surprisingly many answers that at least in some sense can be deemed the rudimentary source of the problems we have with political representation and, consequently, the source of the crisis of representative democracy as well.

4. Entropy of Representation: Teleological Source of Crisis

Political representation has amazingly many meanings. All in all, when speaking of representation and representativity, people can mean very different things and facts. Representation is, by definition, nuanced, unequivocal, complex and, in the end, hard to precisely define.[75] It resembles a sort of labyrinth[76] where one easily gets lost looking for the one and only way out. In the whole mess of ways of looking at representation, there is one thing on which authors are exceptionally unanimous: namely that it is in vain that one looks for a single key to read the sense of political representation. There is simply no such key. So in order to avoid making mistakes, we should clarify at the very beginning what specific sense we ascribe to representation.[77] Otherwise everybody will talk about representation

stable. Cf. N. Urbinati, *Representative Democracy. Principles and Genealogy...*, p. 223 *et seq*.

74 J. Gicquel, J.-E. Gicquel, *Droit constitutionnel et institutions politiques*, Paris 2007, p. 110, 111.

75 Cf. N. Urbinati, *Representative Democracy. Principles and Genealogy...*, p. 20 *et seq*.

76 D. Ryden, *Representation in Crisis. The Constitution, Interest Groups and Political Parties*, New York 1996, p. 13.

77 Cf. H. Pitkin, *Representation...*, p. 132 *et seq*.

using his own language, which will finally make the chaos even deeper, therefore accelerating the phenomenon of crisis. The latter, apart from a generally good diagnosis of the weak mechanisms of correlation and the surprisingly poor procedures of accountability, is also a consequence of what might be referred to as exaggeration of claims to representation. This means that everyone would like to be represented adopting their perspective for assessing representation.[78] The slogan of representation crisis, so popular today, without denying its aptness, is to a high degree a function of entropy of the meaning of political representation. Briefly speaking, it is manifested by a rather simple, almost banal statement that representation is suffering from a crisis, because it is not deployed in accordance with this meaning of representation which we treat as appropriate. With this respect almost everybody accepts that each of the meanings is equal and at least should be taken into account to some extent. And if some of the meanings of representation are refused a *raison d'etre* and, for example, they are applied in practice, this suggests even more strongly a crisis into which representation has fallen by fundamentally changing its sense and meaning. So representation should take into account and possibly fully give effect to all or nearly all possible (or acceptable) ways of understanding it. So what one expects from representation are adequately organized election procedures and sociological sameness of the representative and the represented subject, a correctly functioning mechanism of dialogue, including the right to veto (even if with the use of forms of direct democracy), actions consistent with the intention of the subject delegating the representative (in accordance with the directive of imperative mandate, or otherwise limited mandate), actions taking into account common good or common will (which is in turn envisaged by the well-known construction of free representative mandate) and, for example, a mechanism of inclusion of extra-political (the more so extra-party) interests in the process of making political decisions, which in turn may be a closer reference to the model of polyarchy or the model of functional representation, and finally an effective mechanism of accountability. For this reason, we can say that this is like the famous truth of L. Pirandello, i.e. 'to each his own representation'.[79]

The confusing notion of political representation may, however, or even should, be somehow explained by submitting it to precise insight. Although with respect to political representation we can find a great number of research approaches and points of view and even more developed and elaborate definitions, the first

78 Cf. D. Runciman, *The Paradox of Political Representation…*, p. 95 *et seq.*

79 In line with the slogan *Chacun sa verite…*

and foremost issue is selecting from among them those that can be useful at all, leaving aside those that, even if intellectually attractive, may prove completely useless in terms of praxeology.[80] Of course, the selection is not made easier by the entropy of representation (more precisely, of its possible and permissible meanings), but at the same time, paradoxically, the entropy really forces us to make some divides, schemes and typifications. Thomas Hobbes is right when he says that '[t]here are few things that are incapable of being represented'[81] (especially if we treat representation as fiction and this is, with all the nuances and problems of defining it correctly, how it is treated, because representation is, almost by definition, a fiction once it makes present that which is not literally present. But on the other hand, it *is* obvious that 'although almost anything, and anywhere, can be represented, everything and everywhere cannot'.[82] This is precisely why it is worthwhile to look at how representation is (or at least may be) understood, interpreted and consequently divided, typified, schematised.

One of the ways of interpreting representation which is most frequently present in representation discourse is understanding it as a symbol.[83] Symbolic representation, with reference to the etymology of the very term 'representation', is presenting something, embodying, making current, making the absent present. This meaning of representation is, understandably, the broadest one. It has its equivalents e.g. in constitutional law, but at the same time equivalents going well beyond it and covering not only other branches of law, but also other areas of life. In constitutional law we refer to representation as a symbol when we, for example, describe the president as a representative of the state or when we perceive a member of parliament as a representative of the nation. Even though identification of an MP as a representative is not contained exclusively in the rhetoric of representation as a symbol, but it always remains at the background, being the point of departure for building other, more complex, meanings of representation.[84] Representation in a symbolic meaning is, however, applied much more commonly. It appears almost everywhere, because it happens almost everywhere

80 Cf. P. Pettit, *Varieties of Public Representation*, [in:] *Political Representation*, I. Shapiro, S.C. Stokes, E.J. Wood, A.S. Kirshner (eds.), Cambridge 2009, p. 61 *et seq.*

81 More on this topic: M. Brito Vieira, *The Elements of Representation in Hobbes*, London 2009.

82 D. Runciman, M. Brito Vieira, *Representation* ..., p. 184.

83 Cf. J.-L. Déotte, *Représentation et politique*, [in:] *Représentation et politique*, J.-F. Robic (ed.), Paris 2010, p. 29 *et seq.*

84 More on this topic: F.R. Ankersmit, *Political Representation*, Stanford 2002.

that something is a symbol of, or represents, something and that something is represented (e.g. by graphic sign, symbol, word, gesture, person, etc.[85]).

Another approach to representation is perceiving it as a sort of simulation of what the represented subjects might do in similar circumstances if they were able to take specific measures themselves.[86] This view of representation had, among other things, its constitutive equivalent in the imperative mandate, which to some extent obliged the mandate holder to simulate the behaviour of the represented subject. This simulative understanding of representation is also applied in civil law, where the attorney is expected to simulate the behaviour of the principal. Free mandate only seemingly rejects treating representation as simulation. But it still maintains the fiction that the representative (although without any precise instructions to follow) simulates activities of the represented subject. Because in each form of mandate, the representative acts for the represented subject and his behaviours and actions are seen as behaviours and actions of the represented subject as such.

Representation can also be seen in mimetic terms. In this sense representation should be nothing but a parallelization of the socio-political or other (e.g. economic) characteristics of the represented subject in the representative's structure.[87] With assumptions of this kind, representation should mainly imitate the society, being a proverbial miniature of it. Of course, mimetic representation is by definition a sociological representation (hence, *nota bene* it is often referred to as 'sociological representation'[88]) and its most adequate or precise form is representation which would capture the demographic features of the represented subject and repeat (precisely, represent) them on a micro-scale.[89] A slightly different, today perhaps the most common, way of thinking about representation in mimetic terms is not so much a repetition of the demographic features of the electorate (with regard to parliamentary representation), but rather replication of its political features, the easiest and probably still the best way of achieving

85 More on this topic: K. Stokke, E. Selboe, *Symbolic Representation as Political Practice*, [in:] *Rethinking Popular Representation…*, p. 59 *et seq*.

86 This way of seeing political representation was particularly visible in the origins of Modern understanding of representation. Cf. H.-Y. Lee, *Political Representation in the later Middle Ages*, New York 2008, p. 33 *et seq*.

87 D. Mineur, *Archéologie de la représentation…*, p. 154.

88 M. Duverger, *Institutions politiques et droit constitutionnel*, Paris 1966, p. 81.

89 More on this topic: M. Dogan, *L'origine sociale du personnel parlementaire français élu en 1951*, [in:] *Partis politiques et classe sociales en France*, M. Duverger (ed.), Paris 1955.

which is through proportional electoral laws.[90] It is, consequently, assumed that representation maintains a mimetic shape if the political and party structure of the representative body is a more or less faithful representation of the electorate's political and party structure.

Yet another possible way of interpreting representation is to understand it as a process of redistributing powers. This view was once popularized by Marcel Prélot, in whose view representation is nothing else but a distribution of powers between represented subjects and their representatives.[91] So representation is reduced to distributing powers, because the power of the electoral body (represented subjects) is to designate representatives, whereas the power of representatives is to perform certain public functions, reserved for the representative body. Consequently, representation – and this is a certain version or variety of seeing it as a redistribution of powers – is nothing more but a one-sided grant of the investiture to govern.[92] This approach to the problem is already relatively close to another way of looking at representation, namely a strictly juridical method. Representation in the legal sense (*représentation juridique*[93]) need not be, following the thought of e.g. M. Prélot, seen as just redistribution of powers. It can be treated as a legal principle according to which the function of governing is performed by an authorized subject, acting in the name and on the account of another. From the constitutional point of view, it is not complex to explain the logic of how juridical representation works. It is simply recognized that once the nation does not directly exercise its authority itself, then representatives of the nation exercise it in its name and on its behalf.

What is a kind of mutation of both legal constructions of representation, that is, distribution of powers (first method) and one subject exercising authority in the name and on the behalf of another subject (second method), is seeing it in terms of decision-making. M. Prélot himself believes that apart from the most appropriate – for him – power-based approach (i.e. treating representation as redistribution of rights between the representative and the represented subject) it can also be interpreted as 'legal power enabling making state decisions'.[94] So in this sense, representation is an ordinary decision-making mechanism, which is

90 Cf. A. Lijphart, *Degrees of Proportionality of Proportional Representation Formulas*, [in:] *Electoral Laws and their Political Consequences*, B. Grofman, A. Lijphart (eds.), New York 2003, p. 170 *et seq*.

91 Cf. M. Prélot, *Institutions politiques et droit constitutionnel*, Paris 1957, p. 358.

92 Cf. G. Burdeau, *Manuel de droit constitutionnel*, Paris 1952, p. 88.

93 M. Duverger, *Institutions politiques…*, p. 81.

94 M. Prélot, *Institutions politiques…*, p. 358.

characterized by specific features, i.e. first and foremost by the fact that these decisions are not made by the very subject vested with the attribute of sovereignty (the represented subject) and somebody else (the representative) acts for that subject and in its name.[95]

With slightly different emphases, but generally remaining with the decision-making version of representation, it can be interpreted as the Schumpeterian 'formation of the state's will', i.e. a standpoint determining the state's policy. At its final stage, representation is a process whose result is formulating a 'political will', a 'political standpoint' or simply a decision. Such a decision is, by its very logic, a complex one, because it first requires determining the circle of those who are to be represented; then determining a method of nominating (electing) a representative; later on, the technical manner how the representative makes the right decision; and finally, a mechanism guaranteeing an efficient application of the decision, on the one hand, and control over the actions of the decision-maker (i.e. accountability), on the other.[96] Thus, formulating the final 'political' will is both work-intensive and time-consuming and it, understandably, consists of many overlapping stages. It is also clear that in this approach representation cannot be reduced only to representatives making a decision and subsequently represented subjects being credited with it. 'Formation of the state's will' in this case is a longer, complex and multi-stage process, covering many phases and subjects, while representation covers at least a few steps of reaching the political (state's) decision (will).

In yet another way of looking at the problem, representation may be treated as an interaction of the plural structures, which are typical of contemporary societies. Here we can trace a clear echo of Robert Dahl's thought. For him, representation is mainly an interaction of the representative with various claims made by competing interests revealed in the heterogenic mass of represented subjects.[97] For the American scholar, the essence of representation is not so much the construction of the representative (and e.g. ensuring mimetic representation), but rather the plural structure of the represented subjects, whose various expectations, claims and interests must be adequately aggregated by the representative. Thus a success of representation results not so much from the creation of a pluralist face of the representative (which clearly dominates in the sociological

95 More on this topic: A. Grazia, *Legislative Process, Representation and Decision-Making*, London 1967.

96 Cf. A. Vermeule, *Mechanism of Democracy*, Oxford 2007, p. 143 *et seq.*

97 More on this topic: R. Dahl, *Polyarchy. Participation and Opposition*, New Haven 1971.

approach to representation), but rather from ensuring the possibility of correct, that is, possibly complete, aggregation of plural interests of the represented subject. Certainly, the conception of representation as interaction of plural structures of the represented subject makes sense, because it emphasises the 'other side' of the relationship of representation, namely the represented subject. The earlier approaches, e.g. the symbolic, mimetic or simulative ones, practically ignored the issue of who is represented. Meanwhile, Robert Dahl justly claims that the most important issue in representation is building an optimum mechanism of interaction. From this point of view, the construction of the representative is a secondary matter. It simply has to be such as to ensure the best possible interaction, because only the latter will result in various claims, interests, postulates and expectations being able to be somehow taken into account at the decision-making level. Because we should not forget that interaction is not the goal in itself. It should serve the decision-making mechanism, which will be the better, the more data it takes into account and these data are needed for the final decision to be the best possible one.[98]

Perceiving representation as an interaction of plural structures of the represented subject is already a step away from yet another way of looking at representation. This time it is about thinking about representation in terms of conversion. The whole mechanism of representation, as rightly pointed out by David Runciman and Monica Brito Vieira, may be viewed as a mechanism, where the so-called input is, through conversion, turned into output. In the representation mechanism the key issue is thus, in this approach, the method through which the standpoints, expectations, postulates, claims and hopes of the represented subject (referred to as 'input') become the 'output', that is, the representatives' decision.

If we adopt the perspective of viewing representation as indeed just conversion of input into output, then we should admit that all these views that see representation as just the election process oscillate around it.[99] This kind of view accentuate – in line with the juridical way of perceiving representation – that representation is in fact nothing else, but 'granting the investiture to govern',[100] which takes place via election procedures and the arithmetic mechanisms of

98 From this point of view, Dahl's proposal remains in a broad group of decision-based approaches.

99 Cf. F. Borella, *Élements de droit…*, p. 220 *et seq.*

100 M. Prélot, *Institutions politiques…*, p. 358.

mandate redistribution embedded in them.[101] Recognizing that representation is actually nothing but the election of representatives by the represented subjects stresses at the same time the very strongly fictitious nature of representation, because it anticipates that the electors cannot fully exercise their rights to govern and that they can only do so via their representative.[102] Hence, without a representative selected via the relevant procedure, the very category of the represented subject loses its fundamental sense, because if there is no representative, there is no represented subject, thus there is no representation either.

A variety of both the approaches presented above, both of which suggest that representation is either an election or, more broadly, conversion of input into output, is a view that sees the essence of representation not in the mathematical manner of allocation of parliamentary mandates as such (proportional or majority system), but in defining and precisely delineating the constituency, which plays a considerable role in every model of political representation. This view recognizes the constituency (on which representation focuses in general) as the element which, in a sort of feedback loop, defines the whole representative system.[103] Consequently, the map of constituencies should be determined in such a way as to ensure authentic representativity and this, according to an interesting proposal by Andrew Rehfeld, can only happen by means of abandoning the traditional method of construing constituencies on the basis of localism. Representation should be, in Rehfeld's view, nothing but just a statistical sample of the whole society, not stigmatized in any way and consequently not deformed by territorial, economic, political, religious, nationality or other divisions, which are only petrified by the traditional map of constituencies. Therefore representation should be a chance selection of constituencies, chosen in exactly the same manner as the sociological samples of the society are built for the purpose of various statistical surveys or public opinion polls. Thanks to it, as the author of the idea proposes, ideal representation will be reached and its teleological sense will be reflecting the whole population in the proverbial nutshell, while the pragmatic method of reaching it will be drawing constituencies. The result of drawing will be the so-called random constituency, which is the best guarantee of proper representation, because it has no strengthened features falsifying the image of the

101 Cf. M. Gassner, *Représentations parlementaires: Méthodes mathématiques proportionnelles de répartition des sièges*, Paris 2000, p. 22 *et seq*.

102 Cf. F. Rouvillois, *Droit constitutionnel. Fondements et pratiques*, Paris 2005, p. 239, 240.

103 Cf. A. Rehfeld, *The Concept of Constituency. Political Representation, Democratic Legitimacy and Institutional Design*, Cambridge 2005, p. 30 *et seq*.

represented subject. Because regardless of everything else, the essence of representation is always the mechanism via which represented subjects select the representatives. However, Rehfeld's proposal indicates that the essence of the selection does not lie, as it is usually thought, in the arithmetic formula of redistribution of mandates, but only in the construction of constituencies. The above proposal is important and interesting inasmuch as it unequivocally indicates that the structure of the represented subjects is of fundamental importance for the right determination of political representation. For Rehfeld it is obvious that the so-called random constituency is what best represents the represented subject, revealing the latter's general and universal features, while removing, or at least significantly diminishing, endemic features, strengthened by typical divisions characteristic of the classically construed constituencies. In each representation, as Rehfeld rightly observes, the goal is to reflect the socio-political composition of the represented group in the best and fullest possible way.

This view is seconded by Iris Marion Young, for whom the essence of representation lies in the represented subject and not in the representative. I.M. Young, dealing mainly with the problem of differences within the represented group, proposes considering representation as mainly a method of social dialogue whose basic aim is to maintain social homeostasis.[104] According to this American researcher, representation is a process of constant negotiations as a result of which various interests of the most diverse groups and environments collide, while the true essence of these negotiations is the formation of new constellations of alliances, which comprise – depending on the object of interest – individual interest groups. Representation understood in this way is a mechanism of deliberations of representatives and constituents where in both groups different, sometimes conflicting interests, expectations and demands are revealed. So representation means negotiating all those interests and formation of alliances between individual groups, both among the represented subjects and among constituents, as well as between them.[105] In Young's view, representation, apart from being a negotiation, is first and foremost a relationship, an association of different subjects, within both one and the other group, and – as is clear and as often is the quintessence of representation – between both these groups.[106] The view of I.M. Young is original and interesting in that it departs from a certain one-dimensionality of constituents and representatives, showing the both

104 Cf. I.M. Young, *Justice and the Politics of Difference*, Princeton 1990, p. 183 *et seq.*

105 Cf. I.M. Young, *Deferring Group Representation*, [in:] *Ethnicity and Groups Rights*, I. Shapiro, W. Kymlicka (eds.), New York 1997, p. 249 *et seq.*

106 More on this topic: I.M. Young, *Inclusion and Democracy*, Oxford 2002, p. 124 *et seq.*

the former and the latter are stigmatized by the multiplicity of different, often conflicting interests. Consequently, it is impossible to consider that representation is only a dichotomic division between constituents and representatives. In reality both groups are internally complex and, more importantly, fluid, because the alliances formed within them are often highly temporal and in most cases are prompted by a specific issue which needs to be 'dealt with'. Thus representation is a constantly changing kaleidoscope of the most variegated groups and environments, mixed in various ways, which form a plastic mass.

Young's idea to see representation as the proverbial melting pot of various interest groups covers one more meaning of representation, which is strongly emphasised today; in this case representation is understood as the possibility to veto.[107] After all, the essence of the negotiative or deliberative vision of representation, understood as the formation of alliances between various interest groups, is always, on the one hand, the making of a decision and, on the other one, the possibility of other participants in negotiations protesting against this decision. Some authors even suggest that the main emphasis in representation should be precisely on the latter possibility. Because representation based on the constituents' chance to veto shows that the system of representation works not so much when an alliance is successfully formed between specific interest groups, but rather when no other group remaining outside the alliance's structure questions the decisions made within such an alliance, at least not openly. Importantly, representation identified with veto shows, at the same time, a dimension of representation which is by all means democratic, distinguishing between the representation systems which were or were not democratic and clearly suggesting that representation must imperatively be democratic, since if it loses democratic features it thereby ceases to be representation. At the same time it directs the way of thinking about representation to its yet another meaning.

This is, of course, about understanding representation as control.[108] With this assumption, representation is a form of limiting the discretionary character of authority, while the well-known slogan of a representative government is in fact tantamount to that of a controlled government, that is, to use yet another phrase, one which is accountable to voters.[109] Representation seen that way is, firstly, a general idea, linked with limitation of discretionary character of authority (from where it is fairly easy to link it to democracy as such); secondly, a specific way

107 Cf. I.M. Young, *Deferring Group Representation…*, p. 250 *et seq.*

108 Cf. F. Hamon, M. Troper, *Droit constitutionnel*, Paris 2011, p. 83 *et seq.*

109 Cf. B. Manin, *The Principles of Representative Government*, Cambridge 1997, p. 8.

of applying this general idea, which requires creation of an efficient system of control of the governing by the governed. The latter, as is easy to guess, is by no means easy, because represented subjects have an almost innate capacity for detaching themselves from the governed ones, being led by completely different directives of behaviour, which *nota bene* is the origin of such a popular and moreover resonant slogan of crisis of representation.[110]

Control as a synonym of representation, or at least its main idea or element, is constantly present in all sorts of discourse on political representation, even though, as we have to remember, it hides under very diverse terms. It may be, as Edmund Burke saw it, responsibility.[111] It may also be, as advocated by Jeremy Bentham, *vox populi* correlated with the general interest, or, as John St. Mill wanted it, good government or simply responsibility government.[112] Today, this control-oriented understanding of representation is particularly strongly emphasised for at least two reasons. Firstly, because we notice a slow departure from the idea of responsibility government. So in the popular opinion governments are more and more irresponsible and uncontrolled, which is best summarized precisely in the slogan of the crisis of representation (with all the consequences, e.g. the conception of counter-democracy). Secondly, the current character and popularity of representation as control is grounded in the more and more often noticed 'multi-storey' nature of control as representation, which should be best expressed by two different although at the same time similar expressions, i.e. responsibility and accountability. The former, as we know, refers to the control over the government by the representatives. The latter one, in turn, refers to control of representatives by the represented subjects (precisely, accountability of the former to the latter), thanks to which representation becomes a sort of system of permanent control made up of many links which in various ways connect the person who controls with the controlled one.

Against this background a justified question may arise as to how to actually ensure truly efficient control over representatives? One idea is the conception of public opinion government, which may and should be treated as yet another possible way of understanding representation. According to its recommendations, representation is government by an elite elected through democratic universal election, responsible to the voters for the policy they follow. The

110 Cf. D. Mineur, *Archéologie de la représentation…*, p. 199 *et seq.*

111 H.-Y. Lee, *Political Representation…*, p. 15.

112 Cf. I. Shapiro, *John Locke's Democratic Theory*, [in:] *John Locke: Two Treatises of Government and A Letter Concerning Toleration*, I. Shapiro (ed.), New York 2003, p. 309 *et seq.*

substance of public opinion government is that between the activities of representatives and the expectations of represented subjects there must be a conformity (correlation) of contents, or at least there cannot be a fundamental discrepancy. It is obvious that in order for the conformity of contents to work effectively there must be complex mechanisms of political correlation, that is, looking for and maintaining such conformity, among which elections are naturally an important, but not the most important, or the more so the only one. Mechanisms of representation include also forms of direct democracy (largely focused on controlling the actions of representatives), political parties, which still remain the basic element of articulating and aggregating the will of represented subjects, and in addition to them also mass media, interest groups, associations, trade unions or religious denominations, and – a phenomenon occurring more and more often – various spontaneous, sometimes very short-lived organizational formations, etc.[113]

This set of views, used only as examples, shows that we are indeed dealing with true entropy of representation. All in all, almost everybody proposes his or her own, often strongly subjective, way of looking at representation, considering it from a slightly different perspective, putting the emphasis differently, noticing its other key elements. The multiplicity of views on representation originates not only from the fact that it can be analysed from the historic, doctrinal, philosophical, legal or e.g. sociological points of view, but also from the fact it can be approached both from the representative's side and that of the represented subject, as well as looked at 'from the middle', for example in accordance of the conception of conversion of input into output.

Representation, even though there are so many different possible ways of interpreting it, has nevertheless some common points. The first and most important one is the absent presence, i.e. that its essence is making something that is absent at a given moment present or real. Each representation assumes 'simultaneous presence and absence'.[114] The second common point is certainly what Didier Mineur refers to as 'political communality'.[115] This means that representation, by definition, assumes the existence of a certain group, but not only a group understood in the sociological, hence, at least to some extent, statistical meaning of the word, but precisely a community which, apart from the arithmetic principle of several, has in common something that is the real

113 More on this topic in S.N. Soroka, Ch. Wlezien, *Degrees of Democracy. Politics, Public Opinion and Policy*, Oxford 2010, p. 14 *et seq.*

114 D. Runciman, M. Brito Vieira, *Representation…*, p. xi.

115 D. Mineur, *Archéologie de la représentation…*, p. 55.

substance of communality, that is, certain ideas, identities, views, goals, wishes, features, etc. shared at least by those several. Finally, the common element in almost all approaches to, and conceptions of, representation is recognizing that representation (on the grounds of politics) is a form of exercising power in the name of someone who, for some reasons, cannot exercise it personally.[116] Yet recognizing that someone cannot personally exercise authority or make decisions does not in itself mean establishing the regime of representation. It must be accompanied by, as indeed indicated by I.M. Young, negotiations or deliberations or – in line with R. Dahl's conception – 'causing interactions' between the pluralist structures characteristic of the represented subject. This is not about interactions or negotiations in themselves. They are conducted for a specific purpose, namely in order to achieve a state of agreement demonstrating the conformity of views on both sides of the relationship of representation. Because representation requires (and this is the fourth common point for almost all ways of interpreting it) a correlation between the representative and the represented subject.[117] The correlation need not, of course, be an automatic reproduction of the represented subject[118] in the representative's structure or, all the more so, the two need not be identical (in line with the principle of representation of identity), but it must be a form in which interaction will be constantly maintained, while the represented subject will have the right to veto if they perceive a lack of correlation.

The aforementioned correlation and more precisely lack of it is also what in the eyes of most critics determines the contemporary crisis of political representation. On this occasion it is, however, stressed that the crisis cannot be solved or, the more so, prevented by the entropy of representation, which is visible to the naked eye, because none of the adopted standpoints of looking at representation inspires optimism, smaller or bigger defects being revealed in every single one. If we, consequently, recognize that representation is just replication, it is obvious that today the representative cannot be recognized as a straightforward replica of the represented subject. In the same way we can no longer adopt without dispute the standpoint that the representative only simulates the activities of the represented subject. Also the electoral key of reading representation paints it in rather dark colours, especially if we combine it with the need to guarantee mimetic representation. Representation as control, especially accountability, also

116 More on this topic: H. Pitkin, *The Concept of Representation*, Berkley 1967.

117 Cf. J. Leca, *Représentation*, [in:] *Dictionnaire constitutionnel*, red. O. Duhamel, Y. Mény, Paris 1992, p. 914 *et seq*.

118 Cf. D. Mineur, *Archéologie de la représentation…*, p. 154.

leaves much to be desired, just like representation identified with public opinion government. So it might seem that representation, like before, remains mainly a political idea, axiologically important and very attractive, but teleologically extremely varied and difficult (and perhaps not at all possible).

Chapter II: Theoretical Concepts of Representation

1. The *Principium*: Philosophical Concept of Representation

The Latin term *repraesentatio* meaning representation gained its contemporary denotation of political representation with all its implications in the era of the French Revolution. The earlier terms, such as *mandatum*, *concilia*, *colloquia*, *conventus*, *curiae*, *placita* etc., did not reflect the meaning of the term *representation*, albeit it must be admitted that some of them, such as mandate, were closely related to this term.[1] Notably, the predominant majority of these terms functioned within the limits of private law[2] and found their way into the domain of the public law much later, i.e. after the French Revolution, when the foundations of the modern concepts of constitutional law understood as public law began to form.[3] It was then that the concept of the mandate, and specifically representation, took on its public legal character, becoming in a short time the most fundamental constitutional concept both in the constitutional law theory as well as in legislation at a constitutional level, which more or less openly accepted the principles of political representation construing it into a political principle of a state.[4]

Despite such lingering presence and, what's more, regardless of a certain intuitive understanding of the term, the precise definition of the notion of representation in the constitutional law has continued to pose challenge and elude the rules of accurate interpretation to date.[5] It is easier to analyse the adjective than to pinpoint the exact meaning of the noun from which such adjective was formed. Being *representative* means representing someone or something rather well, having the characteristic features of a representative or, more broadly, of some type of a community. When representation is correlated with an electoral

1 *Cf.* J.L. Gazzaniga, *Mandat et représentation dans l'ancien droit*, 'Droits'1987, no. 5, p. 24 *et seq.*
2 *Cf.* G. Vedel, *Manuel élémentaire de droit constitutionnel*, Paris 2002, p. 134.
3 More on this topic: P. Fournier, *Institutions et représentations du politique:totu Espagne, France, Italie, XVIIe–XXe siècles*, Paris 2006.
4 *Cf.* D. Mineur, *Archéologie de la représentation politique*, Paris 2010, p. 89 *et seq.*
5 *Cf.* J.A. Fairlie, *The Nature of Political Representation*, 'The American Political Science Review'1940, vol. 34, p. 236–248.

procedure (which customarily takes place in constitutional law), *representative* means being consistent with the social process of selecting representatives of some social group, reflecting the composition of the same group (in this sense we would refer to, for instance, a 'representative body') and, *a contrario, unrepresentative* means contradicting this process and distorting faithful representation of vital features of the group. In this sense, *representative* all too often means nothing else than based on general or otherwise democratic elections, while *unrepresentative* means divergent from the model of general elections and following other methods of selecting members of certain bodies such as parliaments, which further implies a distortion of the features or characteristics of a group that is to be representatively (i.e. faithfully) mapped in the composition of the representative body.[6]

Clearly, the terms *representative* and *unrepresentative* contain a highly evaluative component.[7] They suggest that a certain body (such as a parliament) is elected in such a way as to reflect (i.e. to represent) the features of a certain group and therefore be congruent with the accepted model of selecting the said group in order to properly (genuinely) reveal its socio-economic and political heterogeneity or *viceversa*, the said body is elected in a manner that does not allow mirroring, in the membership of the elected body, the specific (essential, relevant) features of the group that ultimately is to be represented, and is thus incompatible with the assumed relationship of representation. The delineation of *representative* or *unrepresentative* assumes *a priori* the existence of a certain relationship, a relation of something to something else.[8] Something is *representative*, once it befittingly (truthfully) represents (reflects, mirrors) the properties of the subject, which is to be represented; something is *unrepresentative* when it diverges from the adopted model of mirroring (representation). What's more, if only the feature of representativeness is fulfilled, then most often the representativeness itself gains a substantial positive value, thus becoming an axiological category and not only, as it could be *prima vista* recognized, a sociological or downright arithmetic category, i.e. envisaging the existence of a certain type of an algorithm

6 Very often the term *representation* is identified with the electoral process. Thus, J. Leca writes: 'La représentation est un processus par lequel quelque chose personnel(s), grepe(s), chose(s), ou abstraction(s) qui n'est pas réellement present est rendu présent par un intermédiaire'– J. Leca, *Représentation*, [in:] *Dictionnaire constitutionnel*, O. Duhamel, Y. Mény (eds.), Paris 1992, p. 914.

7 More on this topic: J. Boulad-Ayoub, P.-M. Vernes, *Aux fondements théoriques de la représentation politique*, Paris 2007.

8 *Cf.* A. Heywood, *Key Concepts in Politics*, New York 2000, p. 144.

whereby the features of a represented subject *vis-à-vis* the representing subject are determined (most often by some proportion[9]). The latter conviction is all the more justified since according to the sociological approach (which is clearly predominant when it comes to the understanding of the term) the attribute of being *representative* is in fact identified with reflecting or actually mirroring (replicating) the features characteristic of the represented group, yet on a lesser scale. Thus, being *representative* simply connotes replicating the features of the said group, and in a certain sense also mapping its structure into another place and into another, reduced, image. The qualitativeness of the formulated views in this case is, easy to guess, a function of two elementary circumstances.[10] Firstly, the notion of being *representative* or, plausibly, *unrepresentative* represents the endorsement of this proportion according to the formerly known mathematical formula. Thus, something will be *representative* (or mimetic in a somewhat different approach or, as seen by Philip Pettit,[11] simulative) when the proportion of certain or desirable attributes of a group and features of group representatives has been attained, while *unrepresentative* will exhibit distortions in the manner of embodiment of this mathematic algorithm of redistributing features (qualities) of the ultimately represented group. In this sense, *representative* means nothing but faithfully or accurately, though on a fittingly smaller scale, representing the essential qualities or features of a subject which is to be represented. Furthermore and secondly, it should be kept in mind that it is quite commonly assumed that if the state of representativeness is attained, even if from a certain angle only (such as from the point of view of the mathematical proportion), then this outcome should, generally and regardless of anything else, be considered positive and *vice versa*.[12] Thus, if the mechanism of allocation of, for instance, the parliamentary mandates deforms the attributes (qualities or characteristics) of the represented group (thus resulting in the parliament being unrepresentative), then the entire mechanism of aggregating the socio-economic or political (or both of these) qualities of the electorate will be adversely assessed, while the parliament will be perceived as unrepresentative, *ergo* non-democratic and non-legitimate. Naturally, it is quite a different issue what criterion is used to differentiate these specific attributes (be it a social, economic or political criterion

9 More on this topic: M. Gassner, *Représentations parlementaires: Méthodes mathématiques proportionnelles de répartition des sièges*, Paris 2000.

10 *Cf.* D. Mineur, *Archéologie de la représentation…*, p. 26 *et seq.*

11 P. Pettit, *The Common Mind. An Essay on Psychology, Society and Politics*, Oxford 1996, p. 284 *et seq.*

12 *Cf.* G. Sibertin-Blanc, *Philosophie politique*, Paris 2008, p. 103 *et seq.*

or, possibly, a potential compilation of all or some of these features).[13] The true essence of representation is actually not what is to be mirrored in a respective scale, but how it must be done in order to preserve the above mentioned relationship between the represented and the representative.[14]

Contrary to the adjective derived from it, the noun *representation* is a term which can hardly be precisely defined, particularly since it is used both in everyday language and in a language of scientific research, and in the juridical studies as well, and in the latter case, the concept of representation takes on a completely different guise against the background of civil law, the international law and the constitutional law.[15] Be that as it may, the term *representation* and the identical notion of presentation is used in yet another sense in humanities, where there exists a vast multi-coloured mosaic of all its possible meanings and connotations, relationships, nuances and suggestions.[16] On the margin, it is being pointed out that this noun, like the adjective derived from it, has at least two basic, yet slightly different meanings. Representation is treated somewhat differently when viewed from sociological and juridical perspectives, albeit these interpretations are not completely contradictory or mutually exclusive, but rather complementary and certainly at least in some sense overlapping.[17]

Irrespective of all the nuances in the understanding of representation, it might be assumed that at the root of all the interpretations and connotations of the term *representation* lies some original common meaning, which is indirectly validated by the use of a single term derived from Latin, namely *repraesentare*.[18] Besides, in all the cases of this term being applied, the semantic content refers to the phenomena of replacing someone or something *vis-à-vis* another subject, the phenomena of symbolizing, substituting, replacing or making present. The actual substance of the verb *repraesentare* boils down to the following definition: 'to

13 *Cf.* P. Bourdieu, *La représentation politique. Éléments pour une théorie du champ politique*, 'Actes de la Recherche en Sciences Sociales' 1981, nr 36/37, p. 3 *et seq.*

14 *Cf.* D. Mineur, *Archéologie de la représentation…*, p. 42 *et seq.*

15 For different approaches to the understanding of the term 'represenation', *Cf.*: L.B. Curzon, *Dictionary of Law*, London 2002, p. 365; *Le Droit de A à Z.Le Dictionnaire juridique practique*, Paris 1996. p. 510–511; G. Cornu, *Vocabulaire juridique*, Paris 1987, p. 712–713.

16 *Cf.* G. Rœsz, *De la représentation au politique*, [in:] *Représentaion et politique*, J.-F. Robic (ed.), Paris 2010, p. 9 *et seq.*

17 *Cf.* M. de Villiers, *Dictionnaire du droit constitutionnel*, Paris 2005, p. 212.

18 More on this topic: G. Leibholz, *Das Wesen der Repräsentation*, Berlin–Leipzig 1929, p. 26.

make present again something that is currently absent'.[19] That is why for instance Gerhard Leibholz perceives in representation the duality of existence, since something is present and absent at the same time. In representation, which is always some form of mutual relationship between two subjects, there are two independent beings as parties of this relationship, albeit distinct, yet always bound and inextricably linked to each other by their relationship of representation. In other words, 'the essence of representation lies in every represented subject living and thinking via its representative, and thanks to the trust in its representative, blending his will with the will of the latter'.[20] Consequently, representation is an expression of unity binding two independent, self-contained and fully separate subjects into an organic whole, unifying the wills of both these subjects into one and the same, and hence always a common, will of the representative and the represented. Therefore, whenever one of these subjects come into play, for instance the representative, then at the same time the second one, i.e. the represented, comes along as well. That is why even though something is absent, it remains present and it exists, although it does not exist. Despite the necessary concurrence, each of the parties of the relationship of representation remains a separate and independent being, and the representative will never identify himself with the represented,[21] yet one would never come to exist without the other and *vice versa*.[22] It is thus only a volitional, but never existential, unity. This way, the substance of representation involves making real something that is not present. Its specific dialectic function is manifested in something being both absent and yet currently existing. At the same time, G. Leibholz clearly highlights that representation understood as *Repräsentation* is only an abstract and ideal category, a certain abstracted theoretical construct, the sole tangible designate of which is representation understood as *Vertretung*. The latter cannot, however, be understood, if not interpreted as *Repräsentation*, since both these concepts treated separately are in fact void and meaningless; only when combined do they merge into a coherent and logical whole. It should further be noted that a model of construing representation such as the one proposed by G. Leibholz breaks apart the equivalence of both these terms, i.e. *Repräsentation* and *Vertretung*, which we have in the constitutional law.[23] In the presented approach, *Vertretung*

19 M. Sobolewski, *Reprezentacja w ustroju współczesnych demokracji burżuazyjnych*, Kraków 1962, p. 64.

20 A. Esmein, *Prawo konstytucyjne*, Warszawa 1921, p. 308.

21 More on this topic: G. Leibholz, *Das Wesen der Repräsentation...*, p. 20 *et seq.*

22 *Cf.* A. Esmein, *Prawo konstytucyjne...*, p. 308.

23 *Cf.* P. Ardant, *Institutions politiques & droit constitutionnel*, Paris 2004, p. 166 *et seq.*

is nothing but an embodiment of *Repräsentation*, its real-life reflection, lacking which it remains merely an abstract notion, both volatile and difficult to define in a clear-cut way. On the other hand, no other method of interpreting the phenomenon of representation touches upon its most rudimentary substance, namely showing that something is both present as well and absent, both existent and non-existent. Hence, the philosophical approach to representation stays very close to its symbolic dimension.[24] Something that is absent, though nonetheless present through representation, remains present via, for instance, either a symbol or a symbolic depiction of presence despite absence. In consequence, philosophical representation is, *mutatis mutandis*, symbolic, since its basic and most elementary sense is a symbolic representation of existence despite non-existence.

2. The *Meritum*: Juridical Concept of Representation

Leaving in the background intricate philosophical digressions, the issue of representation can also be approached from a point of view of pure competence, where representation is trimmed down to a formal legal institution. Viewed from this perspective, it becomes nothing but the demarcation of powers between voters and representative bodies with all the resultant consequences to follow. Under such an assumption, in the most general terms, representation means the 'juridical competence that permits making decisions of the state'.[25] In this case, the relationship of representation is replaced, at least to some extent, by the division of powers between the represented and their representatives. The powers of the voters involve designating of their representatives, while in turn the powers of the representatives involve performing certain public functions reserved for the representative body. As a result, there is no bilateral relationship between the mandator and the mandatary, while representation itself is nothing but a unilateral grant of the investiture to govern.[26] With such an approach to the phenomenon of representation, the elector, i.e. the represented, assigns during the voting his prerogative to make decisions upon the representative who, once

---

24 More on this topic: K. Stokke, E. Selboe, *Symbolic Representation as Political Practice*, [in:] *Rethinking Popular Representation*, O. Törnquist, N. Webster, K. Stokke (eds.), New York 2010, p. 59 *et seq.*

25 M. Prélot, *Institutions politiques et droit constitutionnel*, Paris 1957, p. 358.

26 A similar position is taken by G. Burdeau: 'Le corps électoral est un instrument de désignation, il n'est pas un organe de volonté' – G. Burdeau, *Manuel de droit constitutionnel*, Paris 1952, p. 88.

elected, assumes the general powers and responsibilities previously reserved for electors. Thus, those who engage in the elections waive the exercise of their rights and privileges, at the same time conferring their effective enactment upon the representative. And this exactly is the quintessence of a mandate, meaning an assignment granted by the voter to his representative, subsuming the right to take any and all actions which in their entirety make up a mandate. Under a slightly different interpretation of the juridical concept of representation, which dissimilarly accentuates, though does not contest the very principle of representation as the demarcation of powers, it is assumed that the voter is deprived of any right to manage his own competencies and to transfer them to his representatives. The only competence which is left to him is to make a purely personal, programme-based and eventually political choice of a representative. His will is, therefore, greatly restrained in the sense that he cannot for instance choose his own representatives or to individually take up actions which he assigns within the frame of his *mandatum*. The juridical fiction of representation manifests itself best in this approach, since it turns out that the voter himself cannot fully and effectively exercise his own right to govern and may do so only through his representative.[27] Thus, pursuant to the juridical concept, not only does the voter have the right to confer his rights and powers upon the representative, thus as if voluntarily self-restraining his own potential to exercise them, but in fact his capacity is reduced to granting the investiture only, which means that in the event it is not granted, the powers nominally vested in the voter cannot be effectively exercised by the voter himself. Along such lines, the sovereign (the voter) is not endowed with even a purely theoretical competence to take up and pursue matters reserved for the representative, since those have been permanently and irrevocably delegated to the representative only. The power of the sovereign is thus limited to the mere election (designation) of the representative. It is nonetheless the most vital and in no case transferable power which cannot be subject to any annexation or restriction.

Markedly, such approach to the juridical concept of representation entailing a demarcation between the competences of the mandator and the mandatary is a form of mutation or a version of such structure of political representation that predicates a full omnipotence of the representatives in view of the assumption that their role is to *vouloir pour la nation*. With the passing of time this idea was brought down to its most restrictive form, that is the sovereignty of

27 *Cf.* F. Rouvillois, *Droit constitutionnel. Fondements et pratiques*, Paris 2005, p. 239–240.

the parliament and people's representatives who become members of the parliament.[28] Resultantly, any real will of the people (voters), apart from the one manifested in the representative body, was eradicated. In its most extreme form, this idea gave birth to the assumption that there is no sovereign beyond the parliament, as the very structure of the nation-sovereign is a sort of a legal fiction that can in no way be put into practice within the frame of political action. It thus appears that the juridical concept of representation cogently corresponds with this view, starting from the general statement that a voter does not himself have the opportunity of taking political action and that his competencies can be effectively exercised through a duly authorized representative only. Therefore, the one and only, but also the most vital and – from the point of view of the representation theory – central competence is indeed the voter's right to designate his proxy, which right is exercised anew from time to time during elections, meaning nothing more but granting the investiture to govern.[29] Thus, regardless of whether it is verbalized in a statement that there is no will of the people other than the will of their representatives who are members of the representative body, or in a statement that representation is nothing but redistribution of competencies and is tantamount only to the granting of the title to govern to the representative, the juridical concept of representation boils down to acknowledgment that a representative, within the limits of the attributes assigned to him, is appointed to freely and independently decide on behalf of the nation. This in turn means that his will is an expression of the will of the nation and that his lips are the lips of the very people having the status of the sovereign.

The juridical approach to representation is not only, however, abridged to the principle of redistribution of powers in line with a simple rule that the voter's competence is to delegate a mandatary, while the powers of the latter involve acting for and on behalf of the voter that delegated him.[30] Granting an investiture to govern, and more specifically, to act on behalf of the principal i.e. the voter, is merely one of the aspects – though admittedly often dominant – of the juridical interpretation of the notion of representation. Yet another aspect focuses on substitution as a true bone of representation. As Hans Kelsen wrote: 'In substitution there is always a legal relationship between two legal subjects, one of which acts on behalf of other; the acts-in-law of the substitute are indeed his own actions,

28 *Cf.* I. Nguyen-Duy, *Souverainete du Parlement Britannique*, Paris 2011, p. 35 *et seq.*
29 *Cf.* M. Prélot, *Institutions politiques…*, p. 358 *et seq.*
30 *Cf.* F. Rouvillois, *Droit constitutionnel…*, p. 230 *et seq.*

yet they have a legal effect as if they were the actions of the substituted'.[31] The delegation of powers itself is not so crucial here as for example Marcel Prélot saw it. The bottom line is that as a result of the granted proxy (not coincidentally referring to the civilistic concept of proxy), one subject is substituted by another, but at the same time the former is also made permanently present (i.e. it is precisely represented) by the latter.[32] The true sense of representation is, after all, to act on behalf of another subject that is being replaced, represented, or – in reference to the etymology of the concept of representation – made present, existent and acting, although in actuality, *hic et nunc*, it is absent, non-existent and not acting.

This clearly reveals that a juridical analysis of representation develops in a certain sense in two different directions, yet that does not mean that it is internally antipodal or discrepant. Accents are simply distributed in a different manner and other elements of representation are highlighted as crucial. The first, juridical, perception of representation focuses on the very moment of delegating powers as the key element of representation; while the second approach emphasizes the effect of this delegation, namely the recognition that a delegate acts on behalf of the delegator, that he acts *de jure* as his deputy, personifying the delegator (the voter) within the representative body.[33] Inasmuch as under the first approach there is a real risk that the wills of the representative and the represented may diverge (since the essence of representation lies in the very action of appointing a delegate), under the second approach the delegate is much more associated with the delegator, since the accord of wills of both the parties is assumed *a priori* as the delegate is only a substitute of the delegator. Both the variants of the juridical interpretation of representation do not, however, eliminate the risk of severance of the delegate and delegator's wills and, in extreme cases, even the delegate's will gaining a full autonomy with no regard for the will of the delegator.[34] Insofar as in the first case, this risk can be clearly seen (since representation is only a technical mechanism of granting the investiture), in the second case it is at least apparently minimized, since according to H. Kelsen, substitution means that the 'actions of the substitute have the legal effect of actions of the substituted'. The mere terms 'deputy' or 'substitute' *prima facie* suggest that the substitute is not

31 H. Kelsen, *Podstawowe zagadnienia nauki prawa państwowego*, vol. II, Vilnius 1936, p. 428.

32 *Cf.* G. Vedel, *Manuel élémentaire…*, p. 133, 134.

33 *Cf.* M. Sadoun, *Représentation*, [in:] *Dictionnaire du vote*, P. Perrineau, D. Reynié (eds.), Paris 2001, p. 794 *et seq.*

34 *Cf.* D. Gaxie, *La démocratie représentative*, Paris 2003, p. 79 *et seq.*

endowed with his own will, but acts on behalf of the substituted person pursuant to the principles of proxy known under the civil law. However, the same H. Kelsen wrote that the actions of the substitute are 'his actions' and only their legal effect is such that they are regarded as the actions of the substituted. At this point the legal literature touches upon the fundamental problem, that is the autonomy of conduct of the representative (substitute). It can be assumed that such autonomy does not exist, since it is precluded by the very nature of representation, where the substitute is to merely express the will of the substituted. On the other hand, however, actions of the substitute may equally well be perceived as his own personal actions which, regardless of whose will (view) they express, are always recognized (attributed) as the actions of the substituted. It is well known that in the end both these variants have been accepted; one took the form of an imperative mandate, i.e. a mandate strictly correlating the will of the substitute with the will of the substituted, and the second transpired in the form of an alternative, the so-called free, mandate that breaks apart from the traditional imperative on the part of the substitute to act in a manner compliant with the intentions of the substituted.[35] Both these variants are at the same time merely a function of a theoretical approach to the concept of substitution. The first assumes, after all, not only a pure identicalness or even oneness of the will of the substitute and the substituted, but – above anything else – an actual existence of the substituted. The substituted subject exists, is an actual reality, but for some reason (such as technical reasons) only cannot express his own will. The substituted (voter) is thus in this case the most real, actual and current person, however at that certain phase he cannot personally articulate his view and therefore his view is articulated on its behalf by someone else.

It perfectly corresponds with the thesis by G. Leibholz, according to which representation boils down to something being and not being present at the same time. The substituted and his will, though they cannot reveal themselves personally at any point in time, exist and are continuously present, however, they are present through their substitute who, when acting in a certain way, always acts for and on behalf of the real substituted person (under the imperative mandate approach, lacking *de jure* his own will). According to the second variant, the substituted is a *persona fictia* and his personality is *aliquid representatum* rather than something real. In this case, 'not the fact that certain individuals act for other people, but the fact that a certain person is a fiction and that is why certain

35 *Cf.* M. van der Hulst, *The Parliamentary Mandate. A Global Comparative Study*, Geneva 2000, p. 8, 9.

individuals act "for such a person" lies at the bottom of this structure'.[36] Thus, it turns out that the fundamental problem in the whole representation theory is the issue whether the represented is fictional or non-fictional.[37] Seemingly, two utterly different concepts may be followed in this regard. According to the first concept, the represented or the substituted, despite being a collective subject, clearly exists and is something real and present. According to the second concept, the sheer structure of such a collective subject (and its potential will) is an obvious fiction in itself, and the necessity of representation arises as a consequence of accepting the idea of a fictional existence of the represented. Representation in the first sense is therefore a logical implication of the existence of a collective subject additionally equipped with its own will. It is thus a consequence of a sort of a 'natural state of things'. On the other hand, in the second sense, representation itself comes into play because we consider a certain person (the represented) to be a fiction, and the consequence of such fiction is that the will of this fictional person must be articulated (or perhaps even created) in some way. If hypothetically we were to reject the idea of *fictio iuris*, then representation as a whole would become pointless, because a real, actually existing person would not need a representative to reveal his will.[38] Thus, while under the first variant of representation, the existence of volitional unity (oneness) of the delegate and the delegator is a consequence of the fact that the representative expresses a real will of the represented, under the second variant it is difficult to even talk about the existence of such a unity or oneness, if only the representative exists *de facto* and *de jure*, while the represented is only *aliquid representatum*.

3. The *Accessorium*: Sociological Interpretation of Representation

All types of sociological approaches also contribute to a proper discernment of the meaning and essence of the phenomenon of representation. Furthermore, it seems that nowadays these approaches cannot be ignored in any truly thoughtful and critical discussion on representation. Any clearly juridical approach, unless it is to be a sheer fiction, must – at least to a certain degree – refer to the

---

36 K. Grzybowski, *Teoria reprezentacji w Polsce epoki Odrodzenia*, Warszawa 1959, p. 16.

37 *Cf.* L. Jaume, *La représentation: une fiction malmenée*, 'Pouvoirs'2007, no. 120, p. 6 *et seq.*

38 M. Verpeaux, *Manuel de droit constitutionnel*, Paris 2010, p. 136 *et seq.*

sociological understanding of representation.[39] All the more so, since even *stricte* juridical ideas of deciphering the sense of representation more and more often refer to its sociological interpretation. If some time ago sociological analysis determined only certain juridical approaches (such as the English or, more widely, Anglo-Saxon one), today in fact there are no juridical ideas of representation that would not draw on, even complementarily, to its sociological construction.

Various sociological approaches seem not only fashionable, but above all indispensable. On the one hand they equate representation with 'responsible government', on the other hand with the 'public opinion government'. In the first case, which is more typical for the British legal literature, representation means government by an elite elected in general democratic elections and accountable to the voters for their policies. A critical *novum* is that the concept of representation is complemented by content compatibility between the principles of state policy and public opinions that connects this group of theories with the broad stream of *sensu stricto* sociological theories, i.e. the theory of 'public opinion government'. The latter theories not indirectly or incidentally, but straightforwardly, focus on explaining the phenomenon of representation, i.e. indirect government. In doing so, they in the first place deal with the issue of creating the governing elite, taking the view that this element of diagnosing the political system is the most vital for democracy, as democracy is nothing but a 'government of the people by an elite elected from amongst the people'.[40] Analysis of the act of designation cannot be lessened, as it is the case under the concept of representation-competence, to the sheer technical method of electing representatives or to giving the investiture to the governing ones. Here, emphasis is in fact laid on the substantive relationship between the governing and the governed, on their personal similarities and differences as well as on similarities and differences in their conduct. In the first

39 More on this topic: N. Loenen, *Citizenship and Democracy. A Case for Proportional Representation*, Toronto 1997.

40 M. Duverger, *Les partis politiques*, Paris 1967, p. 466. That is why very often the notion of representation is being reduced down to nothing more than the process of voting – *Cf.* J. Becquart-Leclerc, *Représentation…*, p. 914. *Obiter dictum* it should be noted that the merit of sociological theories is also that they highlight the fact that the ratio of representation is, as it were *ex definitione*, the ratio of the 'masses' (i.e. the represented) to the 'elite' (i.e. the representatives). Both the concept of 'responsible government' and even more so the concept of the 'public opinion government' reveals that – as regards the issues of representation – as a matter of fact this relationship comes down to successive acts of creation of a certain formal group (the elite), without any other additional content.

case, interest is being often focused on the purely descriptive attributes of representatives and their electorate, which is reflected in trimming down the entire issue to the so-called demographic representativeness of representative bodies.[41] Reviewing parliaments' members in terms of their social, professional, age cross-section, etc., and then comparing them with the corresponding proportions in a given society gives an indeed incomplete, and – what's worse – a static image of a representative body. And although it can hardly be described as irrelevant or marginal, it always remains a purely descriptive depiction of the issue of representation, although it must be admitted that very often it is the demographic representativeness, i.e. the proportions of certain socio-economic characteristics of a represented social group being reflected in the representative body, that is identified with representativeness as such.[42]

The second problem, namely the problem of similarities and differences that occur between the governed and the governing in their conduct and actions is, however, by far more important. The key issue here, first and foremost, is whether there is a certain general compliance, or at least absence of discrepancies, between the conduct of the governing, which is to say between the direction of the policy pursued by the governing group and the so-called public opinion. Governing is in fact to be based on public opinion, being a specific form of aggregating postulates and expectations articulated by the public opinion as to how the general state policy should be implemented. Under this perspective, the notions *democratic* and *representative* overlap to a certain extent alike two concentric circles of unequal size. The concept of representativeness is, however, a necessary prerequisite for any democratic system, without which the system would *ab initio* be undemocratic, but at the same time it is merely an initial condition, insufficient for a system to be considered democratic based merely on the attribute of its representativeness.

A specific manifestation (laced up in the bodice of the law) of the special treatment accorded to the public opinion government as a method of interpreting political representation was the nineteenth-century British theory of the mandate.[43] According to it, every meaningful political project, especially innovative, should be subject to a decision by the people, i.e. decision by the represented

41 More on this topic: M. Dogan, *L'origine sociale du personnel parlementaire français élu en 1951*, [in:] *Partis politiques et classe sociales en France*, M. Duverger (ed.), Paris 1955.

42 *Cf.* H. Eulau, J.C. Wahlke, W. Buchanan, L.C. Ferguson, *The Role of the Representative...*, p. 743.

43 *Cf.* P. Magdwick, *A New Introduction to British Politics*, London 1984, p. 275–276.

subject, unless it has previously been the subject of a proxy (granted in the process of elections). The intermediate link, i.e. the representatives, by definition have limited capacity for action and act only on those matters that have been passed over or assigned to them. Hence, if a new relevant issue arises, such an issue should unconditionally become an election issue and, accordingly, become the subject of a proxy (or mandate).[44] After all, representatives should always represent the view of the represented and, what's more, are in advance restrained in their actions, as being substitutes they cannot do more than the substituted. Thus, in the event an issue, particularly an issue of relevance, has not been the subject of a clear mandate granted in the act of investiture (granting a proxy to speak for and on behalf of the represented), then this should mandatorily be the basis for granting a new proxy, whose substantive scope will cover the matter so far not included in the principle of substitution.

Being a manifestation of an applied idea of representation, the theory of the mandate highlighted several matters of importance, particularly from the point of view of political representation. First of all, that each and every, and particularly far-reaching, decision should enjoy political acceptance of the represented. Secondly, that representatives are in principle limited in their actions by the sheer fact that they are *solely* representatives, while the limits of their mandate are clearly set by the investiture. Thirdly, that between the one and the other (i.e. between the representative of the represented) there should exist a relationship of conformity (identity) of wills, since representation is nothing other than an embodiment of public opinion. Fourthly, that due to its inherent limitations and being merely a 'substitute', representation is by definition an incomplete form of democratic government, where the *clou* is the political designation of the substitute by the substituted (which incidentally well shows that institutions of direct or pure democracy are always complementary towards the electorate). Fifthly and finally, that according to the classical theory of the mandate, representation is the only method of citizens' political participation, which in turn excludes the possibility of reverting to the institution of the referendum, even as an accessorial method. The essence of the concept of the mandate was contained, after all, in the requisite to renew the mandate (as the content of representation) rather than deployment of any alternative form of conceptualizing the will of the

44 It must be admitted that this theory corresponded with the majority of classical approaches to representation where the need for unity between the will on the one hand and the action of a representative as a proxy on the other hand was accentuated. More on this topic: C. Pateman, *Participation and Democratic Theory*, Cambridge 2000, p. 22 *et seq.*

represented subject. Hence, if the current mandate being the subject of the proxy proved insufficient for some reason, it was considered necessary to renew such a mandate, i.e. to grant (through elections) a new mandate changing the content of the earlier mandate. Only in this manner, it has been thought, can the idea of representation be reconciled with the idea of sovereignty (heavily accentuated by Albert V. Dicey[45]), the specific logical conjunction of which is the principle of political representation that is nothing but an axiological and praxeological validation of the political position of the parliament.[46]

For obvious reasons, and particularly due to the evident need to legitimize the represented and the entire political process where representation materialises,[47] the theory of the mandate is still valid and gains in attractiveness.[48] Increasingly, also due to the insufficient legitimacy, the need for granting an electoral mandate is recognized (as the British theory of the mandate has put it) in all the key decisions of the parliament in order to enable it to restore its position at least from a political perspective, since the legal devaluation of the role and importance of the parliament nowadays seems an obvious and probably irreversible fact.[49] Hence, if new room is being sought for the parliament within the space of the *polis*, it centers around the very process of representation which should lay emphasis on democracy and legitimacy of action of the contemporary legislative bodies.

It should be kept in mind that the British theory of the mandate corresponds very well with the general principles of political representation, all the while perfectly effectuating the idea of the public opinion government and concurrently a responsible government. It implements the ideal of political representation primarily because it actually constitutes a textbook case, since the mechanism of representation is most fully reflected in the influence of the society upon modelling the policy of the state and those in charge of it. On the other hand, the general idea of public opinion was embedded in the theory of

---

45 *Cf.* A.V. Dicey, *Introduction to the Study of the Law of the Constitution*, London 2012, p. 37 i n.

46 M. Elliott, *Parliamentary Sovereignty and the New Constitutional Order. Legislative Freedom, Political Reality and Convention*, 'Legal Studies' 2002, nr 3, p. 368.

47 *Cf.* A. Rehfeld, *The Concept of Constituency. Political Representation, Democratic Legitimacy and Institutional Design*, Cambridge 2008, p. 13 *et seq.*

48 *Cf.* P. Mair, *Political Parties, Popular Legitimacy and Public Privilege*, [in:] *The Crisis of Representation in Europe*, J. Hayward (ed.), New York 2005, p. 40 *et seq.*

49 More on this topic: D. Judge, *The Failure of National Parliaments*, [in:] *The Crisis of Representation...*, p. 79 *et seq.*

the mandate for the simple reason that under this theory the nation is assumed to designate, in the general elections, the direction of action for the governing for the term of their office. The responsible government component is introduced because the act of investiture makes the governing group responsible for implementing this program in successive elections, in which the group will seek re-election. The theory of the mandate is thus rooted in a 'promise' which the substitute (representative) makes to the substituted (represented).[50] This promise should be fulfilled with reference to the mandate and its substance demarcates the scope of action by the representative that may encounter resistance, should 'breach of promise' be claimed.[51] On the margin, the theory of the mandate also shows very vividly that it is not individual members of parliament but political parties that play the key role in the whole mechanism of representation. After all, the 'promise' today more often than not is the electoral program of political parties, and, more importantly, such a program is a binding commitment for the party. Moreover, the theory of the mandate in its pro-party version clearly ties a deputy with the party, in fact obligating the deputy to carry out the program of the party which he represented when he won the parliamentary mandate. The extreme version has it that the theory of the mandate is limited to saying that members of parliament should be considered party delegates subordinated to the party mandate. This shows that the theory of the mandate attempts to link various aspects of representation together. On the one hand, it combines strictly juridical concepts (the act of investiture and treatment of a representative as a delegate or substitute) with sociological concepts that view representation above all as a special form of public opinion government. On the other hand, it takes up an extremely important issue of the role of a single deputy and attempts to treat him not as an independent member of parliament unrelated in any way to a group of voters or to the organization on whose behalf he eventually became a beneficiary of the mandate, but as a person bound by the 'content' of the party manifesto. Being a manifestation of the 'election promise', the said content no longer binds just two traditional parties to a relationship of representation (i.e. the representative and the represented), but three parties, introducing as the third party

---

50 This by the way underlies the great majority of representation theories, although of course it is differently rendered by them. More on this topic: B. Garsten, *Representative Government and Popular Sovereignty*, [in:] *Political Representation*, I. Shapiro, S.C. Stokes, E.J. Wood, A.S. Kirshner (eds.), Cambridge 2009, p. 90 *et seq.*

51 P. Magdwick, *A New Introduction…*, p. 275.

of such a relationship the political party or any other organization that submits its electoral program for evaluation by the voters.[52]

Being in every respect a sociological concept, the concept of 'public opinion government' applies the term 'representation' to sociological phenomena. In this sense, it is a theory that is ideologically neutral which does not endeavour any axiological, ideological, political or even normative quantification of the notion of representation and representativeness.[53] Representation in this sense is trimmed down only to the similarity between political views of the nation and political views of its representatives. [54] Its true sense is contained in a 'more or less strict congruity between actions of the representative and the opinion of the represented'.[55] The main axis of such cognizance of representation is the convergence between the attitudes of the governed and attitudes and conduct of the governing. Thanks to this, the concept of representation embraces the idea of demographic representativeness, compliance, similarities in opinions and views, positions and actions of the represented and the representative. Furthermore, notably this approach also to some extent falls in line with a juridical view on representation as long as its objective is to recognize that the essence of representation lies in the consistency between the wills of a delegate and a delegator or, to put it in more general terms, the volitional relationship between the substitute and the substituted, which is perfectly corroborated by the British theory of the mandate. After all, an action by the Kelsen's substitute 'on the account' of the substituted also falls, at least partially, within the limits of a sociological concept, provided of course that we recognize that the essence of representation rests in the action for the benefit of the represented subject, and this in turn requires

52 *Cf.* D. Oliver, *The Parties and Parliament. Representative or Intra-party Democracy?*, [in:] *The Changing Constitution*, J. Jowell (ed.), D. Oliver, Oxford 1989, p. 126 *et seq.*

53 Such is the nature of the majority of representation theories, therefore, it is widely hinted in the literature that the principle of representation itself plays an important legitimizing role not only in relation to the parliament, but to the entire political system as well. Contrary to them, the concept of the 'public opinion government' is utterly neutral, not even attempting to transform the notion of representation into a normative rule, much less democratic legitimacy. Also in respect of the concept of 'responsible government', it is more of an empirical concept than a theoretical construct. *Cf.* M. Duverger, *Les partis politiques…*, p. 409. On ideologization of majority of concepts of representation, for instance: A. de Grazia, *Public and Republic. Political Representation in America*, New York 1951; J.A. Fairlie, *The Nature of Political Representation…*, p. 236 *et seq.*

54 *Cf.* M. Duverger, *Les partis politiques…*, p. 409.

55 G. Burdeau, *Traité de science politique*, Paris 1952, vol. IV, p. 267.

minimmum minimmorum of conformity of wills of both subjects (i.e. the substitute and the substituted).

4. Conjunction: Representation as a Correlation

It seems that the sociological interpretation of the meaning of the term 'representation' most faithfully reflects its linguistic sense. It makes its gist most realistic, meaning nothing beyond what is defined in the Latin *repraesentare*, i.e. making present something that is currently absent. The essence of representation lies in reiteration of the electorate's opinion at the level of the state governing bodies. Therefore, representation is best interpreted as the phenomenon of convergence (concordance) between the content of the decisions of the state and the public opinion. Thus, representation is always the relationship of two distinct dimensions. The content of the decision on the one hand and the public opinion on the other hand are in this case the two opposing dimensions which must be reconciled so that the actual content of the state decision falls in line with the content of the social opinions. The process of reconciliation means that representation should never be considered solely in static terms as a particular condition or a state reached as a result of certain action. Compatibility between actions of the representatives and opinions of the represented indeed does not remain constant or unvarying, nor does it hibernate. It is a process[56] during which the status of compliance can be, and usually is, subject to multifarious fluctuations. The phenomenon of representation should therefore be expounded as the process of convergence of the content of state decisions with the views of the governing. Adopting such an assumption is to primarily emphasize the fact that representation is an unceasing process of assimilation of decisions and opinions, and the intensity of this process as well as its effectiveness may be discrepant and fluctuate over time. Being a process and therefore a dynamic phenomenon, representation therefore encircles a whole set of phenomena, social situations and conduct, as a result of which the decisions of the governing and the opinions of the governed converge.

Adopting the sociological interpretation of the term 'representation' should in no case depreciate its normative value. More than that, its full juridical explication becomes possible only once this context is taken in. The opinions of the represented subject, being a point of reference for the process of correlation with the decisions on the state policy, remain after all *la clef de voûte* of the phenomenon

56 *Cf.* J. Becquart-Leclerc, *Représentation…*, p. 914.

of representation. This facilitates, at the same time providing the grounds for, the capacity to assign the will expressed by the representatives to the represented subject. This 'attribution' is in fact the essence of the juridical structure of representation, making the juridical interpretation of the concept of representation largely ideologized, and in any case certainly ideologically non-neutral. Its normative sense lies in the 'legally legitimized exercise of state power on behalf of a collective bearer of sovereignty [...] by constitutionally defined state bodies'.[57] The ideologization of the legal, that is purely competence-oriented approach to the phenomenon of representation, which limits representation to distribution of competences between voters and their representatives, where the voter's competence is to designate his representative, while the representative's competence is to act and carry himself to implement the proxy granted to him, at that it is not associated with just the 'distribution of tasks', but with the legitimization of such a distribution. This legitimization in fact justifies the specific *de jure* expropriation of the voter from performing these tasks and powers, which via the elections are passed upon the mandate holder. It is, after all, this legitimacy that is subsequently conveyed into specific concepts of the mandate, either free or imperative, non-restricted or bound, which always has a strong ideological dimension. A simple example of far-reaching ideologization of the discourse on representation is the opposition between a free and imperative mandate. From an ideological point of view, the first of the two corresponds to all those ideas that discern deliberation in representation. Manifestly, firmly reflected here is the thought of E. Burke for whom the freedom of action of the representative was the starting point of deliberation in which the common good was 'forged'. The imperative mandate in turn is a radically different conception of approaching representation in terms of aggregation. The mandate holder himself can do nothing, nor has a free will, as he is only a cogwheel in a specific political arithmetic. The general will (which, after all, should always remain in the focus regardless of the possible perspectives on representation) in this case is the sum of individual specific wills. Therefore, it is the proverbial 'large number' achieved through aggregation. This is the way of thinking about representation promoted by J.J. Rousseau and his followers, who consistently believe that representation cannot trigger any other will that would differ from the will of the represented, and this in turn is conceptualized through mathematics, that is adding up one individual will to another. The source of conflict between the two designs of the mandate is thus ideology, and more specifically the manner in which it treats the general will, which is to

57 B. Banaszak, *Reprezentacja*, [in:] *Słownik wiedzy o Sejmie*, Warszawa 2001, p. 176.

be expressed (or perhaps only reflected) through representation.[58] In the event of the free mandate, it is deemed that the general will is not identical with the individual will(s) and that it is formed as an outcome of political deliberation of the representatives. Quite the reverse, the imperative mandate recognizes that the general will is merely the sum of individual wills, which is in no way created, but merely recreated and disclosed through the process of aggregation.

The concept of proportional or majoritarian representation[59] or, in another sense, democratic and, on the contrary, undemocratic, conservative, backward, and even reactionist representation has the same *par excellence* ideological dimension. In particular, the question whether representation should be proportional or perhaps majority representation (deploying an algorithm to redistribute seats in the parliament) entangles representation from an ideological point of view. By all means, the paradox of social differentiation is ideological. Furthermore, the aspect whether or not the structure of the representative body should express the primitive in fact principle of majority or perhaps the principle of multiplicity and variety of structures, features and characteristics of the subject, which ultimately is to be represented, is ideological as well.[60]

Ideological and certainly strong political undertone of the concept of representation is curbed, at least in some measure, by a sociological analysis of representation that binds representation with the concept of 'public opinion government'. Therefore, it cannot be unequivocally said that representation stands for either delimitation of competence (the juridical approach) or merely appointment of a substitute (another variant of the juridical approach) or, another perspective of a juridical concept of representation, the volitional unity of the representative and the represented, or – last but not least – the process of convergence of the content of the representative's decision with the content of the opinion expressed by the represented (sociological approach). The true, genuine sense of representation is expressed only in those concepts that combine the *strictly* juridical approach with the sociological approach, which is perhaps best articulated in the concept of responsible government and its special form, that is the theory of the mandate.[61] This is because on the one hand it accentuates the juridical sphere, providing for the exercise of the public authority by authorized representatives of the people, yet on the other hand it lays emphasis on the importance of the

58 *Cf.* A. Waśkiewicz, *Paradoksy idei reprezentacji politycznej*, Warszawa 2012, p. 207.

59 *Cf.* C. Émeri, *Représentation proportionnelle*, [in:] *Dictionnaire constitutionnel…*, p. 917 *et seq.*

60 *Cf.* A. Waśkiewicz, *Paradoksy idei…*, p. 279.

61 *Cf.* W.I. Jennings, *The British Constitution*, Cambridge 1966, p. 195.

sociological context of representation, assuming the need for an even minimum *iunctionis* of the decisions of the governing with the views of the governed. It follows that representation must be seen, first, as a sociological phenomenon which boils down to substantive reconciliation and the consequent convergence of all decisions pertaining to the policy of the state with the views of the represented subject, i.e. individuals and social groups prevailing in the society that are the point of reference for the process of correlation with state decisions. Secondly, representation must be assessed through the lens of the constitutional principle established under the strictly juridical approach by the idea or principle of political representation.[62] In this second, constitutional and juridical sense, representation is contained in the competence of exercising the powers of the state on behalf of the collective bearer of sovereignty by the constitutionally designated authority of the state, 'whereas from this principle one may infer the existence, on the part of the governing, of the obligation to create conditions and provide the means needed to promote the process of assimilation of the prevailing social views with the decisions of the state'.[63]

The principle of representation finds its reflection in the wording, according to which the people exercise power through representatives, thus it is manifestly complementary to the principle of popular sovereignty of the nation.[64] In this sense, it also plays the role of democratic legitimization of not only the representative body itself, but also the *tout court* political system, since it conjoins the principle of sovereignty with powers of sovereign state authorities, including

62 *Cf.* P. Sarnecki, *Zasada reprezentacji*, [in:] *Prawo konstytucyjne*, P. Tuleja (ed.), Warszawa 1997, p. 26 *et seq.*

63 B. Banaszak, *Reprezentacja…*, p. 176.

64 Therefore, among others, the view that representation is an essential element of popular sovereignty and that both these concepts, i.e. representation and sovereignty, are inextricably paired, is accepted as indisputable. Many authors find it impossible to ponder upon the question on the content of the principle of popular sovereignty without considering the content of the contemporary principle of representation. Therefore, chronological precedence of the principle of popular sovereignty, on the basis of which the principle of representation was construed, is rather widely accepted. The views reversing chronological relationship between these two principles are quite rare – *Cf.* P. Avril, J. Gicquel, *Droit parlementaire*, Paris 1988, p. 25. However, regardless of the degree of correlation between both these principles, the fact of their interpenetration and complementarity is beyond dispute – *Cf.* e.g. P. Avril, *Les origines de la représentation parlementaire*, 'Commentaire' 1985, no. 30.

above all the parliaments.[65] Its normative nature manifests itself most fully in the legal relationship that is established through it between citizens (the sovereign) and their representatives. On the part of the governing, it triggers the duty to create conditions for the establishment and maintenance of this relationship throughout its duration. Hence, the objective is to ensure the existence of measures necessary for a proper implementation of the process of assimilating the prevailing social opinion with the decisions taken by the state.

The ultimate adoption of precisely this approach to representation transpired as a result of a long-lasting process that generally speaking embraced four major and perhaps central types or models of representation (representing). Chronologically, under the first of those models the representative was the owner of his function (such as the hereditary monarch); under the second, a certain political order was represented by community members or groups that construed this order (such as the estate assemblies; while the third of the models assumed bound representation under an imperative mandate and the right to recall the representative by the represented. Finally, the last, i.e. the fourth model has introduced free representation, under which the 'representative is not bound by any instructions and remains the master of his actions,[66] but at the same time it is anticipated that he is by no means a 'free electron', but enjoys political empowerment by the represented. The underlying idea of representation in any of the forms in which it does or may occur is that the representative (the delegate or the substitute) is perceived exactly as the representative, which means that he cannot be regarded as the owner of his specific function in line with the assumption that he expresses only his own interests and position.[67] Representation (or the relationship of representation) is nonetheless always a relationship, the parties whereof are the represented subject and the representing subject. Even today, under the universal formula of representation bearing the representative (free representation) signs, it is accepted that an MP is not legally bound by instructions, orders or bans (as it used to be in the case of the earlier structures of the imperative mandate), but at the same time expresses someone's interests[68] and it is not so that he represents himself only. The modern formula of the representative (free) mandate ripped free the relationship between the representative and

65 *Cf.* S. Pierré-Caps, *Le constitutionnalisme et la nation*, [in:] *Le nouveau constitutionnalisme. Mélanges en l'honneur de Gérard Conac*, Paris 2001, p. 67 *et seq.*

66 M. Granat, *Zasada reprezentacji politycznej*, [in:] *Polskie prawo konstytucyjne*, ed. W. Skrzydło, Lublin 2010, p. 116.

67 *Cf.* A. Rehfeld, *The Concept of Constituency...*, p. 19 *et seq.*

68 *Cf.* M. van der Hulst, *The Parliamentary Mandate...*, p. 8.

the principal of the mandate, yet it did not eliminate any mutual relationships. So, it still remains the essence of representation with a reservation that it reverses the direction of its interpretation in its own way. Today, on the assumption of a free mandate, it is not the MP who is bound by the will of the voters. It is rather the electorate of the given MP that identifies itself with the interests presented by the MP, considering these interests their own and therefore voting for him during the elections.

Of course, such structure of the concept of representation assuming consequently that the representative is independent from the represented, while at the same time expressing not his own will, but the will of the represented, was not an autarkic product, detached from wider processes and phenomena associated with the development of parliament and parliamentarism. On the contrary, it was closely tied to them, co-forming them and constituting their natural follow-up and progression. This slow, though steady evolution of such a thoroughly modern concept of representation has been particularly impacted by attainments of the Middle Ages, particularly the emergence of the English formula of the 'King-in-Parliament'.[69] It was the positioning of these two mutually conjugated authorities, i.e. the monarch and the parliament, at the top of the system of state power that laid the foundations for the newly interpreted institution of the mandate (representation). And although in the feudal England the backbone of representation was not the proxy granted to the representative by the represented, but the legal unity between the representatives and the represented,[70] nonetheless, elevating the parliament (composed of the King, the House of Commons and the House of Lords) as a representative body to the position of the sovereign authority in the state, where decisions were made upon the consent and with the participation of representatives, made the actions of representatives (although at the time they represented *stricte* estate privileges, but nonetheless were representatives) actions of clearly political representation.

The parliament did not become *par excellence* representation right until the moment of transposing of the concept of sovereignty from the monarch to the nation,[71] when the exercise of power by the sovereign himself became technically

69 *Cf.* H.-Y. Lee, *Political Representation in the later Middle Ages*, New York 2008, p. 34 *et seq*.

70 *Ibidem*, p. 35, 36.

71 At this moment it became obvious that the monarch had to be deprived of the right to oppose the will of the parliament, which expressed the will of the true sovereign, i.e. the people. *Cf.* C. Clavreul, *Sieyès et la genèse de la représentation moderne*, 'Droits' 1987, no. 6, p. 56.

undoable.[72] Then the representative system in which power is exercised by representatives, but on behalf of a collective bearer of sovereignty, that is the nation (the people), became the rule. It is not the same as the civilistic concept of representation, namely an action *per procura* and with a direct effect for the represented person, but representation understood as a concept opposed to the principle of legal identity (unity) of the representatives with the represented. Thus understood principle of representation set against the doctrinal background of Edmund Burke, Emmanuel Sieyès or Gerhard Leibholz is built on the concept of national community as a spiritual, indirectly perceived social oneness.[73] The will of this oneness is, however, absent on account of the fact that the nation (the sovereign) itself is absent as a whole *hic et nunc*, and so its will must be incarnated as a unity by the social substratum, i.e. by the elected representative body. Thus, representatives of the sovereign who sit in the parliament serve by their word and action to find a supra-individual general will, whereas the necessary correlate of this value, embodied by the representatives, is a wholly determined self-value of the representative, which means that only the very best and most qualified personalities are appointed to the most prominent office of a member of the parliament. Representation in this traditional classical approach is therefore a legal structure that entails assignment of the will expressed by the deputies to the represented subject, that is the nation. In other words, public authority is not exercised directly by a subject equipped with an attribute of sovereignty, but in his name and on his behalf by his representatives, whose will is identified with the will of the sovereign represented by these representatives.

This attribution to the sovereign of the will of its representatives boils down to the fact that the whole nation gives a collective and impersonal mandate to all its representatives.[74] The common good is thus conceptualized by the

72 *Cf.* Y. Mény, Y. Surel, *Politique comparée. Les démocraties*, Paris 2009, p. 239, 240.

73 *Cf.* H.-Y. Lee, *Political Representation…*, p. 13 *et seq.*

74 It is the so-called classical concept of representation. Differently, under the non-classical approach, every citizen grants an individual mandate, i.e. a personal mandate, to a selected representative. This way the representative accumulates mandates from a large number of citizens (his voters). Hence, the non-classical concept of representation brings the concept of representation closer to the concept of a proxy under civil law. In this case, being unable to perform an action himself, the voter grants to another person a proxy to execute such action in his name and on his behalf. Thus the powers of the mandator are clearly limited on the one hand by the possibility of revoking the proxy and, on the other hand, by the limited – individual after all – scope of the proxy. Evidently, this structure is the starting point for an imperative mandate

representatives of the people, who according to the well-known metaphor by E. Sieyès were the lips of the nation and were capable of expressing its sovereign will. This is exactly where the recognition of identity between the mandate holders and the mandate came from, and the identity that was at play was juridical, fictional. It was assumed that the mandate holder acted as a mandator or even was a mandator himself[75] and therefore it was accepted that the mandator was the same person as the person granting the mandate. In connection with the foregoing, the representative endowed by the sovereign with the mandate expresses the will, yet not the real will, but the legal will of the nation–sovereign, by his actions and conduct in the representative body. Therein lies the essence of the so-called juridical fiction of representation. It is based on the assumption that the collective bearer of sovereignty (equated with the whole electorate) grants, through the act of designation, a mandate to representatives elected by himself to represent its will, and the will of the representatives is then attributed to the nation. In this perspective the nation is not endowed with any specific will; this will is only formulated by its representatives acting in the representative body, whereas the said will is not apportioned to representatives, but to the sovereign itself. In consequence, the juridical fiction of representation precluded the existence of some real, actually existing will of the people, separate from that formulated by the authority appointed to do so, i.e. by the parliament.[76] Thus, not only was the nation denied the existence of a separate will other than the will expressed by its representatives, but in addition the existence of the nation beyond the parliament was negated as well, from which followed the nation's legal identification with its representatives.[77] Thanks to this structure, mandate holders elected in general elections which, as we know, are the basic form of

of various types, restraining the freedom of the representative by demarcating the limits of his authorisation.

75 This is exactly where the identification of the concept of the mandate and representation comes from – *Cf.* J.L. Gazzaniga, *Mandat et représentation...*, p. 28.

76 *Cf.* M. Hauriou, *La souveraineté nationale*, Paris 1912, p. 33 *et seq.*

77 Inevitably, this led to the independence of deputies (this is where the modern concept of the representative mandate originated from) and the recognition of the sovereignty of the parliament. The parliament was, after all, the sole exponent of the will of the people, therefore *ex definitione* it had to be on top of the state bodies, and the actual sovereign (the nation) was devoid of any opportunity of challenging the decisions of the representative body (it was logical, since the nation as such was not endowed with its own will). It also impinged on other issues, such as the principle of sovereignty of an act of parliament, which in England finds its fullest expression in the statement that the Parliament can do anything except turn a man into a woman and woman into

correlation, i.e. reconciliation of position between the representatives and the represented, become *de jure* substitutes of the people empowered to have the will on behalf of the people (*la puissance de vouloir pour la nation*).

5. Limits of Representation: Forms and Means of Correlation

However, a question arises whether there exists any criterion of representativeness in the above-accepted meaning of representation as a process of convergence of attitudes and views of the society with attitudes and views of representatives, whose will is then transposed as the will of the sovereign itself? And if so, what criterion is it? In other words, is there a certain limit beyond which the relationship between the content of the representatives' decisions and the attitudes and views of the represented ceases to qualify as the relationship of representation? It seems that an efficient system of correlation, i.e. the mechanism for reaching convergence between decisions of the state and social opinions, is such a limit. This mechanism is contained in the process of reconciliation between the content of public opinion and the content of a state decision by way of mutual interaction. The basic formula of this mechanism is of course comprised in the general elections, during which the people make a personal and program-based choice of their representatives to the representative bodies, granting to them, in a *stricte* competence-wise approach, the investiture to govern. It is therefore the prerogative of the sovereign to grant approval, i.e. give a vote of confidence to a certain group of people to hold a public office and the right to reiterate such approval during the next elections. At the same time, the sovereign is endowed with a contrasting right, i.e. the right to refuse to give the vote of confidence and to transfer the approval to another group of persons, thus asserting disapproval.[78]

The right to assert approval (or, contrariwise, disapproval) seems to be the key factor of the juridical approach to the phenomenon of representation. Therein lies the competence of granting investiture to the governing, i.e. acting for and on behalf of the represented (according to the Kelsen's idea of a substitute). Besides, the duality contained in the right of approval and disapproval, making up the concept of investiture, is the basis for the phenomenon of alternation of power, which is, after all, the substance of every democratic system. Without

a man. The most well-known promoter of the concept of the Parliament's sovereignty was Carré de Malberg.

78 More on this topic: E. Kaufmann, *Zur Problematik des Volkswillens*, Berlin 1931, p. 13 *et seq.*

the right of disapproval, each and every investiture granted through the act of voting would be constrained to the repetition of the right of approval expressed in the earlier elections, which in turn means that the trust that exists between the representative and the represented, the said trust being the true substance of the representative mandate, would dwindle. Therefore, it is not only the formal right of designation, but the right of disapproval – closely correlated therewith – that predetermines the actual substance of representation. Without the approval/disapproval alternative, there is really no representation and, what follows, no democracy.[79] This is the reason why the concept of being representative and democratic are too often treated as synonyms or, in any case, similar terms. No real alternative is so characteristic for all sorts of authoritarian systems, or in broader terms non-democratic regimes, as these systems reject the essential fundamentals of representation, namely reconciliation of positions between the represented and its representative. This shows best the weight of the sociological analysis of the phenomenon of representation that accentuates the need for convergence of views and approaches by the sovereign with the views and approaches of its representatives. This means that the necessary substratum of representation, naturally over and above the technical appointment of representatives by general elections, is the public opinion, which thanks to representation is to be transformed into a content of a decision of the state.[80] Representation signifies not only and is not limited to the sheer formal procedure of granting the investiture or, in a slightly different perspective, designation of a substitute or a deputy, but also, or perhaps above all, the convergence of view of the represented with the view of the representative. Convergence or even oneness of views (positions, opinions and approaches) of the representative and the represented (even without going into details as to who actually is to be represented) is, after all, the true essence of every political representation, best reflecting the general idea that representation aims at making the absent present. It seems that it is exactly this opinion, though often defined and understood differently, is the most vital, i.e. the material attribute of the concept of representation that gives it a real and actual, rather than merely procedural, content.[81] Apt mirroring of the public

79 Although it should be kept in mind that the issue of mutual relationship between terms such as representation and democracy remains a complex and controversial issue. More on this topic: D. Runciman, M. Brito Vieira, *Representation*, Cambridge 2008, p. xii *et seq*.

80 More on this topic: G. Burdeau, *L'evolution des techniques d'expression de l'opinion publique dans la démocratie*, [in:] *L'Opinion publique*, Paris 1957, p. 140 *et seq*.

81 *Cf.* C. Pateman, *Participation and Democratic…*, p. 22 *et seq*.

opinion, and more precisely, of the opinion of the whole electorate, takes place via the process of general elections and therefore elections remain the principal form of correlation, at the same time constituting the *clou* of the whole process of representation. What is revealed during elections is the purely competence-oriented, i.e. juridical aspect of representation alongside with its social or sociological nature. On the one hand, elections comprise a process where the power to elect and to be elected and, what directly follows, the power to take all the actions provided for under the law on behalf of the electors is subject to strict delimitation. On the other hand, and perhaps most importantly, elections are the same procedure through which political or ideological options are rightly translated into the membership of a representative body, whereby the parliament is, or at least should be, a kind of a mirror reflecting the sentiment of the public opinion. Thus, it is not until the two conditions for the right choice are jointly met, i.e. a purely juridical, competence-oriented requirement offering a real opportunity of choice thanks to the approval/disapproval alternative, and the sociological condition, thanks to which the whole heterogeneity of the represented subject will be mapped, that the representation elected during the given elections process can be deemed full, perfect or perhaps simply democratic.[82]

Remaining an elemental form of correlation, elections are thus a certain, legally institutionalized way of manifesting the existence of a specific view on a given aspect, of exerting direct pressure on the addressee of this manifesto in order to have it considered. A series of correlation means, i.e. public institutions aimed at articulating public opinion, of which the most important are undoubtedly political parties, back up this mechanism.[83] Party interference is so far-reaching at this point in time that it substantially modifies both the very concept of representation as well as the consequent concept of the representative mandate and, last but not least, the work of the parliament itself. Hence, the legal literature makes more and more frequent references not only to the so-called 'particracy' or 'party democracy' (*démocratie de partis*)[84] or 'party government', but to *Parteienstaat* as well. In consequence, the image of a representative representing the sovereign is replaced with the image of a representative representing a political party, thanks to which he could have been elected to parliament, and only then, via the party, as if in the second place,

82 *Cf.* R. Eckrsley, *Representing Nature*, [in:] *The Future of Representative Democracy*, S. Alonso, J. Keane, W. Merkel (eds.), Cambridge 2011, p. 236 *et seq.*

83 *Cf.* I.M. Young, *Inclusion and Democracy*, Oxford 2002, p. 164 *et seq.*

84 D. Mineur, *Archéologie de la représentation…*, p. 210.

representing the proper sovereign, that is the people.[85] It obviously affects the perception of the bearer of sovereignty and its rights, since in a democracy of a party state the will of the majority of the parties at the given moment is put on par with *volonté générale*.

Monopoly of political parties in the process of founding and maintaining the process of representation is indisputable these days.[86] It is also probably the greatest reason for challenging, at least occasionally, the pure or theoretical concept of political representation that presumes representation, by free and unconstrained mandate holders, of an abstract will of the overall represented subject (regardless of the fact that, after all, the issue how to conceptualise this will was most contentious one). Nonetheless, the phenomenon of other subjects, including pressure groups or even narrower lobby groups, competing with political parties that have so far remained the main – if not the sole – means of correlation becomes increasingly discernible. Consequently, although the present role of political parties remains uncontested, yet 'non-party' circles, groups and organizations play an increasingly vital role in the process of correlation. Hence, as it seems, the phenomenon of representation deepens or at least potentially may deepen even further in the sense that reconciliation of views of the representatives and the represented is more and more across-the-board and ever more faithful. Thus, besides political parties, the articulating and aggregating of public opinion becomes the domain of a variety of movements and groups, both formal and informal, and associations, organizations, pressure groups *sensu stricto* and, finally, lobbies. This phenomenon reflects the tendency of forming a consensual, participatory and finally neo-corporatist democracy,[87] in which more and more centres that formulate diverse demands, views and opinions appear. In such a democracy, these groups are increasingly taking on a decision-making role, while not only the means of correlation via which the views of the represented and the representatives are reconciled, but also the forms of correlation are substantially expanded and enriched. Although elections remain the central mechanism of creating the

85 *Cf.* Y. Mény, Y. Surel, *Politique comparée…*, p. 241.

86 *Cf.* J.-L. Déotte, *Représebtation et politique*, [in:] *Représentaion et politique…*, p. 29 *et seq*.

87 More on this topic: A. Lijphart, M.M.L. Crepaz, *Corporatism and Consensus Democracy in Eighteen Countries: Conceptual and Empiricial Linkages*, 'British Journal of Political Science' 1991, vol. 21, no. 2, p. 235 *et seq.*; A. Lijphart, *Democracy in Plural Societies. A Comparative Exploration*, New Haven–London 1977, p. 25 *et seq.*; G. Tsebelis, *Veto Players. How Political Institutions Works*, New York 2002, p. 67 *et seq.*

relationship of representation, since they result in investiture being granted as well as personal and program-based designations of substitutes being made, yet they have ceased to be the fundamental, and certainly the sole, mechanism of seeking convergence between the will of the represented and the representative. Apart from them, a growing number of procedures come up (such as strikes, demonstrations, pickets, various kinds of *ad hoc* bottom-up initiatives, mass media), as a result of which the genuine will of the represented comes to light, thus turning the whole mechanism of representation into an everlasting process that continues to unfold itself, and is not time-censored by the ticking of the electoral clock. These – other than the elections – forms of correlation are particularly important when the juridical concept of representation (regardless of whether it is applied only to the redistribution of competence, act of investiture, appointment of a delegate, or merely the 'attribution' of will) is supplemented by a sociological outlook upon representation, requiring convergence between the views of the represented and their representatives. Regardless of the details, representation as political agency is always focused on one and the same, that is action for the benefit of the represented subject, which in turn requires consideration of the views, opinions and interests of such subject.

Thus, it turns out that the presently observed clear reorientation of the conditions for realization of the idea of political representation need not necessarily question or otherwise undermine it. For instance, party dominance in the process of correlation, often identified with the idea of *Parteienstaat*, did not challenge representation understood as the process of unifying attitudes of the represented and their representatives. If we were to refer even to the British theory of the mandate, the opposite is true. Only the political party and its election manifesto constitutes the content of the 'promise' which becomes the *meritum* of the mandate (i.e. in other words, of the representative relationship). It is a fact, however, that regardless of the degree to which we accept and carry out the theory of the mandate in practice, at some point a representative became in the first place the representative of the party or a fraction which he represents or at least is somehow related to. It is also a fact that this party bond of the representative (obvious and natural for the theory of the mandate, yet less obvious, and sometimes downright embarrassing in some sense for other theories) has been successfully compensated for by giving rise to a number of groups, communities and organizations that, like parties, have grown to be the means of political correlation. Forms of correlation have nowadays outgrown the electoral arena, often in a different way articulating (though no longer necessarily aggregating) the will of the represented. Consequently, representation as such has not only remained undisputed, but at least to a certain degree it has grown even deeper due to the emergence of a polycentric system of centres of formulating public opinion,[88] the proper articulation and aggregation of which in the representative body is, after all, the essence of representation.

The involvement of political parties and other organizational structures alongside them (such as trade unions, employers' organizations, associations, foundations, etc.) in the process of representation makes political representation, also that dressed in the form of a constitutional norm, more and more often viewed through the prism of sociology.[89] Personal and political compositions of representative bodies are therefore expected in the first place to be representative, i.e. to reflect, at least roughly, the socio-political cross-section of the electorate. Notably, today this is the elementary criterion for assessing political representation and whether it is appropriate and accurate. At the same time, considering the sociological cross-section of the represented, it is acknowledged that the process of representation is fuller, better and more accurate if various kinds of representative fora emerge beyond the parliament itself. Therefore, in this regard, 'an extra-parliamentary "continuation of the politics" that goes beyond the realm of widely understood parliamentary and cabinet connections'[90] is said to come into play. What is meant by this covers all kinds of bodies representing particular social, professional and economic interests which, grouped together, are to complement the process of political representation at the level of the *polis*, thereby recreating an authentic, namely sociological cross-section of the represented groups.[91] The emergence of interest groups, quite broadly understood, opened up the process of representation, but also changed its political importance. Previously political representation had been identified with national representation, that is, with the parliament. Alternatively, today it is acknowledged that a true representation, thus a representation that reflects the sociological image of the represented group must inexorably be complemented by other representative structures that

88 What in a sense corresponds with the concept of polyarchy, which contemporary democracy embodies today. More on this topic: R. Dahl, *Polyarchy: Participation and Opposition*, New Haven–London 1971. *Cf.* also A.H. Birch, *Concepts and Theories of Modern Democracy*, New York 2007, p. 133 *et seq.*

89 *Cf.* M. Duverger, *Institutions politiques et droit constitutionnel*, Paris 1966, p. 81.

90 R. Herbut, *Reprezentacja*, [in:] *Leksykon politologii*, A. Antoszewski, R. Herbut (eds.), Wrocław 1995, p. 344.

91 *Cf.* R. Mouriaux, *Syndicats, organisations professionnelles et groupes d'intérêt*, [in:] *Institutions et vie politique*, ed. J.-L. Parodi, Paris 2003, p. 115 *et seq.*

will reveal the entire sociological heterogeneity of the represented subject.[92] For the sociological composition of the group to be as faithfully represented as possible in the representative body, such forms of correlation which will actually allow achieving it to the maximum possible extent must be applied. Hence, this is the origin of the natural weight of electoral procedures, which should be arranged in such a way so as not to cause an excessive deformation (in the form of over-representation or under-representation) of the electorate's will.[93] Therefore, sociological interpretation of representation, perceiving it as a replication of the socio-political composition of a group within a body representing this group stems from a purely 'technical' understanding of representation. Pursuant to its etymological meaning of representing someone or something, the latter treats representation as a mechanism for the redistribution of the mandates;[94] whereas very often connecting the technical meaning of representation with its sociological connotation makes only the proportional electoral system to be perceived as being representative.[95]

Ireespective of which of the electoral systems we ultimately believe to be much closer to the sociological concept of representation or even, in more extreme cases, which one *is* representation, it is a fact that representation (apart from the above described philosophical, juridical and sociological approaches) may be approached in technical terms only. In such case, representation will denote a system allowing to select the 'few' who will act on behalf of 'many', represent their interests and beliefs and take care of their implementation at a wide, institutionalized forum. Nonetheless, it should be kept in mind that the 'technical' outlook on representation does not always and not necessarily need to refer to electoral procedures only, although admittedly it is probably the most common case.[96] However, in the technical sense, representation can also be reduced to its institutional dimension, namely to the parliament. Under such an assumption, representation will be tantamount simply to the representative body of the people.[97]

---

92 *Cf.* C. Haguenau-Moizard, *Les systèmes politiques européens*, Paris 2009, p. 74.

93 *Cf.* A. Lijphart, *Degrees of Proportionality of Proportional Representation Formulas*, [in:] *Electoral Laws and their Political Consequences*, B. Grofman, A. Lijphart (eds.), New York 2003, p. 170 *et seq.*

94 *Cf.* P. Blachèr, *Droit constititionnel*, Paris 2009, p. 79.

95 *Cf.* B. Pauvert, Élections et modes de scrutin, Paris 2006, p. 12 *et seq.*

96 More on this topic: Ch.R. Hayward, *Making Interest: On Representation and Democratic Legitimacy*, [in:] *Political Representation…*, p. 111 *et seq.*

97 *Cf.* P. Laundy, *Les parlements dans le monde contemporain*, Lausanne 1989, p. 28.

It is clear that the technical meaning of representation is strongly simplified, and – as such – failing to denote all the nuances cloaked in the phenomenon of representation. Thus, apart from the technical meaning, also its normative significance is highlighted. At the same time it should be noted that normative approach to representation is not at all identical, as it might seem, with the juridical approach as proposed by G. Burdeau or M. Prélot. For the latter, as well known, representation denoted nothing more than competence or, more specifically, a form of division of powers between the two subjects in a relationship of representation, i.e. the representative and the represented. Meanwhile, a normative perception of representation means its recognition as a constitutional norm alone (properly articulated), allowing for reconciliation of the basic canon of constitutionalism, which is the supremacy of a collective subject (the people, the nation) with the fact that in reality it cannot function in a direct way, except in situations which are by definition exceptional.[98] Thus, in this case representation signifies an indication or manifestation of the constitutional principle of sovereignty of the people (the nation) and a specific mechanism of its practical application.[99] If, however, the issue is to be approached more broadly, representation in a normative sense would mean nothing but an indirect method of exercise of sovereign rights by a collective subject, that is, the nation, hence in other words the establishment of a regime of indirect (representative) democracy.[100]

Bringing out the technical and normative sense of political representation, does not, however, exhaust all its conceivable meanings. In the proposed system (besides representation in technical and normative terms), representation can be classified in the so-called functional meaning. What is understood by it is such a mechanism of political decision-making that can be shared by dominant segments of social, political and economic divisions. Thus, under the functional understanding of representation, the final decision is to be a decision that subscribes to various points of view, taken in a multi-phase procedure of involving different bodies, both formal as well as informal, which together will present the most significant structures (cleavages) coming to light in the represented group. The functional approach to representation thus lays emphasis on the mechanism of public decision-making, which must be designed in such a manner so that it can disclose (present) different views and positions. The ultimate decision

98 *Cf.* M.-A. Cohendet, *Droit constitutionnel*, Paris 2008, p. 435, 436.
99 *Cf.* M. Verpeaux, *Manuel de droit…*, p. 87 *et seq.*
100 *Cf.* M.-A. Cohendet, *Droit constitutionnel…*, p. 436.

need not, of course, take into account each and every view and opinion (which would be impossible anyway), but must offer an opportunity of unveiling these differences, so that the decision can be rational in the fullest sense of the word, taken in a methodically and pragmatically optimal manner.[101]

Regardless of the adopted positions and points of view, every representation is merely a form of arranging a decision-making mechanism. Representation, no matter how defined and implemented in practice, is to offer grounds to present specific reasons, views, positions and opinions, and hence to organize the decision-making procedures in a way that will simply ensure that a good decision is made (whatever that means). Such a decision can potentially be made by, for instance, taking a philosophical perspective on representation. Then representation will be a presentation of values, ideals and principles that should be taken into account when making a decision, a specific form of care applied to ensure that certain imponderables are respected and remain intact. However, such a decision can be made under a strictly juridical interpretation of representation, which means the division of tasks between the represented and the representative. On the other hand, focusing on the sociological point of view, representation will mean taking a decision in such a way that the decision-maker is a kind of 'social cross-section' of the represented or, from a slightly different angle, that different positions or different, yet relevant social groups are taken into account in the decision-making mechanism. If we approach representation from a technical perspective, in the decision-making mechanism we will be laying emphasis on the procedure of selecting the decision-maker bearing in mind that this procedure will have to link up self-contradictory values such as representativeness and effectiveness. If we were to treat representation in a normative way, we would be suggesting that the decision is taken by a narrower body, but always with an effect that is binding upon all, because it is what the essence of indirect democracy is all about. Further, the functional approach to representation will require including all or almost all important social and political divisions, which divulge themselves in the political system, into the decision-making mechanism. Yet always, no matter what approach to representation we ultimately choose to adopt, it will only be a kind of a variant of a decision-making mechanism, which should be constructed in the best possible manner from axiological, praxeological and, last but not least, political points of view.

---

101 More on this topic: I.M. Young, *Deferring Group Representation*, [in:] *Ethnicity and Groups Rights*, I. Shapiro, W. Kymlicka (eds.), New York 1997, p. 249 *et seq.*

Chapter III: Historical and Doctrinal Embodiments of Representation

1. Multivariant Applications of the Idea of Representation

In its historical peregrinations and practical embodiments in which it was implemented, the principle of representative government changed shapes and hues, consequently becoming just as much a general principle as a capacious one, understood and interpreted differently, expressed in many, not necessarily identical or even similar ways.[1] Moreover, it often turned out that different approaches, which, despite their divergence, did have some sort of common denominator at the point of departure, in the end produced very different application variants of the principle of political representation, proving that a single idea can be turned into reality in many different ways. The reverse happened sometimes, i.e. at the outset ideas were given different meanings, their practical implementations also differed, while the final approaches to representation proved surprisingly convergent, similar or even identical.[2]

The variety of perspectives from which the principle of political representation was read and then arranged[3] is explained for instance by the fact that, as we know, representation can be understood either philosophically, or sociologically or, finally, strictly juridically, which by no means excludes combined approaches, where the original concepts are mixed.[4] In addition, one has to bear in mind that the three proposed general patterns of thinking about representation do not exclude more detailed approaches, cutting across the existing ideas and concepts, which are predominantly a product of political sciences in the broad sense, where political representation is one of the basic

---

1 More on this topic: J. Boulad-Ayoub, P.-M. Vernes, *Aux fondements théoriques de la représentation politique*, Paris 2007.

2 *Cf.* J. Krynen, *La représentation politique dans l'ancienne France*, "Droits" 1987, no. 5, p. 31 *et seq.*

3 *Cf.* P. Pettit, *Varieties of Public Representation*, [in:] *Political Representation*, I. Shapiro, S.C. Stokes, E.J. Wood, A.S. Kirshner (eds.), Cambridge 2009, p. 61 *et seq.*

4 More on this topic: A.-M. Le Pourhiet, B. Mathieu, F. Mélin-Soucramanien, D. Rousseau, *Représentation et représentativité*, Paris 2008.

notions.[5] In this context, what distinguishes politology-based approaches is that they call for departure from the pre-existing, strongly separative and dissociative, individual meanings of representation and consider representation to be so complex, multivariant and pyramid-like that it cannot be treated just like a philosophical idea, a legal structure or e.g. a sociological replication, because it is a bit of everything. This is so especially if we believe that, apart from being an idea – certainly an attractive, but inherently abstract one – it is also by all means a real, in the full sense of this word, current systemic institution. The latter, as Hanna Pitkin observes, may be viewed in at least four different thinking patterns, i.e. formalistic representation; symbolic representation; descriptive representation and substantive representation.[6] Under the first of those patterns, that is, formalistic representation (one most strongly associated with the juridical approach to political representation), the status of a representative is analysed in two meanings or aspects, i.e. the authorization he has received from the constituents to act on their behalf and his accountability to them. Symbolic representation, in turn, refers to the meaning of the act of authorization and accountability of the representative seen in formal terms. It gives the formal procedure of authorization and accountability an axiological and teleological dimension, thus determining the systemic status of accountability as such. So in this sense it is a continuation of the former, i.e. formalistic, understanding of representation. Meanwhile sociological representation is a descriptive form of representation that emphasizes the need for the representative's representativeness of the subject in whose name and on whose account he acts. Finally, substantive representation puts emphasis on the fact of acting in somebody's name at all times, which entails the need to take into account the represented subject's interest.[7] The standpoint of H. Pitkin demonstrates conclusively that a single political institution, such as representation (let alone the notion or idea of representation, which is by definition abstract[8]), is a point where many very different meanings of representation come together, but actually it is only all of them taken together that determine its actual, authentic and universal substance. The view of H. Pitkin is a kind of

5 More on this topic:: H. Pitkin, *The Concept of Representation*, Berkley 1967; M.P. Hall, *Facing the Future: A New Theory of Political Representation*, Whitefish 2007; F. Ankersmit, *Political Representation*, Stanford 2002.

6 H. Pitkin, *The Concept of Representation*..., p. 11 *et seq.*

7 *Ibidem*. Also: P. Pettit, *Varieties of Public Representation*..., p. 71 *et seq.*

8 *Cf.* J. Mansbridge, *Rethinking Representation*, "American Political Science Review" 2003, vol. 93, p. 515 *et seq.*

further elaboration of the three general intellectual constructs of representation (juridical, philosophical and sociological). It also shows conclusively that it is in principle impossible to approach representation in isolation, because its various meanings always resonate, regardless of how one thinks about it. Nevertheless the historical embodiments of political representation prove irrefutably that in nearly every case, despite the numerous meanings and the whole repertoire of interpretations, some of them were adopted, recognized as the major, most important or dominant ones, and that it was them that determined the final shape of representation, which was translated in a specific place and time from a general idea into a specific political institution.

Adopting a certain perspective on representation meant that, understandably, it could have been eventually implemented in practice in a completely different way. The principle was indeed implemented in certain ways at times when it was ascribed exclusively or mainly philosophical substance and completely differently when it was seen merely as a legal category. It looked different still when it was reduced to a sociological principle of similarity or replication, in the belief that representation was mainly the represented subject in the proverbial 'nutshell'. This latter case in turn gave rise to the important problem of what features were supposed to be reflected (replicated) in that 'nutshell'. Should these features include only political ones (in line with party representation, the most common form nowadays) or perhaps also socio-economic ones, or rather territorial, ethnic or professional features? The plethora of representations based on the sociological rule of 'replication' opened, as one can see, a very broad room for manoeuvre. So in the end, the idea of representation could be woven into the framework of the representation system using very diverse methods, which by no means eliminated combined solutions in various variants and proportions.[9]

Thus the concept of representation has not been in any way standardized from the very beginning.[10] Suffice it to mention the example of the philosophical view of representation, according to which representation consists in expressing certain ideas, values, incontestable and objective truths, timeless contents important from a specific point of view[11]. In such case the representative may even be a single person, the only condition being that he express those important contents.[12] *Nota bene* the original understanding of representation did not at

9 *Cf.* C. Haguenau-Moizard, *Les systèmes politiques européens*, Paris 2009, p. 36 *et seq.*

10 *Cf.* J. Krynen, *La représentation politique…*, p. 31 *et seq.*

11 *Cf.* D. Mineur, *Archéologie de la représentation politique*, Paris 2010, p. 42 *et seq.*

12 *Cf.* E. Gasparini, E. Gojosso, *Introduction historique au droit et histoire des institutions*, Paris 2011, p. 232.

all exclude the representation manifested through a monocratic authority. Certainly, once kings were also representatives, their majesty expressed a certain philosophy of the state and power. A monarch was perceived as a depositary of the relevant values, a kind of totem pole of statehood, a factor which not only unified the heterogeneous socio-political community, but also expressed (thus represented) certain values and imponderables. It is also in the philosophical perspective that we should approach representation of a certain systemic order by members of societies or groups constituting the said order, as was the case in traditional estate assemblies. In both cases (i.e. monarchs and estate assemblies) the representative personified mainly a certain order of things, externalized a certain socio-political order and all these values taken together constituted the complex edifice of the state. This political representation in the purely philosophical dimension was a representation of values, ideas and ideals that were deemed a necessary component of the state; its elementary substrate without the presence of which the state undermines the very foundations of its existence. In addition, the key notion in the philosophical view of representation was that of a 'political community' (*communauté politique*), which was at the same time expressed, protected and, through a sort of feedback loop, guaranteed by representation. So representation referred to a political community was representation of the principles on which this community was built, its axiological system and, finally, the goals that the community intended to achieve.[13] Here too, representation was a certain fiction, just like the very notion of a political community. *Communauté politique* expressed much more than just the state or, even more so, the state's apparatus (authorities). It was a synthesis of various elements without which one cannot imagine proper functioning of a political system, i.e. the institutional structures, social structures and, finally, axiological structures.[14] Such comprehensively conceptualized political community was the object of representation, which means that it was in itself an important value. Consequently, it was believed, the various values contained in, and expressed by, the political community were represented, but at the same time there was also representation of the community seen as an independent value, a value *per se*, a different and separate value from the ontological point of view, which was not a simple sum of the values of which the political community consisted. In view of the above, the philosophical approach to representation set aside the subject which was to become the target representative and as such represent the

13 *Cf.* D. Mineur, *Archéologie de la représentation...*, p. 55 *et seq.*

14 *Cf. ibidem*, p. 42–43.

political community. What mattered was only the subject of representation, that is, what was to be represented, and not by whom or how it was to be represented. Consequently, representation in the philosophical aspect did not at all assume identicalness of the representative and the represented (which is true of the juridical concepts, where the requested identicalness is expressed by the hypothesis of attribution[15]) or any correlation between the represented subject and the representative (which, in turn, is envisaged in the sociological interpretation of representation). It only assumed that representation was about expressing (externalizing) a certain state of affairs (i.e. principles, values, ideas, ideals and concepts) which was for some reason relevant and required a certain protection, mainly in the name of maintaining a homeostasis of the state or system. Thus the aim of representation it its philosophical dimension was not acting for and on behalf of the represented or achieving convergence of wills of the two parties of the relationship of representation, but maintaining the *status quo*. Hence representation in the philosophical dimension is, first and foremost, a form of presenting, but also petrifying the existing legal and political order; a method of upholding the social, economic, legal, political and, finally, axiological order recognized for some reasons as fixed and inviolable. Representation perceived this way, unlike its subsequent embodiments, is also by definition global, not particular, in its nature. What is represented is not the individual parts of a political community or even its structural features (to which attention is drawn in the sociological aspect of representation), but the *communauté politique* as a whole, consisting of structures, the functions allocated to them and, finally, the values which describe the community and its individual component parts. In this context, it is highlighted that in the philosophical view on representation it is not treated as a specified mechanism through which the people exercise power, which is nowadays a permanent fixture in definitions of representation in general. The philosophical point of view leaves aside the question whether representation is simple, in line with the assumption that people make political decisions in their own names (*gouvernement du peuple par lui-même*), or whether it is perhaps distorted by the actions of representatives (*gouvernement du peuple*

15 According to which hypothesis the will expressed by the representative on the forum of the representative body is hypothetically treated as the will of the represented. So a hypothesis is assumed that the representative thinks, speaks and acts like the represented, which in extreme variants led even to questioning the existence of the represented subject's will, once the will of the representatives was the sole, authentic and real will. *Cf.* J. Barthélemy, P. Duez, *Traité de droit constitutionnel*, Paris 2004, p. 324 *et seq.*

par ses représentants).[16] Because here representation is not a certain 'governing technique', but a form of accreditation of the political community.[17]

The juridical understanding of representation, which was subsequently adopted, first based on private law and then in public law, radically changed the sense of representation. From this time, representation became a mechanism of governing, a particular method of making decisions in the public sphere. The juridical sense of representation, in which it is reduced to a certain entity acting in the name and on the account of someone else, had its roots in two different theories. One of them was the so-called transfer theory, which perceives the essence of representation in one entity transferring its rights to another one, deemed to be the representative (delegate, deputy, member of parliament, etc.). The other theory, i.e. proxy theory, treated representation as proxy of a special nature, for which the point of departure was civil law agency. Whereas in the former case, representation was perceived mainly as a mechanism legitimizing actions of representatives who, paraphrasing E. Sieyès, 'willed for the represented', in the latter one representation was a certain kind of justification for the represented being unable to exercise themselves and directly the rights vested in them, but with the proviso that in representation as such the rights are never assigned, it is only the right to exercise these rights that is assigned to another entity. This in turn suggested that a person acting on behalf of the represented never acted *sua sponte*, but was expressly commissioned and, in addition, controlled by the proper depositary of these rights.[18] Both approaches generated, as a consequence, two concepts of representation, which were by definition completely different and may be referred to in brief as the French and English concepts.[19] Both concepts, plausibly, had completely different starting points. The French one respected the belief that the represented subject transferred rights to the representative, recognizing that not only was the former physically unable to exercise itself the sovereign rights vested in it, but that its very existence was problematic, because it was a certain fiction, since even though the sovereign as a collective entity could hypothetically exist, it lacked a will which would be a different, independent will, not reduced to a simple sum of wills of members of the entity.[20] Thus representation is a consequence of adopting an abstract assumption that the people

16 J. Gicquel, J.-E. Gicquel, *Droit constitutionnel et institutions politiques*, Paris 2007, p. 110.

17 *Cf.*: D. Mineur, *Archéologie de la représentation...*, p. 42 *et seq.*

18 *Cf.* F. Hamon, M. Troper, *Droit constitutionnel*, Paris 2011, p. 83 *et seq.*

19 B. Manin, *The Principles of Representative Government*, Cambridge 1997, p. 94.

20 *Cf.* C. Haguenau-Moizard, *Les systèmes politiques...*, p. 24.

(nation) are the represented and that in line with the principle of sovereignty the people (or nation) they have sovereign rights. Meanwhile, though the existence of such a people (nation) can still be actually accepted, it is already impossible to maintain that it have a will as such and that sovereignty is no more than an expression of such a will and actions consistent with it.[21] In view of the above, the concept of transfer, as an explanation of representation, is based on a general thesis that the very sovereignty of a nation, understood as realization of its will, is a certain legal fiction, a theoretical construct adopted exclusively in order to justify the phenomenon of power.[22] The will of a collective subject of sovereign rights, such as the people or nation, simply does not exist and has to be formulated.[23] It is formulated precisely by the representative onto whom the right to conceptualize the will of the nation-sovereign is transferred. Of course one of the foundations on which this assumption is based is a sort of its continuation, namely the recognition that the representative's will is in turn treated as the will of the nation-sovereign. It is precisely here that the hypothesis of attribution, suggesting that when expressing a will the representative never acts in his own name, but in the name and on the account of the collective sovereign (which in H. Pitkin's terminology is expressed by the notion of 'substantive representation'), proves useful. So he only acts instead of the nation-sovereign in order to formulate the latter's will, which will simply does not exist physically.[24]

2. The French Concept of Political Representation

The concept of representation based on the transfer theory was developed on the French soil in a direction which was not at all expected initially, i.e. towards separation of the will of the representative and that of the represented. It had its roots in idealizing the category of nation-sovereign, which was very French in nature. The nation-sovereign has never been a real community of people, but a certain theoretical axiom serving, first and foremost, to explain and democratically justify authority. The nation-sovereign understood in this way never acted independently and was placed outside representation and outside the apparatus of state power. Yet it was a super-democratic category, sufficiently legitimizing

21 More on this topic: A. Haouet, *Le concept de souveraineté en droit constitutionnel français*, Paris 2003.

22 *Cf.* D. Mineur, *Archéologie de la représentation…*, p. 127 *et seq.*

23 *Cf.* C. Haguenau-Moizard, *Les systèmes politiques…*, p. 24.

24 *Cf.* S. Pierré-Caps, *Le constitutionnalisme et la nation*, [in:] *Le nouveau constitutionnalisme. Mélanges en l'honneur de Gérard Conac*, Paris 2001, p. 67 *et seq.*

the mechanism of functioning of the state, for which reason it helped change the way of looking at representation. A representative, formerly sitting on the Estates General, by his very presence represented a certain order of things, endorsing the system of socio-economic relations that existed at that time and were deemed to be true, authentic and sacred, of which relations he was an exponent and at the same time a 'tangible' proof.[25] After the experience of the Great Revolution a representative – this time sitting on the parliamentary benches – became the exponent of the will of an ideal entity, i.e. the nation-sovereign, by whose election he received the mandate, however not in order to confirm the *status quo* with his presence, but in order to 'have will for the nation', i.e. to express a will to be attributed later on to the sovereign itself. As it happens, when the matter is put this way, the chronological relationship between the sovereignty of the people (nation) and representation is reversed. Because after all it was not the sovereignty of a collective entity, the nation, that finally generated representation, but the other way round: i.e. representation was 'fitted in' with the modern concept of sovereignty.[26] Thus representation transpired as a primary category, one that had been present in public law almost since time immemorial, whereas sovereignty attributed to the nation proved to be just a pretext for modifying the idea of representation and, consequently, giving it a new, previously unknown shape. The concept of representation was merely interpreted by the post-revolutionary project of popular sovereignty, which gave it a democratic, hence acceptable, shape. Before that a representative was an exponent of his own interests, being the owner of either his own function or, much later, the function of a guardian epitomizing a certain order or state of things, but – regardless of the differences – he was never treated as a medium for another entity's will.[27] He always expounded his own, completely unencumbered will, acting on his own account.

The revolution project, although, as Raymond Carré de Malberg put, it was mainly a philosophical abstraction, gave representation a completely different foothold. It placed at the centre a collective body (nation) provided with the attribute of sovereignty. Nevertheless that project was based on the conviction that the nation could not have any other voice than that of its representatives, because it was only through them that it could speak and act. It was precisely here that the key thesis of transfer appeared. After all, it was recognized that the nation's

25 *Cf.* E. Gasparini, E. Gojosso, *Introduction historique au droit…*, p. 226.

26 *Cf.* P. Avril, *Note sur les origines de la représentation*, [in:] *La représentation*, F. d'Arcy (ed.), Paris 1985, p. 102 *et seq.*

27 *Cf.* J.L. Gazzaniga, *Mandat et représentation dans l'ancien droit*, "Droits" 1987, No. 5, p. 24 *et seq.*

sovereignty, in order for the idea to turn into reality, must be somehow reconstructed, given a tangible shape. And this shape was the sovereign's will, which could only manifest itself in the will formulated by the sovereign's representative. Consequently, the will expressed by the representative was the sovereign's will, because the latter transferred its will onto the will of its representatives. And this quickly led to recognition that apart from the will articulated by the representative there was no other authentic, pre-existing, original will of the nation-sovereign, once the latter was just a theoretical abstraction. This is why it was considered, by the way quite rightly, that representation carried by the nation-sovereign became nothing else but a springboard for recognition that there was no sovereign apart from the sovereign's representative.[28] And this – as we are well aware – established the regime of sovereignty of representatives, once the represented subjects were just a theoretical construct, treated as a fiction from the very beginning.[29]

What becomes apparent here is probably the biggest paradox of representation being linked to the post-revolution project of national sovereignty.[30] As we are well aware, this link aimed mainly to give representation a democratic dimension. From this moment a representative was to express not his own will, which he conceptualized fully independently and personally, but the will of another collective entity, which could not be voiced in itself only for 'technical' reasons. But the issue is that this other will, namely the will of the collective entity to which sovereignty was attributed, was problematic from the very beginning once the very entity was *a priori* treated as a certain fiction. Consequently, the will of this inherently fictional entity, which did not exist in reality, was perceived as a fiction as well. An additional argument in favour of the fictional nature of the nation as a sovereign and the fictional nature of the nation's will was that neither the nation was a statistical sum of individuals of which it is made up nor, even more so, the will of this nation was by any means a result of adding up the individual wills of persons forming the collective body of the hypothetical nation-sovereign. The fictional nature of the whole structure, including especially the nation and, subsequently, the will of that nation, generated in the end something which is typical of the French approach: putting an equation mark between the hypothetical will of the nation and the will of its representatives. The path to this statement was not a complex one altogether and it was best recapitulated by

28 *Cf.*: D. Mineur, *Archéologie de la représentation…*, p. 114 *et seq.*

29 *Cf.*: P. Ardant, *Institutions politiques & droit constitutionnel*, Paris 2004, p. 172.

30 *Cf.*: D. Chagnollaud, *Droit constitutionnel contemporain. Théorie générale. Les grands régimes étrangers*, Paris 2005, p. 171.

the famous thesis of an act of parliament being an expression of the general will (i.e. the will of the nation-sovereign). Because once *la loi expression de la volonté générale*, it was only a question of time before a solution was adopted in which it is the entity passing the law that became *de facto* (and even *de jure*) not just the exponent of the *volonté générale*, but the *volonté générale* proper.[31] As a result, the French theory reached a point when both the nation as the bearer of sovereign rights and the will of that nation were questioned since they had been a fiction from the very start. What was not a fiction was the parliament, which grouped representatives of the imagined will of the nation-sovereign, who were by all means real, present and tangible. This being the case, it was considered a simpler solution to assume that there was no nation outside the parliament and the will of the representatives was not only treated *as* the nation's will, but simply *was* the nation's will. So there occurred a certain 'deformation of the regime of political representation' and 'representative absolutism'[32] (*absolutisme représentatif*) emerged, actually questioning the sense of modern representation, as it brought to the fore the representative, not the represented subjects. Thus the regime of sovereignty of the parliament, so typical of the French theory of the late nineteenth century, very quickly replaced the regime of sovereignty of the people, once the latter had been treated from the very beginning as a fundamentally abstract category, a hypothesis adopted exclusively for legitimization purposes.[33] It is worth observing that at this point the French concepts unexpectedly converged with the English ideas, which – as we know – originated from completely different assumptions, but eventually also led to the supremacy of the parliament's will in the name of the principle of its sovereignty.[34] Of course it does not mean that both concepts were by and large similar or, the more so, identical. If they have anything in common, this is only the point they both arrived

31 *Cf.* E. Gasparini, E. Gojosso, *Introduction historique au droit...*, p. 344.

32 G. Vedel, *Manuel élémentaire de droit constitutionnel*, Paris 2002, p. 141.

33 Which suggests that the categories of representation and sovereignty need not meet at all. Moreover, for a long time they coexisted side by side, overlapping only sometimes and only in specific contexts. This was so e.g. in the case of sovereignty of the monarch, who at the same time represented the values and principles forming the systemic order or simply the crown. Another 'meeting' of both these categories was precisely in the post-revolutionary project of popular sovereignty and modern political representation. More on various interpretations of sovereignty and its 'meetings' with representation: M. Hogga, *Souveraineté; concept et conflit en Occident. La quête infinie de la liberté*, Paris 2007, p. 7 *et seq.*

34 *Cf.* I. Nguyen-Duy, *Souverainete du Parlement Britannique*, Paris 2011, p. 237 *et seq.*

at, namely recognition of the parliament's preponderance, with the concluding slogan of its sovereignty. But we should remember that the background for the French concepts was mainly disputing the reality of existence of the nation-sovereign and, consequently, of its imagined, mythical will. In view of that the idea of *volonté générale*, which was intended to be represented in the parliament, had only a 'moral character',[35] but according to the provisions of law it was a complete fiction, a clever figure of speech, thanks to which the whole idea was dressed in a super-democratic bodice. But this bodice was, to quote for example the view of R. Carré de Malberg, not a super-, but a pseudo-democratic one, because this very idea of representation is, according to critics, completely misconceived unless representatives' will is counterbalanced by the will expressed directly and simply by the represented subjects themselves.[36] So unless there are established mechanisms providing for political participation of the nation-sovereign, even if they are applied only in an auxiliary and limited form, the grand project of representation is one which enacts not only a legal fiction, but also a legal forgery or even fraud. Therefore the beautiful and noble idea of popular sovereignty and the matching idea of representation have to assume forms of direct and simple participation of the collective bearer of sovereign rights.[37] Otherwise the idea of representation contains, from the very beginning, some form of fraud, because it gives the illusion that decisions are made by the will and in the name of the represented, whereas in actual fact decisions are made by the representatives who are perfectly aware that in reality there are no represented subjects, because the latter are just a legal fiction, nothing more than a theoretical assumption. Hence, sooner or later, representation always leads to a transfer of sovereignty from the represented to the representatives, with the parliament – as the representative

35 D. Chagnollaud, *Droit constitutionnel contemporain…*, p. 170.

36 This is why R. Carré de Malberg does not question political representation 'as such' believing it to be 'irreversible'. Yet he assumes that representation reflected in the parliament inevitably falls into absolutism, by the same token threatening the idea of democracy as government of the people. Thus he postulates that power of the parliament be under a sort of guardianship of the sovereign, which – through a referendum – will eventually be able to decide about the most important matters. As a consequence, the representative system was to be supplemented with a system of sovereign's direct interventions, making the whole construction of the system respect the mythical will of the people (nation) and minimizing its juridical fictional character. *Cf.* : R. Carré de Malberg, *Considérations théoriques sur la question de la combinaison du referendum avec le parlementarisme*, "Revue du Droit Public" 1931, vol. 48, p. 234 *et seq.*

37 *Cf.* D. Mineur, *Archéologie de la représentation…*, p. 214.

body – replacing the proper sovereign.[38] This is where, among other things, we can detect what is possibly the biggest peril of the concept of representation. The beauty of a democratic idea becomes in reality a screen obscuring the undemocratic ugliness of the system. The sovereignty of the fictional nation, having a fictional general will, takes real shape of the real sovereign, by all means having a real will, yet not the general will, but quite the contrary: particular, often separate and sectional one.[39]

Consequently, withdrawal from sovereignty of the parliament, as contradicting the very essence of representation, had to be a two-track process in the French theory. Firstly, it had to involve reaching for the forms of direct democracy as an alternative to parliamentary absolutism and, secondly, it had to entail reduction of the parliament's excessive powers, which it had scooped or rather appropriated, through a snowball effect, referring to its special sovereign status.[40] One should bear in mind that the supremacy acquired by the parliament in the name of its sovereignty generated a situation in which it was the parliament that clearly dominated the system of state authorities, becoming a practically unrivalled institution, which, by the way, also unsettled other constitutional principles, not only that of popular sovereignty.

However, retreat from parliament's sovereignty à la *française* did not reject what, at least at the starting point, gave the French model of representation and sovereignty its peculiar finish.[41] We have already indicated that the French point of view, even though with completely different assumptions than those made *outre-Manche*, led to an altogether very similar finale, namely the thesis of the parliament's sovereignty (once the nation-sovereign is just an abstraction whose aim is to give the whole intellectual construct a democratic accreditation). A similar, or even identical finale, of both approaches (i.e. the French and English one) did not mean, however, that everything else – apart from their starting points – converged too. The differences in details are very noticeable and, more importantly, they remain visible, at least in some sense, or at any rate reverberate until this very day. Naturally, one of the differences is the emphasis on the 'community character' of representation in the French approach.[42] What the representative expresses is, after all, the thoughts, will and opinion of the

38 *Cf.* P. Ardant, *Institutions politiques…*, p. 172.

39 *Ibidem*, p. 171.

40 *Cf.* M. Lascombe, *Le droit constitutionnel de la Ve République*, Paris 2010, p. 107 *et seq.*

41 *Cf.* C. Haguenau-Moizard, *Les systèmes politiques…*, p. 24.

42 *Cf.* B. Manin, *The Principles…*, p. 98, 99.

nation-sovereign and not its individual parts and sections. The fictional nature of the construct of the nation and its will by no means excluded the belief that a representative is, or at least is assumed to be, the exponent of the general will, the more so that his actions are supposed to express the *volonté générale*. This in turn, in a sort of feedback loop, generated pressure for extending the category of 'active citizen,'[43] that is, a citizen who participated in the matters of the *polis*, i.e. had electoral franchise. And this, as one can easily guess, exerted pressure towards extending the group of persons having electoral franchise, thus making up the so-called active country, which was in turn reflected in parliamentary representation.[44] The fictional nature of the nation-sovereign was believed not to collide so much with the fact that at least in some sense the nation, though still fictional, revealed itself in elections in the form of the *corps électoral*. An assumption was made that extending this electorate would minimize the fictionality of the nation and its will, thanks to which it would become 'more bearable' and acceptable, considering that the whole construct of representation was based on a super-theoretical, hence abstract, foundation.[45] The clear community-oriented character of the French concept produced, in the end, several important consequences. The first one was the willingness to significantly extend the group of people with electoral franchise, *ergo* to treat the principle of universal suffrage seriously.[46] The second one was the division of the country into the 'active country', i.e. those having and exercising the right the vote and – *a contrario* – the passive country, which did not enjoy the possibility to participate in elections. The category of 'active country' minimized the fictionality of the assumption of the nation as a sovereign, making the nation a more imaginable and real entity. Nevertheless, one should remember that it never equated the nation-sovereign with the elector. True, it did show that the elector in a certain way made the sovereign real, being a form of diminishing the abstractness of its nature, but there has never been full equivalence between the nation-sovereign and the elector or, the more so, between the nation-sovereign and the 'active country'.[47] Finally, the last consequence of the community character of representation à la *française* was

43 *Ibidem*, p. 98.

44 More on this topic: P. Rosanvallon, *Le Peuple introuvable: Histoire de la représentation démocratique en France*, Paris 2002.

45 *Cf.* D. Mineur, *Archéologie de la représentation…*, p. 127 *et seq.*

46 *Cf.* F. Bluche, *Manuel d'histoire politique de la France contemporaine*, Paris 2008, p. 211 *et seq.*

47 *Cf.* J.-L. Richard, *Corps électoral,* [in:] *Dictionnaire du vote*, P. Perrineau, D. Reynié (eds.), Paris 2001, p. 264 *et seq.*

its obvious aversion to imperative mandate as one being in stark contrast with the community character and with representing the general will, even a fictional one.[48] This matter is of such importance that it is often perceived as yet another, but very distinct, difference (apart from the community character) between the French project of political representation and its English counterpart.

Therefore the idea of representative (free) mandate is yet another pillar of the doctrine of political representation developed in France. It is a logical consequence of the assumption of expressing *volonté générale* ascribed to the nation, which is provided with the attribute of sovereignty. Once everything fits in nicely with a strongly 'community-based' conception,[49] then its keystone must be the standpoint that representation has a general nature and is not in any way bound, ordered, specified in advance or otherwise determined by imperative mandate. Later on, when the French project evolved into the sovereignty of the parliament as such, free mandate became simply a necessity, a solution without any alternative, although it has to be observed that it also played an important role in the formation of parliamentary absolutism, which means that there is absolutely no simple cause-and-effect relationship. All in all, making one more step and recognizing that there was no sovereign apart from the sovereign's representative was motivated by two circumstances. The first and starting one was the fictional character of the sovereign, which was assumed upfront. The other one was providing the representative with free mandate, which was indeed in harmony with the idea of general will and treating the sovereign as something more than a simple arithmetic sum of all individual components, but at the same time it was the driver for autonomization of the representative's will. Regardless of all other causes and effects, free mandate was the core of the French view on political representation, an element which, together with the principle of popular sovereignty and the general will articulated by representatives, gave a coherent and logical picture of the relationship of representation.[50]

Of course, one has to remember that every doctrine has its nuances, points of dissent, views cast sometimes from a completely different perspective. In line with the above, also the ideal of free mandate was by no means, at least not on the French soil, an unchallenged solution to which no alternative would be proposed. Free (representative) mandate finally won as the one which corresponded better to the general idea, but had its excellent adversary in Jean Jacques Rousseau, who

---

48 *Cf.* G. Vedel, *Manuel élémentaire*..., p. 135.

49 *Cf.* D. Mineur, *Archéologie de la représentation*..., p. 70 *et seq.*

50 *Cf.* J. Barthélemy, P. Duez, *Traité de droit*..., p. 103 *et seq.*

consistently advocated the need for imperative mandate. The idea of J.J. Rousseau was, however, linked with a completely different view of representation, which the author of *The Social Contract* believed to be a not very fortunate attempt at making a match between the nation's sovereignty and the need for real, day-to-day governance. According to J.J. Rousseau, the famous *volonté générale* is incapable of representation at all, because it always has to manifest itself personally, as otherwise it gets deformed and distorted, *ergo* it no longer is – from the logical point of view – a general will. Therefore such will can only reveal itself in a simple and direct way (which means the need to apply forms of simple democracy). This follows from the very assumption of its universal character and, according to J.J. Rousseau, the *volonté générale* is universal in at least two senses. In the first sense, this 'universal character' concerns its scope, because it refers to the general interest, precisely the universal one, thus excluding any individual, particular or otherwise defined sectional interest, not being the general, common and universal interest. In the other sense, the universal character of the will concerns the subjects, because it is the will of 'every citizen'. Nevertheless, in J.J. Rousseau's view it is by no means the sum total of private and individual pursuits, thus it is not the will of everybody: *volonté générale* is certainly not *volonté de tous*. It is only the former, *volonté générale*, that takes into account the general, common and supra-individual interest, while the latter, i.e. *volonté de tous*, is guided by particular interest and is composed of the pursuits of individual persons. Moreover, for J.J. Rousseau, the attribute of sovereignty belonged precisely to the general will and not its material medium, the nation.

This is why the thinker from Geneva understood the nation in a completely different way. Unlike the majority of scholars he did not think it to be abstract and, according to the law, even fictional, but the most real social body (society) composed of specific individuals. Yet it was its complexity that presented the greatest difficulty in making real the sovereign general will, which could not be externalized daily. Hence J.J. Rousseau's conditional approval of the representative system, which is, however, *ab initio* imperfect, because it is fictional.[51] The will of the representatives never is or can be the general will, because it is always a deformation of this will, its reflection, yet one carrying the error of a 'distorting mirror'. Thanks to it, J.J. Rousseau somehow reverses the assumption of fictionality in the construct of political representation. It is not the nation-sovereign and

51 Naturally if one accepts the assumptions of J.J. Rousseau concerning the sovereign general will, which is inalienable, indivisible, infallible and, finally, absolute. *Cf.* J. Touchard, *Histoire des idées politiques*, vol. II, Paris 1959, p. 425–426.

its will that are a legal fiction, because only the representative and his will are real, but just the reverse: representation is a fiction, because the only true and authentic thing is the *volonté générale* formulated by the people comprising all the actually existing, by all means present and real people. In order to diminish the fictionality as much as possible, J.J. Rousseau proposed imperative mandate, which was indeed a condition for recognition of the existence of the whole representative system. As he claimed, only imperative mandate, excluding independence of the deputies' activities, guaranteed that the will of the representatives and the represented subjects would not diverge. Nevertheless, it should be observed that imperative mandate, of which J.J. Rousseau was such a fervent supporter, differs slightly from the traditional form of imperative mandate known in the literature before.[52] It follows from a basic assumption made by the author of *The Social Contract* that in an act of delegating or transferring, which is the 'core' of appointment of a representative, it is not the will that can be transferred, but only the power. Once the will is a sovereign one, it is not transferred or reassigned in any way, nor is it e.g. divided. The nation is still its depositary and therefore representatives have to be absolutely bound by its will, of which imperative mandate is a legal manifestation. This is why deputies are not and cannot in any case be representatives of the people, which should conclusively demonstrate the fragility of the whole conception of representation. Representatives are, both *de facto* and *de jure*, no more than just 'envoys' or, as Konstanty Grzybowski once neatly put it, 'ambassadors' of the nation, in addition ones without the power to make final decisions. The right to make the latter is always vested with the nation expressing a sovereign *volonté générale*.

The view of J.J. Rousseau is certainly attractive and, on many counts, probably correct, but it remains an absolutely utopic project.[53] It is noteworthy that it is democratic through and through in that is exposes probably the greatest weakness of the classical approach to political representation, namely the risk of mismatch between the wills of the represented and their representatives.[54] No wonder it became some point of departure for subsequent critics of representation and at the same time a reservoir of arguments for pushing forward ideas to establish simple democracy in its various forms, perceived – whether rightly or not being another issue – as a remedy for the flaws of representative

52 *Cf.* P.-H. Zaidman, *Le mandat impératif. De la Révolution française à la Commune de Paris*, Paris 2008, p. 7–8.

53 J. Touchard, *Histoire des idées…*, p. 420.

54 *Cf.* P.-H. Zaidman, *Le mandat impératif…*, p. 9 *et seq.*

democracy.[55] Also the criticism of R. Carré de Malberg can be trimmed down to upholding J.J. Rousseau's main argument, namely that classical representation does not guarantee the sovereign power of the nation. This very same canon of criticism includes also the – otherwise attractive – project of constitutional democracy, founded on the assumption that it should guarantee true respect for the will of the nation-sovereign, which gets deformed and distorted by the mechanisms of representation in its classical understanding.

The French project of representation does show some degree of complexity. On the one hand, its mainstream can be identified with, and reduced to, the slogan of defining representation as transfer of sovereign rights from the nation-sovereign to its representatives, accompanied by the conviction that both the nation-sovereign and its will are indeed a fiction which takes real shape only upon election of the representative, who formulates the true, actual will, which is subsequently attributed to the fictional bearer of sovereign rights. This way of looking at representation was correlated with the perfectly-matching free mandate, which finally, in extreme versions, led to adopting the thesis that there was no sovereign apart from the parliament, while the mechanism of political representation was just a method of democratic legitimization of the power vested in the representative assembly. The second thread, identified with J.J. Rousseau, reverses the above standpoint by 180 degrees. Its point of departure is the belief that the nation is by no means an abstraction, but a truly real and tangible entity. Moreover, the will formulated by the nation is also real and it is that will, precisely because it is the general will and not just the will of everybody, that has the attribute of sovereignty. The sovereign will understood this way cannot be transferred or assigned to anybody else. Thus the assumption of transfer of will (and consequently sovereignty) is fundamentally false and preposterous. Nevertheless, as it is impossible for the people to exercise general will on a daily basis, representatives are appointed. But such representation is an unwanted necessity and as such it should always be perceived in a minimalist way. Hence the accompanying conviction that the representative is 'just' an envoy of the people, not its 'substitute', and that he is given imperative mandate, because the will which is the object of representation cannot be transferred by any methods and always has to correspond to the *volonté générale*, which can only be guaranteed by imperative mandate.[56] So the project of J.J. Rousseau, as a theoretical dress of representation, is a paradoxical one, because it treats representation as the

55 More on this topic: F. Rouvillois, *L'avenir du référendum*, Paris 2006.

56 *Cf.* P.-H. Zaidman, *Le mandat impératif…*, p. 7, 8.

necessary evil. It is invented only because the sovereign general will cannot reveal itself in the mundane, daily mechanism of running the affairs of the *polis*. This is why representation appears here as the 'unwanted child', being from the very beginning something inadequate and inconvenient, accepted only out of necessity. Therefore the ideas of the thinker from Geneva are sometimes considered to be a complete opposite of representation. They are an apotheosis of direct democracy and treat its intermediate embodiments with noticeable reluctance and caution, perceiving them to be a real minefield for the true, authentic and sovereign general will. For this reason, when analysing the French perspective on the representative regime, these ideas are sometimes omitted because they are considered not to be part of the theory of representation, but rather the theory of anti-representation. So proper representation à la *française* is often associated only with the former project, i.e. the idea of legal fiction and the conception of attribution, supplemented by free mandate.[57]

3. The English Idea of Representation

Apart from the French conception, the second great model embodiment of the idea of political representation is the English concept.[58] It started with a slightly different set of assumptions than the French model, but, interestingly, it finally converged with the latter at the point where it preached the slogan of the parliament's sovereignty. The English concept has a few defining features. First and foremost, representation is treated as a manifestation of responsible government. Representation (representative or, in other words, responsible government) is then a *sui generis* form of control of those governed over those governing. It was assumed that the key to good government – whatever this was supposed to mean – was a systemic homeostasis, which did not allow any element of the state to gain a dominant or otherwise privileged position. This was prevented not by the separation of powers which, as was often claimed, was ill-suited to the conditions of the UK system,[59] but by an efficient system of control. Hence control was to be the tool giving those governed the possibility of enforcing responsibility of the governing ones. And the latter, which we should treat as the second feature identifying the English version of representation, is representation understood

57 *Cf.* C. Haguenau-Moizard, *Les systèmes politiques…*, p. 24.

58 *Cf.* B. Manin, *The Principles…*, p. 95.

59 The disputable nature of adoption of the division of powers in the UK is such that some say the division of powers is a myth in this case. *Cf.* M. Charlot, *Le povoir politique en Grande-Bretagne*, Paris 1998, p. 49.

almost literally as the representative repeating the opinion of the represented subject, that is, a certain coherent set of views, judgements and beliefs, which via the mechanism of representation are transferred from one entity to the other in order to eventually generate a position respecting the will expressed at the very beginning of the government mechanism, i.e. the will of the elector himself. This shows very well that, unlike in the French approaches, the most important thing in London was not creating complex juridical or, the more so, philosophical constructs, but putting emphasis on the natural (sociological) idea of convergence or similarity between the attitudes of the governed and the governing. It was consistently held that the key to responsible government was the existence of representative government, that is, precisely government representing (replicating, mirroring) opinions of the two sides of the relationship of representation, i.e. the representatives and the represented. A representative, thus also responsible, government is one which reiterates the views, opinions and demands of the represented, while being also similar to the represented, which was particularly important at the very beginning of the English representation. At that time it was believed that proper or true representation had to be correlated with the sociological group of which the represented subject was a rendition and that this correlation had to be full (i.e. concern both the social features and the views held).[60] So, while the French doctrine from the very start was rather inclined towards the more juridical understanding of representation (i.e. representation as a legal fiction), its English equivalent was definitively closer to the sociological approach, showing that true representation consisted mainly in aligning the wills of the representative and the represented. Therefore, responsible government had to be representative, which was understood almost literally, that is, similar to the subject to which it was responsible, namely, at the end of the day to electors and before them, members of the parliament. Thus a representative system was achieved by establishing similarity (convergence) of opinions of electors, their representatives (MPs) and finally the government, which should not act *sua sponte*, but in the name and on the account of electors. So the ideal solution was electing representatives in such a way that, first, their composition and views matched those of the electorate and, secondly, they made decisions consistent with the intentions of those whom they represented. What logically followed from this was the third key feature of the English view of representation. It was, especially at the very start, when the representation model was only beginning to take shape, the close link between the representative and the specific social

60 *Cf.* B. Manin, *The Principles…*, p. 96.

group.[61] This shows yet another time the very clear sociological correlation of representation 'made in England'. This representation was to express the interests of specific social groups, from which stemmed the postulate that the representative body should faithfully and precisely mimic all, or at least the key, socio-economic and political features of the represented. Thanks to it, reference was made to the most rudimentary and primary substance of the principle of representation, according to which representation means representing a certain systemic or social order, which is best done by the very members of communities or groups constituting this order. By the way, it shows that the English project of representation was much more 'atomist' or rather 'individualist' than its French equivalent in that it perceived the represented subject not as a general category of the people or the nation, but as a socio-economic group, whose interests and systemic status were to be protected thanks to representation.[62] Thus in the English version of representation, at least at its early stages, emphasis was placed not on the nation or the people, but on the interests of a social or economic group which the MP was to represent. In the subsequent model this social group was replaced, at least in some sense, by the constituency, however, this did not change the clearly particularized pattern of representation at all.

Yet another 'genetic' feature of the English variety of political representation – which was nothing but a simple consequence of the aforementioned features – was therefore the imperative mandate. The expectation that the representative will represent the views of his own group of electors, mainly the constituency where he acquired the mandate, had to lead to a legal obligation on the MP's part to conscientiously execute the electoral orders formulated by his constituents. This is confirmed by the frequently quoted case of poet Andrew Marvell, an MP for Hull in 1660–1678. He kept regular correspondence with his constituents concerning mainly the errands the MP was supposed to 'make' in the parliament. In one of his letters A. Marvell wrote expressly: 'I desire that you will […] consider whether there be anything that particularly relates to the state of your town, or of your neighbouring country […] whereof you may think fit to advertise me, and therein to give me your instructions to which I shall carefully conform.'[63] We can see clearly that the English doctrine was much closer to the concept of representation seen in terms of proxy than representation as transfer, which was

61 *Cf.* M. Kishlansky, *Parliamentary Selection: Social and Political Choice in Early Modern England*, Cambridge 1986, p. 229.

62 *Cf.* B. Manin, *The Principles…*, p. 96, 97.

63 L. Radice, E. Vallance, V. Willis, *Member of Parliament. The Job of a Backbencher*, London 1990, p. 4.

how the French doctrine saw it. A member of the House of Commons was for a long time seen as a 'trustee' of his own constituency, legally bound to represent the interests of the constituency in line with the instructions received from his constituents. Moreover, in a certain sense, upon delegation to the parliament he entered into a sort of 'contract', whose essence was, on the MP's part, representing the interests of the constituency, while on the constituency's part, ensuring means of subsistence for the MP.[64] The latter was a very important component of the English concept of representation, actually upholding the close cooperation between the MP and the constituency and conclusively demonstrating the particular character of representation 'made in England'. The basic issue, as is rightly pointed out, was the MP's loyalty to those whom he represented. This helped preserve the fundamental idea of representation, i.e. responsible government. What was a major element for a very long time was constituencies bearing the costs of having their MPs, which resulted in an obligation of a financial nature to represent the will of the payers. For all those reasons, a member of the House of Commons was perceived as a representative of his constituency, living therein and maintained thereby, which resulted in a simple and, in this case, somewhat obvious principle of imperative mandate, which for a long time was one of the foundations of the English concept of representation. In addition it was believed that the imperative nature of the mandate received by a Member of the House of Commons was not only an ideal match for the mechanism of a clearly atomist version of the relation of representation, but it also excellently corresponded to the general idea on which the English model of political representation was founded: the idea of responsibility (responsible government).[65] An inherent feature of imperative mandate was the principle of representation, which in this case was no longer an abstract and rather general one, but one clearly referring to a named, individual and single representative who – if he disobeyed the electoral instructions – could be deprived of the mandate through withdrawal from the electoral contract.

The model of exceedingly sectional or particular representation, based on a social group or, later, a constituency, additionally supplemented with imperative mandate, was sturdily preserved by the provisions of electoral law, which, firstly, closely correlated the MP with the constituency (place where mandate was gained) and, secondly, bypassed the principle of universal suffrage, thus

64 *Cf.* B.M. Charlot, *Le povoir politique…*, p. 150 *et seq.*
65 *Cf.* M. Knights, *Participation and Representation before Democracy: Petitions and Addresses in Premodern Britain*, [in:] *Political Representation…*, p. 35 *et seq.*

cultivating the highly elitist nature of electoral law.[66] Later on, after emergence of the specific British party system, which centred around the two main parties, the original connotations of an MP associated with particular interests and his own constituency became even more fixed, despite the fact that at a certain moment the concept of imperative mandate was rejected. Yet the surprising strength of electoral rules, despite the obviously numerous and sometimes quite far-reaching changes and the visible bipartisanism still upheld the belief that the English, and then British, representation had a strongly particular profile.[67] So the representative was still perceived as a 'trustee' of the constituency or, later on, of his own party. And what was expected of him was still – first and foremost – commitment to his constituents or, more precisely, principals of the mandate.

The direction towards autonomizing the representative function, which, as we have mentioned, is an element of the peculiar English model of representation, is manifested not only or not mainly by a member of the House of Commons expressing individual interests, i.e. those of his electors, party or constituency. The direction is also, to an equal extent, the reverse, which in turn encourages perceiving the representative (MP) as a leader. So an MP is not (and, the more so, was not) perceived as a member of a collective body (group of MPs), but as a holder of an independent function of a representative (although obviously, in the historical perspective, his role evolved from the erstwhile gentleman to a party player[68]). Hence the expression 'Member of Parliament', which has clearly individualist connotations. Thus an MP was always a leader, an independent player, a real winner, in line with the *winner takes all* principle. Because, for obvious reasons, the clear profiling of an MP as a leader has been fostered almost since time immemorial by the rules of electoral law, including especially the majoritarian system and the traditional voting for a person (although not always in single-seat constituencies, because previously two-seat constituencies were the rule, while single-seat ones became the standard as late as in the second half of the nineteenth century). Another factor contributing to a perception of an MP as a leader, for obvious reasons, was the historically-entrenched treatment of an MP as a representative of a specific, precisely defined socio-economic group (even though the subsequent conception of the so-called virtual representation

66 *Cf.* I. Nguyen-Duy, *Souverainete du Parlement…*, p. 349 *et seq.*

67 *Cf.* M. Charlot, *Le povoir politique…*, p. 59 *et seq.*

68 More on this topic: M. Rush, *The Role of the Members of Parliament since 1868. From Gentleman to Players*, Oxford 2001.

slightly disavowed this assumption[69]). So traditionally, a member of the House of Commons was honoured as 'the "natural leader" of the local community'.[70] This role was additionally and very strongly confirmed by the technical method of voting, which for a very long time assumed open ballot, in effect giving the elected person a very strong mandate of social trust, as well as authentic respect and prestige.[71] As a consequence the members (representatives) formed true social and political elite of the state, which – especially in the British conditions – generated a situation in which MPs were treated as a certain pool of professional civil servants and, at the same time, a mandatory step in the career of each politician or civil servant.[72]

Like in the case of the French doctrine, also in the English doctrine there were sometimes different currents, against the 'mainstream'; and some of them were so strong that with time they caused revision of the main elements of the previous standpoint. Among them were the ideas of Edmund Burke, the main promoter of the idea of free mandate.[73] In his famous Bristol speech Edmund Burke gave a lecture on free mandate, claiming among other things that the parliament was by no means 'a *congress* of ambassadors from different and hostile interests; which interests each must maintain, as an agent and advocate, against other agents and advocates; but [...] a *deliberative* assembly of *one* nation, with *one* interest, [...] not local purposes, not local prejudices'.[74] And although the voters delegate a member from a specific constituency, once they do so, 'he is not a member of Bristol, but he is a member of *parliament*'.[75] This is why, in E. Burke's view, the binding instructions, imperative mandates, which the member has to obey blindly, are completely illogical and contrary to the idea of representation, especially in all those cases when they are 'contrary to the clearest conviction of

---

69 A member of the House of Commons, according to this conception, represented not only those who voted, not even those who had electoral franchise, but also all the remaining people, deprived of electoral franchise. In this context it is easy to observe that the theory of virtual representation aimed mainly to provide democratic legitimacy of the whole system.

70 B. Manin, *The Principles...*, p. 96.

71 *Cf.* M. Kishlansky, *Parliamentary Selection...*, p. 3, 4.

72 *Cf.* M. Charlot, *Le povoir politique...*, p. 194 *et seq.*

73 More on this topic: J. Conniff, *Burke, Bristol and the Concept of Representation*, "The Western Political Quarterly" 1977, no. 3, p. 329 *et seq.*

74 E. Burke, *Parliament as Representative of National Interest 1774*, [in:] *Democracy in Britain. A Reader*, J. Lively, A. Lively (eds.), Oxford–Cambridge 1994, p. 93–94.

75 *Ibidem.*

his judgement and conscience'.[76] The belief that a member of the House of Commons holds a free mandate was accepted with time. Consequently it was thought that a member was not directly a representative of a specific group of his voters and could not receive any orders or instructions from them as to the manner of voting or other behaviour in the parliament. During the terms of the granted proxies, from the legal point of view, he is not subject to any orders or any forms of control as to how he executes his mandate. But the most important thing is that 'members are not mere representatives of their constituents'.[77] In view of the above, a constituency – when the concept of free mandate was applied – acquired only 'technical' features; it became a unit of territorial division, but only for electoral purposes, which means that legal mechanisms of authorizing the mandate are not tied to it anymore. Because regardless of the 'place of acquisition of the mandate', a member of the House of Commons has a duty to follow the general interest and no longer treats himself as a sort of 'envoy' or 'ambassador' of his own constituency.[78]

Of course, such a reconstruction of the model of representation did not automatically entail abandoning other elements typical of the traditional approach to mandate 'made in England'. Thus in the UK context we can rather speak of adjusting the free mandate to pre-existing features and solutions.[79] Undoubtedly, the most important one of them is the concept of responsibility, treated as the basic component of representative mandate, while the resulting principle of responsible government is still perceived as the 'golden' rule of the British system.[80]

Adjusting representative mandate to pre-existing standards of political representation in the British conditions is not, however, limited to merely maintaining the bond between the representative and his constituency, although admittedly this bond is exceptionally strong in the UK.[81] Nevertheless, in no case does it

---

76 *Ibidem.*

77 W.I. Jennings, *The British Constitution*, Cambridge 1966, p. 84.

78 Which naturally does not cancel in practice the relatively strong ties between MPs and their constituencies, additionally and rather strongly legitimized by the rules of the electoral system. More on this topic: *Back from Westminster: British Members of Parliament and Their Constituents*, P. Norton, D.M. Wood (eds.), Lexington 1993.

79 *Cf.* H.-Y. Lee, *Political Representation in the later Middle Ages*, New York 2008, p. 15 *et seq.*

80 *Cf.* A.H. Birch, *Representative and Responsible Government. An Essay on the British Constitution*, London 1969, p. 226 *et seq.*

81 *Cf.* P. Pettit, *Varieties of Public Representation…*, p. 66 *et seq.*

result in a legal obligation to fulfil the constituents' will, although it obviously does not prohibit it. However, the representative's strong authorization in the constituency does provide, at least implicitly, for some form of political and ethical responsibility in a situation when the representative acts against the will of the constituents or the interests of the constituency.[82] But the responsibility is natural and undisputed and cannot absolutely be contrary to free mandate, because it is by all means in line with the rudimentary sense of representation. In addition, in the British conditions, is it fully consistent with the concept of responsible government, on which that model of representation is based. One should, however, bear in mind that 'responsible government', the essence of the English version of political representation,[83] had at least two meanings. The first was the pivotal one and boiled down to the idea of responsibility of the executive power before representatives, generating the general and, as a matter of fact, the most important idea of control of power. The second meaning had a smaller scale and referred to the member's responsibility before his own voters (constituency). And both of them were identified by the Burkean trust, responsibility and public interest, on which the whole concept of representation as responsible government was founded.[84]

But the factor which probably corrected the British concept of representation to the highest extent was the mandate theory. Initially, it was formed in a *soft* version, which consisted in the traditional perception of the MP as a representative of the constituency, but also – and this was the heart of the mandate theory – required the member exercising a mandate not to go beyond the election promises he had made. So an election promise was still seen as a contract, a kind of agreement with the constituents.[85] Naturally, free mandate could not promote any legal obligation to obey by instructions or other kinds of orders from voters, but it could – and did so in the mandate theory – bind the member by the contents of his election promises. Thus an election promise was a *sui generis* vow that the member, in his activities, will not go beyond its contents and, above all, he will not promote any ideas which were not favoured by the voters or were not submitted to them for consideration at all, because they were not the topic of the election appeal. With the mandate theory tailored this way, almost all traditional components of the English conception of representation were maintained, while the idea of free (representative) mandate could at the same time be approved. In

82 *Cf.* A. Adonis, *Parliament Today*, Manchester–New York 1990, p. 42.
83 *Cf.* J. Conniff, *Burke, Bristol and the Concept…*, p. 330 *et seq.*
84 H.-Y. Lee, *Political Representation…*, p. 15.
85 *Cf.* M. Charlot, *Le povoir politique…*, p. 139.

the British theory of mandate, the principle of binding, which is typical of the imperative embodiment of mandate, was somewhat reversed or, in other words, given a negative sense. The MP was no longer obligated to fastidiously respect the orders from his electors or to act upon their request (as in imperative mandate), but was obligated not to act in a manner which he had not previously disclosed in his election appeal. This approach to the issue helped uphold certain solutions perceived as the essence of the British, and previously the English, conception of representation. Firstly, there was express responsibility of the MP before the constituents; secondly, there was an interpersonal relation between the representative and the represented; thirdly, this did not prevent the MP being perceived as a leader who was linked to his constituency by a special kind of relationship, even if the relationship was not determined by laws and its features were more of a political, moral or ethical nature.

A soft mandate theory was subsequently replaced with a hard version. This happened mainly because of political parties, which monopolized elections with the passing of time and became, like elsewhere, the basic component of the conception of political representation and the correlation between the wills of the represented and the representatives, which is established within its framework. However, in the British case it was not the party as such that gave the pretext for modifying the mandate theory, but the specific, quite endemic party system, which boiled down to the existence of two big parties. The lasting character of the British bipartisan system and the evident monopoly of political parties generated in the end a hard, or strong, version of the mandate theory. It started with the conviction that when choosing their representative '[t]he electors do not want men of independent views, but good party men'.[86] So at a certain point electoral manifesto was no longer assessed as the individual candidate's manifesto, but became the manifesto of a political formation, under whose name that particular candidate applied for a mandate. Thus the possible electoral success began to be perceived as an obligation of the elected MP to implement the manifesto which, though he endorsed it with his name, was not at all his own, but that of the party on whose behalf he was running.[87] This enabled also the 'severing' – by all means in line with a free mandate – of the link between the MP and his

86 W.I. Jennings, *The British Constitution…*, p. 82.

87 It is indicated that this was what E. Burke himself thought. He was a 'party man' and his idea of political representation was actually tailored to the party ideology. More on this topic: H. Eulau, *Changing Views of Representation*, [in:] *Contemporary Political Science: Towards Empirical Theory*, I. de Sola Pool (ed.), New York 1967, p. 72 *et seq.*

constituency. The link between the MP and the constituency was replaced by a link with the political party.[88] Over time, this connection resulted in recognizing that the MP was obliged to respect the party's election manifesto, while the party – in accordance with the mandate theory – cannot promote ideas which did not previously gain electors' approval.[89] At this point the mandate theory, in both its varieties, turned out to be particularly resilient. Consequently, nowadays the 'hard' or 'party' version of the mandate theory assumes that in a general election the nation determines the direction for actions of the government, i.e. the group acting on behalf of the party and its parliamentary subgroup, for the government's term of office. For understandable reasons, this makes the governing group responsible for the programme's implementation in the next election, when they seek re-election. Incidentally, the essence and permanent element of the mandate theory, regardless of its various embodiments, is that the programme, both as to the principle and in details, should be submitted to the electors for consideration and implemented after gaining their approval expressed in the general election. The mandate theory designed in this way neatly combines the key elements of the English way of looking at representation, i.e. the concept of responsible government and the emphasis on the convergence of wills of the represented and the representative. As a result, once again, it turns out that the English and then the British model of mandate refers mainly to the sociological approach to representation, noticing in it mainly the need for the representative to convey the views of the represented.[90]

It should, however, be observed that the British way of viewing representation, in spite of its seemingly completely different angle, does, at a certain point, approach the ideas conceived on the other side of the English Channel. Both doctrines come close to each other at the point where they recognize the parliament's sovereignty. As we know, in France the conclusion was reached as a consequence of accepting the thesis that there actually was no sovereign outside of the parliament, once the nation and its will were no more than a legal fiction. As far as the House of Commons is concerned, even though the logic of thinking was different, the final conclusion turned to be the same and found its expression in recognizing the sovereignty of the representative

88 *Cf.* W.I. Jennings, *The British Constitution…*, p. 84.

89 This is why representation in its British variety is nowadays very often called 'party government', because the theory of the mandate in its strict, hard or strong form is also a theory of institutionalizing the role of political parties. A. Wright, *British Politics: A Very Short Introduction*, Oxford 2003, p. 64 *et seq.*

90 *Cf.* P. Magdwick, *A New Introduction to British Politics*, London 1984, p. 275.

assembly as a consequence of electoral accreditation. So an MP, and subsequently the party, were authorized to govern in accordance with the principle of responsible government, thus being given discretion to act within the limits of powers granted to them. These actions, being nothing else but a form of implementing the 'election promises', enjoyed full approval and recognition and this was in fact a shortcut to the assumption that the parliament (grouping representatives selected according to the key of their 'election promises') could do anything.[91] This is why we can probably venture the statement that the British parliamentary sovereignty was a consequence of recognizing the realness of the nation as the sovereign.[92] The parliament could do anything not because the sovereign did not actually exist, once its fictional character was assumed upfront (like in France), but precisely because the nation-sovereign was by all means a fact, something present, whose visible will was manifested in elections held on a periodical basis. Hence parliamentary sovereignty was a logical consequence of the nation's will being strictly respected. The universal, final and undisputable character of decisions made by the House of Commons was nothing else but a consequence of the fact that the nation, in an election, expressed support for a specific manifesto presented by a candidate (in the 'soft' mandate theory) or by a political party (in the 'hard' mandate theory), as a result of which there had to arise a legal obligation to keep an earlier 'election promise'.[93] Thus sovereignty of the parliament, understood to mean that no power on this earth could reverse what the Parliament had done, resulted from the fact that decisions of the parliament were backed by social acceptance and were nothing else but an implementation of ideas on which electors' opinion was sought in universal ballot. This way, also on the British soil, an act of parliament emerged as an expression of the nation's will, while legislative sovereignty – adopted as a dogma in the House of Commons – was a consequence of its earlier election origin.[94]

It turns out that the sovereignty of the parliament originated from the conviction that in its decisions it simply expressed the electors' will and the latter was

---

91 *Cf.* J. Goldsworthy, *The Sovereignty of Parliament. History and Philosophy*, Oxford 2001, p. 229 *et seq.*

92 *Cf.* R. Weill, *We the British People*, „Public Law" 2004, summer, p. 380 *et seq.* A very similar standpoint was presented also by Albert V. Dicey. *Cf.* A.V. Dicey, *Introduction to the Study of the Law of the Constitution*, London 2012, p. 37 *et seq.*

93 *Cf.* P. Magdwick, *A New Introduction…*, p. 275.

94 *Cf.* I. Nguyen-Duy, *Souverainete du Parlement…*, p. 295 *et seq.*

sacred and inviolable.[95] Despite its sovereignty, the parliament is not completely free and unbound in its activities. The framework of its activities is delimited by the sacrosanct 'election promise' determining the scope of permitted measures, including legislative ones. Thus, changing them and, consequently, also introducing new substance, always requires obtaining a new proxy, which can occur only through an election.[96] As we can see, the parliament's sovereignty is, at least in some sense, subject to dual limits. Firstly, it is limited by the substance of the 'election promise', because the sovereign right of decision covers only those areas where there is no conflict with that promise. Secondly, it is limited by the term of proxies, because no promise is unlimited in time. The time of exercising the mandate is thus the period during which the parliament moves within the perimeter of matters covered by the promise, which means that a new proxy, that is, a new term of the parliament, may cover with the scope of its regulation also a new 'election promise'. An election promise confirmed by the votes of the electorate is, however, an arena for free manoeuvres of the parliament, and this is how its sovereignty is expressed.[97]

The assumed structure, while respecting the will of the electorate as the source of powers of the parliament or, more broadly speaking, the governing ones, matches the traditional English way of viewing representation from the sociological perspective. Various modifications of the model of political representation which occur in the British doctrine[98] all converge at one point: namely that representation should always take the form of repetition of wills of the two entities in the relationship of representation, i.e. the will of representatives and that of the represented. So we can venture a slightly simplified statement that the English model of political representation has almost always been much closer

95 This is why we could confidently say that the principle of popular sovereignty was and is one of the main principles of the British system of government, even though it is usually not expressly articulated. It is, however, assumed to be the true essence of the British system and that it is the foundation of such (logically derived) principles as e.g. the principle of responsible government or precisely that of sovereignty of the parliament. *Cf.* I. MacLean, *What's Wrong with the British Constitution*, Oxford 2010, p. 313 *et seq.*

96 *Cf.* W.I. Jennings, *The British Constitution...*, p. 195 *et seq.*

97 *Cf.* J. Goldsworthy, *The Sovereignty of Parliament...*, p. 236 *et seq.*

98 Which, in their details are extremely separate and 'dispersed' and consequently are embedded in various solutions, from imperative to free mandate; from treating the deputy as a 'trustee' of the constituency to the theory of the mandate in its hard version, correlating the will of the majority with the will of the party that won the election.

to sociological approaches, perceiving in representation the need to make the will of the represented and the will of their representatives more coherent (duplicate, repeat or translate it). Therefore true representation was treated as the representative (delegate, MP, deputy) reflecting the will of the represented, perceived more literally as the *corps électoral.* The French model was definitively more sophisticated. It did not provide for a faithful, sociological correlation, but sought the sense of representation in the legal mechanism of attribution, which consisted in assigning the will of the representative to the represented subject; the latter was not equated with the elector, but treated much more abstractly as, precisely, the hypothetical nation-sovereign. Yet both models, despite major differences, had several things in common. The first one was treating electors as the true quintessence of the representative regime. While in the English model elections were mainly a mechanism of forming a true correlation between both parties of the relationship of representation,[99] in the French one they were a form of distribution of power[100] or – in other words – a mechanism of distribution of powers between two entities linked by the relationship of representation[101]. But in either model they were a point of departure for the regime of political representation, being a certain 'spawn' or the proverbial *clé de voûte*[102] of such representation. The second one was recognition of the representative assembly's sovereignty. This conclusion was drawn either because the notion of nation-sovereign as something actual, existing in reality, was questioned (France), or because it was acknowledged that the parliament, whose composition reflected the socio-political and economic features of the electorate and its will, had no rival in the mechanisms of aggregating and articulating the will of the nation-sovereign.

4. Andrew Heywood's Retrospective Model of Representation

Yet the French and English views on representation do not exhaust all the possible theoretical approaches to the phenomenon of political representation, nor, the more so, do they reflect all the changes in the perception of this phenomenon that occurred over time. This is why, apart from those two models, which are

99 *Cf.* B. Coxall, L. Robins, R. Leach, *Contemporary British Politics*, New York 2003, p. 73 *et seq.*
100 *Cf.* P. Parini, *Régimes politiques contemporains*, Paris 1991, p. 73 *et seq.*
101 M. Prélot, *Institutions politiques et droit constitutionnel*, Paris 1957, p. 358.
102 I. Nguyen-Duy, *Souverainete du Parlement…*, p. 237.

probably presented most frequently,[103] different divisions and classifications of models of political representation can be attempted, taking into account historical experiences and transformations of that representation. Here, a good example may be Andrew Heywood's proposal, in which he identifies four types (kinds) of political representation.[104] The first one is trusteeship model; the second one – delegation model; the third one – the mandate model and the fourth and last one – resemblance model. According to the trustee model of representation the representative is a trustee, i.e. 'a person who is vested with formal responsibility for another's property or affairs.[105]' It is recognized that the promoter of viewing representatives as trustees was E. Burke, for whom the essence of representation was serving the constituents through 'mature judgement' and 'enlightened conscience'. According to E. Burke, the essence of acting *pro publico bono*, as the quintessence of representation, was precisely that the representative-trustee was not blindly obedient to the instructions of his electors, but served them with 'his mature judgement'.[106] Thus the trustee was a better being, with better education, able to look 'farther' and 'deeper' and additionally provided with a rare ability of rising above the particular divisions and interests. As a result of being elected he became a trustee of his electors precisely due to his virtues. It was not accidental, as is observed, that the selection of such citizens, by definition better, more enlightened, more experienced or simply wiser was fostered by the clearly individualistic election system, which generated voting for a leader, a local authority.[107] Here we can trace very strong elitist inclinations. The elected representatives should be free in their judgements and decisions (thus provided with a free mandate) not because the law so requires, but because this is their moral obligation, since they are fundamentally better beings.[108] Hence they should 'think for themselves and exercise independent judgement on the grounds that the mass of people do not know their own best interests'.[109] Thus the feature which typifies the trustee model of representation is a very strongly marked elitism and the belief that the essence of representation is by no means the mere 'technical' representation of the constituents' interest, but rather determining the 'general

103 *Cf.* e.g.: B. Manin, *The Principles…*, p. 95 *et seq.*; C. Haguenau-Moizard, *Les systèmes politiques…*, p. 24.
104 *Cf.* A. Heywood, *Politics*, Houndmills-New York 2013, p. 197 *et seq.*
105 *Ibidem*, p. 198.
106 H.-Y. Lee, *Political Representation…*, p. 18–19.
107 *Cf.* B. Manin, *The Principles…*, p. 96.
108 *Cf.* H.-Y. Lee, *Political Representation…*, p. 15 *et seq.*
109 A. Heywood, *Politics*, p. 198.

good' according to the criterion of common sense. In addition to E. Burke, it is John Stuart Mill and Thomas Paine who should be seen as the promoters of representation perceived as trusteeship relationship. The former, as we know, supported elite democracy and acknowledged that not all judgements and opinions are of the same importance and equal value, although naturally all of them, for the sake of the ideal of democracy, require representation.[110] Yet representation does not mean representing all ideas and concepts to the same (equal) extent.[111] Some of them, even if only because they are more professional, experienced, substantively elaborated, etc., should rank definitively higher, which means that in the process of representation they should be present more strongly than the remaining ones. Consequently representation should refer to all of them, but certainly not according to the principle of equality. This encapsulates the elite character of the approach proposed by J.S. Mill, namely a sort of 'weighting' of representation according to predefined criteria (education).[112] In turn, T. Paine agreed with J.S. Mill on one thing: that education was the essence of true representation. But while J.S. Mill believed that the differences in the level of education should 'naturally' translate into representation, recognizing that it was not and could not be egalitarian, but precisely elitist, as we know, T. Paine did not want to place a barrier to education and, consequently, representation. Moreover, he was convinced that a well-educated society will have better representation and the latter will reduce egoistic, particular interests. Therefore, good universal education is the essence of representation for T. Paine, because at the point of departure it will make it more oriented towards the general good than the good of individuals. Education eliminates the sectional and individual point of view, instilling a 'sense of social responsibility'[113]. Consequently, educated citizens-electors have the much-needed common sense, which should be the essence of political representation and, consequently, the decisions taken on the public forum.[114] In conclusion it should be stated that the project of representation as

---

110 *Cf.* H.-Y. Lee, *Political Representation…*, p. 24 *et seq.*

111 *Cf.* A. Zakaras, *John Stuart Mill: Individuality and Participatory Democracy*, [in:] *J.S. Mill's Political Thought. A Bicentennial Reassessment*, N. Urbinati, A. Zakaras (eds.), Oxford 2007, p. 200 *et seq.*

112 In electoral law it was reflected e.g. in the technique of plural voting, which meant that electors had different number of votes depending on their 'value' (with extra votes for electors with better education or wealthier ones).

113 A. Heywood, *Politics*, p. 199.

114 More on this topic: G. Claeys, *Thomas Paine. Social and Political Thought*, London 1989, p. 42 *et seq.*

trusteeship assumed that although the representative expressed the will of the represented, he was not at all bound by the latter's judgements and opinions. More than anything else, his role is that of a 'trustee', someone who knows better, has a broader view of public affairs, but also someone who does not act being guided by his own, thoroughly particular, interest. A representative has free will (so in the legal sense he holds free mandate), but cannot (should not) use it to pursue his own selfish interests. Free will should rather make him immune to the lobbying of particular opinions and result in the common good prevailing in the final decisions, when various reasons and counter-reasons clash with one another.

Another model proposed by A. Heywood is the so-called delegate model. It assumes that a representative is a delegate, hence a person 'who is chosen to act for another on the basis of clear guidance and instruction.'[115] In this model, the delegate is consequently not expected to be independent in formulating assessments and views, or other kinds of *pro publico bono* activities, but rather acting in someone's name and on someone's account. This is why a delegate is 'a person who acts as a conduit for the views of others, while having little or no capacity to exercise his or her own judgement or preferences.'[116] So we can see that delegate model of representation is actually nothing else but representation based on imperative mandate.[117] It perceives the representative as, firstly, a representative of a relatively narrow group (identified with the people who actually voted for the delegate or, slightly more broadly, with his constituents) and, secondly, as a person provided with specific directives determining the manner of voting and conduct in order to possibly faithfully translate the will of the principal. On this occasion, Andrew Heywood remarks that the true delegation representation should establish a mechanism of recalling a delegate if he should act at variance with the mandate (election instructions). In his view – which is incidentally in line with the classic assumptions of imperative mandate – representation based on the logic of delegation forms a logical progression, namely: election of the delegate (as the first step); providing the said delegate with a mandate whose contents concern how the delegate should act and conduct himself (second step); the possibility of recalling the delegate if he fails to execute the mandate granted to him (third step). Recall of a delegate is here, like in every version of imperative mandate, a sanction for wrong (incorrect) exercise of the mandate and at

115 A. Heywood, *Politics*, p. 199.

116 *Ibidem*.

117 *Cf.* Y. Déloye, *Mandat impératif*, [in:] *Dictionnaire du vote...*, p. 611 *et seq.*

the same time a warranty of preserving the essence of the delegation model, in which the delegate is obliged to express the will of the principal instead of formulating his own judgements and assessments. As we can easily observe, the presented approach strongly resonates with the ideas of J.J. Rousseau, who never treated the deputy as the proverbial 'free electron', but as a 'necessary evil', which by definition had to be contained and mitigated somehow. What guaranteed this mitigation and respect for the authentic sovereignty of the people (nation), was precisely the imperative mandate, which, in the view of J.J. Rousseau, ensured respect for the will of the represented. Hence e.g. A. Heywood expresses the opinion that delegate representation corresponds to the idea of popular sovereignty and in general it is probably the most democratic one, of course if democracy is understood as the classic government of the people, for the people and by the people. According to that author it is so because delegation ensures sameness of wills of the representative and the represented and efficient control of the represented over their representatives, which is particularly well-illustrated by the possibility of recalling the representative. Nevertheless this does not mean at all that delegation model of representation is fault-free. The most serious drawback is certainly the danger of conflicts bred by the promotion of narrow, particular interests. It is precisely here that the fundamental dilemma of representation, once mentioned by E. Burke, becomes apparent. It is the conflict of two different and, more importantly, mutually exclusive roles of the deputy, i.e. that of the 'ambassador' of his own constituency, and that of a member of parliament. The former role, as we know, gives priority to particular, individual interest, while the latter focuses on the general and universal interest. Therefore the parliament as a representative body should always have in mind the universal interest of all, yet this cannot be achieved in a situation when a parliamentarian is expected to represent individual interests. The above contradiction is one of the basic topics in any discussions on political representation, revealing its truly astonishing durability, but also its rudimentarily problematic nature.[118] The delegate model of representation reveals its weaknesses in one more area. Treating a representative as a delegate, tightly bound to election instructions, reduces his importance as a leader. All in all, a delegate is not expected to have mobilization skills, the ability to promote his own ideas and conceptions, to be active and to act according to the common sense cannon. Quite the contrary, an ideal delegate is a person without any ambitions of his own, without the ability to think independently,

118 More on this topic: N. Urbinati, *Representative Democracy. Principles and Genealogy*, Chicago 2008, p. 35 *et seq.*

precisely executing the orders of his principals. A delegate representative cannot become a statesman for one simple reason: 'professional politicians are not trusted to exercise their own judgement'[119]. So politicians are forced to represent the ideas of their electors in constituents or even flatter them, thus they are unable to mobilize the public or provide it with vision and inspiration.

Therefore, the delegation model of representation proves just as problematic as the earlier trusteeship model of representation. In view of the above, one should seek for other, even better models of representation, or at least more faithful ones (for example to the reality). Therefore yet another type of representation is proposed: this time it is the mandate representation. The starting point for this model are political parties, which in practice are known to have considerably changed the model of representation. Both the trustee and the delegate models were shaped in the practice of political action even before the appearance of modern, well-organized, efficiently operating political parties. So the earlier representation models regarded a representative as an independent actor, an autonomous subject in every sense of the word, without any organizational affiliations. Regardless of whether the representative was provided with a free or imperative mandate, each time he was perceived as an independent, separate and individual entity, under no circumstances as part of any other, bigger organization (e.g. political party, professional union, association, etc.). Actually the only manifestation of some sort of 'organizational' connection of the deputy (and only in delegation based on the principle of imperative mandate) was a constituency, of which the representative felt an 'envoy', 'ambassador' or emissary. No other structures were known or envisaged at that time yet. But at a certain moment the electoral and parliamentary arena of political rivalry was dominated by parties and it was them that gradually seized the representative. This very fact is accentuated in the mandate model of representation, which, with good cause, refers to the British theory of the mandate in its 'strong', i.e. party version. The mandate model indicates that 'candidates are rarely elected on the basis of their personal qualities and talents', much 'more commonly, they are seen as foot soldiers for a party and supported because if its public image or programme of policies'.[120] This is why it should be deemed that 'in winning an election, a party gains a popular mandate that authorizes it to carry out whatever policies or programmes it outlined during the election campaign'.[121] Thus the mandate model of representation

119 A. Heywood, *Politics...*, p. 200.

120 *Ibidem.*

121 *Ibidem*, p. 283.

links the deputy not with an abstract *corps électoral*, not with a constituency where he gained the mandate, but with the political party under whose banner the deputy successfully stood for election. Consequently the mandate model is closely correlated with the phenomenon of party discipline, because according to it 'politicians serve their constituents not by thinking for themselves or acting as a channel to convey their views, but by remaining loyal to their party and its policies'.[122] The mandate model has several important consequences. Firstly, it understandably fosters the introduction of a proportional mandate allocation formula, once it is fairly commonly assumed that proportional representation is the pro-party representation. Secondly, it institutionalizes the role of political parties whose electoral monopoly is consequently petrified and becomes not only a question of practice (as it was before), but also a question of law. Thirdly, it makes it easier to introduce the mechanism of party discipline, thus linking the deputy with his political party, which *mutatis mutandi* puts on the agenda the question about the renaissance of the conception of imperative mandate. Fourthly, once it obliges the party to implement the election manifesto, at the same time it ensures consistency of opinions of representatives and the represented, which is the goal of political representation in every instance. Finally, fifthly, it puts on the agenda an important question about who or what the actual agent of representation is. It is still the individual deputy or perhaps the political party which obtained the mandate of public trust on the basic of the presented election manifesto? One can easily guess that the mandate model suggests rather the second answer.

It should be noted that the mandate model, though certainly attractive, does not fully reflect the true picture of the relationship of representation. Although the role of a party is not questioned today, it is still an open question to what extent the election manifesto of a political party is the sole criterion for the electors' choice. We know that the manifesto is taken into account as one of the criteria, but not necessarily in the first place, especially nowadays, at the time of greater importance of various election marketing techniques, which shift the elector's attention to other elements of the election offering. Another thing to be considered is the dilution of election manifestos, which is observed with growing frequency. Thus manifestos cease to be treated as party identification labels. Their capacious and general character means that in actual fact various parties could subscribe to them, which phenomenon is observed particularly in majoritarian systems, where the election game is based on a simple 'zero-one' system and where every

122 *Ibidem*.

vote is worth its proverbial 'weight in gold'. Finally, the issue which casts doubts on the theory of representation seen as the mandate is the fragmentary character of the election manifesto with respect to the questions which are really tackled. Most election manifestos of political parties fail to cover all matters, which in turn results in a situation when the very mandate, understood as determining the scope of matters commissioned to be implemented by the winning political party, becomes highly controversial. If in this context we can speak of mandate at all, it is to a limited extent, usually referring to generalities.

Questioning the mandate model of representation makes the resemblance model constantly? valid.[123] It is based not so much on the way representatives are chosen, but rather on whether they typify or resemble the group they represent. So the key notion for the model is that of 'representative cross-section',[124] according to which the representative body should be built. It is easy to notice that the resemblance model refers to the sociological view of representation. In accordance with it, representation means nothing else but capturing in the representative body the inherent, relevant features of the represented group, which goal is best, that is, most faithfully, served by the proportional algorithm of distribution of mandates.[125] Representation as a resemblance is thus creating the personal substratum of the elected body in such a way that is reflects all, or at least the most important, features identifying the group which is to be represented. In extreme cases representation as a resemblance is an expectation that representative bodies will be created in such a way that they mirror all sociological features of the electorate (e.g. gender, education, place of residence, income bracket, etc.).[126] Consequently it is often referred to as 'demographic', 'sociological', 'mimetic' or 'microcosmic' representation.[127] And sometimes the sense of proportional representation is reduced to resemblance representation. In this context, Andrew Heywood suggests – by all means correctly – that resemblance representation is convenient in many ways, because it eliminates to a large extent the controversial issues which were raised with respect to other, earlier representation models. In this case there is no fundamental dispute about the nature of the mandate (free or imperative) or dispute about the individualistic or collectivist, or somehow mixed character of the whole relationship of representation; nor is there a

---

123 *Cf.* A. Heywood, *Politics...*, p. 201.

124 *Ibidem.*

125 *Cf.* M. Duverger, *Institutions politiques et droit constitutionnel*, Paris 1966, p. 81, 82.

126 *Cf.* M. Dogan, *L'origine sociale du personnel parlementaire français* élu *en 1951*, [in:] *Partis politiques et classe sociales en France*, M. Duverger (ed.), Paris 1955.

127 A. Heywood, *Politics...*, p. 201.

dispute as to whether the representative should or should not be the leader of his constituency. Here, the problem of representation is reduced to the requirement of the sociological rule of resemblance, which, once fulfilled, gives a generally satisfactory picture of political representation.

5. Other Diachronic Models and Scenarios of Representation

The typology proposed by A. Heywood, where the author distinguishes trusteeship representation, delegation representation, mandate representation and, finally, resemblance representation, proves that political representation need not be divided traditionally and rather conventionally into the French and English varieties.[128] The historically developed models are undergoing constant changes, modifications and accommodations, but also they at all times remain somewhere in the background, providing support for other, differently established classifications. Among those other classifications it is perhaps worthwhile to mention one more, where changes in representation are viewed mainly (though not exclusively) in the historical perspective. Consequently, it identifies: 1. monocratic representation, where the ruler was the sole representative; 2. classical parliamentary representation, consisting in selection of a deputy who, together with other deputies, forms a collective representative body; 3. party representation, in which the deputy and even the parliament itself are replaced in the representation process by political parties according to a well-known concept of *Parteienstaat*; 4. pluralist representation, in which the parties lost their monopoly in representation and various other structures act as representatives alongside them; these structures include e.g. pressure groups, trade unions, associations or e.g. civic groups formed *ad hoc*.[129]

A certain variety or variant of the above view is found in the proposal to distinguish three basic 'representation models', i.e. parliamentary representation, party representation and, finally, corporate representation.[130] The main criterion for distinguishing those three pure, or – looking at the problem differently – the clearest models of representation is the so-called space of public debate[131], that is, the place where various, often mutually exclusive interests, clash and where – in the name of preserving the systemic homeostasis – some consensus has to be reached. The parliament was the original space, regardless of whether it only

---

128 *Cf.* B. Manin, *The Principles...*, p. 94 *et seq.*

129 *Cf.* T. Debard, *Dictionnaire de droit constitutionnel*, Paris 2002, p. 269, 270.

130 *Cf.* D. Held, *Models of Democracy*, Stanford 2006, p. 158 *et seq.*

131 *Ibidem*, p. 182.

grouped 'freelancers', that is, parliamentarians without strong and unequivocal party affiliations, or persons linked by strong ties of membership with a party or another organization having political features. So the model of parliamentary representation indicates that there is practically no other place, apart from the parliament, where interests are disclosed. Thus social, political and economic requests are sufficiently aggregated and articulated in the nationwide representative body, which remains not only the basic forum of political representation, but actually the only one. In case of party representation, the space for debate shifts. The place where various ideas are confronted with one another is no longer just the parliament, but the whole *de facto* party system (referring both to parties in the parliament and outside it), while the complex rivalry among parties (on election, parliamentary and cabinet levels) becomes the proper area of representation understood as expressing various interests. So in the party representation model, the parliament is just one of the arenas for political and party rivalry, whereas representation of various judgements, views and opinions has a much broader dimension and refers to all parties, which, taken together, form the party system. But as we know, in times of advanced socio-economic differentiation this model devalued and was replaced by corporate representation, in which the key element is the tripartite relationship between organizations of employers, employees and the state. In this model, understandably, both the parliament and the political parties lose their importance, because they are simply unable to correctly recognize, aggregate and finally present all the relevant social issues. Yet the corporate profile of representation demonstrates not only, and not even predominantly, a change in the very space for public debate, but also a change in the debate's agenda. In this model, traditional political issues, though still important, give way to social, economic and (particularly nowadays) ecological issues, which turn out to be much more important and, at the end of the day, politically more significant, because they influence almost all the possible political cleavages.[132]

Going further along this path, Pierre Rosanvallon, also approaching the problem of representation in a diachronic way, identifies its two basic types or kinds. The first one is 'political representation', which takes place in the parliament and its area is the space of inter-party rivalry in the broad sense; the other one, which is a sign of the current times, is 'post-political representation', which, firstly, is no

132 *Cf.* H. Best, *Cleavage Representation in European Parliamentary History*, [in:] *Democratic Representation in Europe. Diversity, Change and Convergence*, M. Cotta, H. Best (eds.), Oxford 2007, p. 292 *et seq.*

longer parliamentary representation and, secondly, is no longer representation which becomes apparent only in the inter-party competition. The latter representation, which, in P. Rosanvallon's view, is realised today, is reflected not only by organized and institutionalized interest or pressure groups, but also by grassroots, often spontaneously formed, free groups of citizens who want to achieve a specific, usually short-term, goal. 'Post-political representation' understood in this way includes also the more and more enthusiastically used instruments of direct democracy, which in view of the above is no longer treated as a traditional antonym of representation, but perceived as its complementary and accessory variety.

Representation can also be defined and, consequently and subsequently, an attempt can be made at classifying it as 'institutional means for translating segmental cleavages into the political realm'.[133] In other words, representation can be perceived as a method thanks to which a complex socio-political and economic reality, which determines the heterogeneity of the represented, will be mimicked at the level of political institutions. In this context the aim is not to translate the reality exactly and faithfully; what matters is rather the very method of such translation and the results it yields. Taking this train of thought further, Arend Lijphart proposes two basic models of representation, relevant for the current times, i.e. the Westminster model and the so-called consensus model.[134] The former model is characterized by the majoritarian electoral formula, an orderly two-party system, a clear socio-political cleavage, usually marked by a single basic determinant, and exclusively representative democracy. On the other hand, the model of representation with consensus features is characterized first and foremost by the multi-dimensionality of the party system, which means a multiplicity of issues that finally determine the political, social and economic cleavages within the electorate; continued existence of the multi-party system (as a consequence of the first feature) and – as is logical in view of the above – application of the proportional formula. It is easy to notice that what is the axis of representation for A. Lijphart is the party system plus, on the one hand, what shapes it (i.e. social and political cleavages within the electorate) and, on the other hand, what allows it to be expressed in an institutionalized way, that is, the electoral system. Socio-political cleavages and the issues which arise around them determine the cross-section of the represented, which should be expressed somehow,

133 A. Lijphart, *Democracy in Plural Societies. A Comparative Exploration*, New Haven and London 1977, p. 83.

134 *Cf.* A. Lijphart, *Democracies. Patterns of Majoritarian and Consensus Government in Twenty-One Countries*, New Haven–London 1984, p. 1 *et seq.*

including through political representation. The electoral system is, in most cases, an effect of the persisting cleavages and has – at least in general terms – a stabilizing effect upon them. Therefore A. Lijphart is of the opinion that it is impossible to imagine modern political representation without political parties and that all representation is indeed party representation,[135] which supposedly is the single most important factor distinguishing it from all earlier types and models of representation and which currently (depending on the number of the relevant parties) determines each individual model of representation. According to A. Lijphart even if there are other organizational structures and even if they function in the mechanism of representation of individual interests, not only are they unable to replace parties, but they cannot even be a real competition for them. Therefore, despite the evolution of political representation, elections are still the basic form of the so-called correlation, that is, obtaining the convergence of judgements and views of the represented and their representatives, while political parties are a means of such correlation.

A. Lijphart believes that the decisive factor why contemporary representation is fundamentally different is precisely the political parties, which have dominated or even appropriated representation both at its election stage and at the parliamentary stage. This is why representation, in both of its current variants, i.e. the Westminster and consensus models, should be contrasted with 'non-party' or 'extra-party' representation, which was characteristic until modern, efficient, organizationally and electorally strong political parties appeared. Today such 'non-party' or 'extra-party' representation remains a certain political wish, which in all sorts of searches for the best model of representation still wants to find a pure, unadulterated relationship between the representative and the represented. This, however, seems to be an ideal which has never been actually or completely achieved. Between the representative and the represented there have always been elements that disturbed the process of political correlation. They included particular interests, pressures from highly sectional groups and circles; similarly individual interests of the constituency; or, finally, interests formulated (changed) by political parties or other similar formations. All models of representation, in all versions and varieties, only attempted to describe the continuity and change in representation understood as identifying the interests that link the representative and the represented.

---

135 *Cf.* A. Lijphart, *Democracy in Plural Societies…*, p. 83 *et seq.*

Chapter IV: Constitutional Expression of Representation

1. The Content of the Constitutional Principle of Representation: *Rei Compertae*

The general idea of political representation or, following a different linguistic convention, of political agency is an systemic solution that most often finds its constitutional manifestation, very strongly emphasised at that. What's more, the basic principle of political representation in a sense tests or tackles (not suggesting a confrontational nature of such testing) other constitutional principles and solutions. These other principles, including above all else the constitutional principle of sovereignty of the nation (or, in other words, national supremacy) and, secondly, the constitutional principle of a representative (free) mandate, are regarded as supplementary or resultative *vis-à-vis* representation. Political representation is without a doubt the key political principle of the state; in addition it is strongly correlated with the principle of sovereignty, whereby both these principles (or perhaps one, but interpreted in two ways or having two variants[1]) become a fundamental principle when it comes to defining the axiological foundations of the political system that every fundamental law aims to reflect. Its axiological dimension surfaces in that it offers some sort of a punch line for the already classical definition of democratic government being the famous Lincoln's 'government of the people, by the people, for the people'. Under such an approach, the principle of sovereignty of the people (the nation) tallies with the 'government of the people' (*le gouvernment du peuple*), while the principle of representation is rooted in, explicably, in the said power being exercised 'by the people' (*gouvernment par le peuple*) and at the same time 'for the people' (*gouvernment pour le peuple*).[2] It reflects the most rudimentary understanding of representation as acting in the name of someone or something and as representing (expressing) somebody's position with an effect for somebody or something. Holding on to this convention, the principle of political representation laced up in a bodice of a constitutional principle tones with mainly the juridical approach to representation, according to which its substance lies in the powers of the

1 *Cf.* M. Verpeaux, *Manuel de droit constitutionnel*, Paris 2010, p. 87 *et seq.*

2 *Cf.* J.-M. Denquin, *Introduction à la science politique*, Paris 2001, p. 63.

nation (the people) being exercised by their duly authorised representatives. Accepting such a line of reasoning invokes a number of consequences. First of all, power is held by a collective subject in the form of people (the nation). Secondly, for certain reasons this collegiate body cannot personally or independently exercise this power. Thirdly, in the light of the foregoing, the said subject delegates its substitutes or representatives to exercise power on his behalf, which power is *de jure* exercised by a group, such as the people (the nation). Fourthly, actions of the substitute will be perceived and regarded as actions of those who delegate the substitute. It is so, since regardless of who 'physically' exercises power, i.e. be it the people (*le peuple*) or the representatives of the people (*par le peuple*), at any time and place such power will be exercised on behalf of the people and with an effect that is binding upon the people (*pour le peuple*). Accordingly, the constitutional principle of representation has it that the entire nation grants a collective and impersonal mandate to all its representatives, by virtue of which the task of determining the welfare of the people, the general good or the general will – which is the basic idea of political representation[3] – and subsequently decision-making on public affairs was entrusted to nobody else but representatives who, according to a well-known metaphor by E. Sieyès, became the lips of the people and could articulate their sovereign will. Expression of this will by representatives was on the other hand ascribed to a collective bearer of sovereign rights, which *summa summarum* coined quite a simple structure, whereby representatives speak on behalf of their nation, yet the voice of representatives in regarded as the voice of the nation as a whole. This is how a certain legal fiction of a nation acting through its representatives came to exist, via which the governing and the governed have been coalesced in a way. By all means, this fiction has from the very outset been abstract and it remains so till now, alike the general principle of representation that envisages the presence of the absent, meaning that a representative of the people acting *hic et nunc* personifies the absent, that is, the represented.[4]

It is worthy of note, nonetheless, that a strictly juridical analysis of the principle of political representation is much more nuanced that it might have appeared at the outset. Indeed, its essence stems from a legal fiction according to which the will of representative is synonymous with the will of the people, alongside with other equally vital elements which, once merged, only then make up the juridical construct of political representation and its essentially abstract form. For

3 *Cf.* C. Pateman, *Participation and Democratic Theory*, Cambridge 2000, p. 22 *et seq.*

4 *Cf.* D. Mineur, *Archéologie de la représentation politique*, Paris 2010, p. 127 *et seq.*

obvious reasons, its pivotal point is the act of delegating the representatives, i.e. designating the substitutes whose actions will be regarded as the actions of the substituted, and even more precisely, will be equated with those actions or will simply be – at least from a formal point of view – the actions of the substituted.[5] It plain to see that the emphasis is placed primarily on the act of delegating the substitute, and the essence of representation lies in granting the investiture.[6] From the point of view of the substance of representation what is important here is not so much the subsequent assignment of the features of the represented to the representative, but naming the representative. Such approach to representation demotes the represented (the substituted) only to a subject that indicates who is to make, on his behalf, pertinent decisions that were nominally assigned to him. The granting of the investiture (a proxy) is this case lies at the very heart of the principle of representative government, while the key role in this government is vested in elections as the only process via which investiture can be granted.[7] Hence, it is highlighted that it is the general elections (regardless of their adjectival descriptions and definitions) that constitute the salient (and at times the one and only) form of civic participation, while at the same time being the mechanism via which the constitutional principle of representation is implemented to the greatest extent.[8] In line with this approach, elections are seen as a legal form of awarding the mandate, that is – in a word – an instruction to represent the electorate at the level of the national representative body.[9] Narrowing down the matter even further, it is sometimes said that representation is nothing but certain choices made by the electorate, while political agency is the will of the voters only (*volonté des* électurs).[10] Beyond doubt, adoption of such a view devalues the voter (the represented) to a subject that simply specifies who will exercise the mandate on his behalf.[11] As it is rightly pointed out, governance thus is not – with this type of assumption being made – the essence of representation.

---

5 *Cf.* F. Robbe, *Démocratie représentative et participation*, [in:] *La démocratie participative*, (ed.) F. Robbe, Paris 2007, p. 11 *et seq.*

6 M. Prélot, *Institutions politiques et droit constitutionnel*, Paris 1957, p. 358.

7 *Cf.* P. Türk, *Théorie générale du droit constitutionnel*, Paris 2010, p. 103 *et seq.*

8 *Cf.* J.-M. Denquin, *Introduction à la science politique…*, p. 66. More on this topic: F. Rouvillois, *Droit constitutionnel. Fondements et pratiques*, Paris 2005, p. 230 *et seq.*

9 According to the rule that 'l'élection sert à désigner les représentants' – P. Avril, J. Gicquel, *Lexique de droit constitutionnel*, Paris 2004, p. 103.

10 P. Leroy, *Les régimes politiques du monde contemporain. Introduction générale*, Grenoble 2001, vol. I, p. 63.

11 *Cf.* P. Avril, J. Gicquel, *Droit parlementaire*, Paris 2004, p. 29, 30.

It is merely an indication who will be the substitute, thus invoking the proverbial saying, who would be 'willing for the nation' (according to the well-known definition by E. Sieyès that representation is nothing but 'willing for the nation' (*vouloir pour la nation*) and thus expressing its anticipations and aspirations).

In yet another, slightly mutated, perspective on the juridical approach to deciphering the sense of the constitutional principle of representation, representation is viewed as 'delegating rights of some sort upon someone else'.[12] Representation in this case thus means merely 'delegating power',[13] which is another of the possible meanings of the separation of powers, except not traditional, i.e. horizontal, but vertical, between the sovereign and its specifically understood emanation, that is, the representatives. The distinctive regime of representation is, after all, the regime of a divided government, where the proper sovereign, that is the nation, cannot itself exercise power and therefore a transfer of power takes place, and even more specifically, a transfer of exercise of power.[14] Naturally, such transfer is made during each and every election, hence in a sense this meaning of representation coincides with the one previously described. However, inasmuch as previously the sense of representation *de facto* laid in elections as an act whereby the represented subject indicates (designates) his representative, here representation has a much more abstract dimension. Indeed, elections are always a concrete embodiment of the principle of political representation, yet the principle itself has mainly the dimension of a certain theoretical project, explicating the sense of popular sovereignty which, after all, cannot in most cases be deployed via means of direct democracy. It is thus not the point that elections stand for the delegating of powers, which are transferred from a collective subject upon the representative, but that regardless of the form in which each and every time the principle of representation is applied by designating the representatives, the essence of representation always is the exercise of sovereign powers by the nation-sovereign that never acts *per se*, but via its representatives. Representation is thus a distribution of power in the sense that it splits up the power of delegating and the delegated power.[15] The powers of the sovereign lie within the first of these spheres and involve transfer of power to another, smaller subject. On the other hand, delegated power is exercised by this other, smaller

12 P. Ardant, *Institutions politiques & droit constitutionnel*, Paris 2004, p. 167.
13 B. Chantebout, *Droit constitutionnel*, Paris 2004, p. 84.
14 *Cf.* P. Ardant, *Institutions politiques...*, p. 167.
15 *Cf.* P. Parini, *Régimes politiques contemporains*, Paris 1991, p. 73 *et seq.*

subject, yet always in the name of former subject.[16] Given this extremely abstract interpretation of the principle of representation, the essence of a specific regime of political representation (*régime représentatif politique*) is therefore *a priori* division of the sovereign power, which in fact is the 'power to delegate power'.

In a slightly different variant of the juridical approach to the constitutional principle of representation, emphasis is laid not on the investiture as the very heart of representative government (and thus on elections, at the same time devaluing them to merely the technical act of designation), but on the distribution of competencies amongst both the parties of the relationship of representation.[17] It is assumed that representation connotes two utterly different, yet mutually conditional, competences. Both the competences are closely linked to each other, since one follows after the other, and one is nothing but a consequence of the other, thus both follow a logical sequence, and are conditional on each other. What's more, representation cannot in any way be pondered upon by examining each of these competences one by one. It is only the two of them jointly that determine the content of the principle of representation, while representation examined individually though each of these competencies, and even more so, though only one of them, ceases to be representation, both *de facto* and *de jure*. Therefore, when viewed from this angle, representation is nothing but a distribution of competencies interconnected both logically and chronologically. Election of representatives, thus granting the investiture within the frame of the electoral process, is the competence of the represented. The representatives, on the other hand, rely on their competence of acting for and on behalf of the represented.[18] The rudimentary sense of representation therefore always lies in the distribution of competencies between two subjects (parties) of the relationship of representation.[19]

Appointing the representatives – the first of those competencies in terms of chronology – is thus nothing but designation via elections. Yet representation itself does not end there, since it cannot be scaled down to the polling place, and hence to the purely technical or procedural process of voting in the light of the principle that representation is merely *choix de l'élctorat*. Indeed, what is central is the effect of this choice, that is the granting of the proxy to represent (substitute) the subject exercising the first of its competencies, and therefore imposing

---

16 *Cf.* B. Ackerman, *The New Separation of Powers*, "Harvard Law Review" 2000, no. 3, p. 633 *et seq.*

17 *Cf.* J.-C. Acquaviva, *Droit constitutionnel et institutions politique*, Paris 2005, p. 39.

18 *Cf.* G. Burdeau, *Manuel de droit constitutionnel*, Paris 1952, p. 88.

19 *Cf.* M. Prélot, *Institutions politiques…*, p. 358.

an obligation upon the representative to act on behalf of the represented. Along these lines the second competence, inherent in representation 'as such', is a certain kind of reverse competence, which could not have been exercised without the first of these competencies. On the contrary, the first competence, unless followed by the other one, would not have much sense and would be in a way 'lacking', 'undone' or suspended in a vacuum. Thus, only both these competences jointly render the principle of representation really genuine, finite, and above all axiologically and praxeologically complete and perfected in the full sense of the word. To retain its basic, the most elementary sense, every representation must, after all, be a combination of two elements: first, the election of the representative; secondly, the representative acting on behalf of the represented.[20] The election alone may prove ineffectual, since – if not followed by a recognition that the elected expresses the will of the electors – it could deny representation and trigger a situation in which the representative gains full independence, thus in fact conjoining the role of the representative and the represented. From a historical perspective it in many instances led to various versions of sovereignty of the parliament. Their main support axis was the assumption that the role of the elector ends with the designation, while the representative in fact becomes the one who not only aggregates the general will, but articulates it himself. In extreme cases this meant equating the general will with the will of the representative, as opted for, among others, by Raymond Carré de Malberg.[21] It is said that that his doctrinal ideas embody a certain paradox. On the one hand, they affirm popular sovereignty making it – most rightly so – the axiological foundation of the whole principle of political representation, yet on the other, in fact devalue it by putting sovereignty of the representatives in place of sovereignty of the represented.[22] Although it determines the standpoint of the representatives, the will of the represented (*volonté du peuple*) is in fact replaced with the own will of the representatives in daily reality of the political life,[23] which puts on the agenda the question of who actually is the controller of sovereignty, especially if sovereignty is to be perceived as the right to conceptualize the *volonté generale*.[24] The issue at

---

20 *Cf.* D. Mineur, *Archéologie de la représentation…*, p. 106.

21 More on this topic: E. Maulin, *La théorie de l'État de Carré de Malberg*, Paris 2003.

22 *Cf.* D. Chagnollaud, *Droit constitutionnel contemporain. Théorie générale. Les grands régimes étrangers*, Paris 2005, p. 171.

23 Which was sometimes however considered a legal consequence of representation, particularly when combined with the concept of legal fiction.

24 More on this topic: A. Haouet, *Le concept de souveraineté en droit constitutionnel français*, Paris 2003.

stake here is whether representation stands for a mere designation of representatives and nothing beyond that or whether such designation does produce some far-reaching consequences? An extreme approach which can be deciphered from ideas of R. Carré de Malberg, according to whom the key representation is to recognize the will of the representative as being the will of the represented without even a token acknowledgment that there must exist at least some slightest accordance between these two wills, would, after all, lead to 'sovereignty being confiscated by the representatives'.[25] It will always be the case, were one to assume that the will of the representative is to replace rather than express the will of the represented.

Hence, parenthetically, we come quite close to the next of the meanings of the constitutional principle of representation. According to this approach, representation is perceived as a principle according to which representatives of the nation-sovereign simply have a monopoly to express the will of the sovereign (*représentants disposent du monopole de l'expression de la souverainté nationale*).[26] Under this approach, which is some modification of the earlier ideas, the centre of gravity of the principle of representation itself has been shifted. It is recognized, after all, that representation is a constitutional method of applying the general idea of sovereignty; while the idea of real sovereignty expressed through the will of the representatives is brought into being in place of moral sovereignty.[27] Notably, following this type of reasoning R.Carré de Malberg and others reach the tipping point. They argue that the constitutional principle of representation alone is not the guarantee of a proper implementation of sovereign powers of the nation-sovereign. In fact, political representation conceived as a mechanism in which representatives formulate the will which is then ascribed to the represented cedes sovereignty, curbs the rights of the represented and removes efficient control of the representatives who place themselves at par with the represented.[28]

In line with another, modified and, above all, much milder version of this approach it is recognized that the essence of representation lies in the representative (the deputy) expressing the will of the represented (the voter). It worth noting that this approach estranges representation from the elections or – more precisely – the sheer technical process of designation. Consequently, it gives priority not to the mere granting the representative a proxy to act (as it happens in

---

25 D. Chagnollaud, *Droit constitutionnel contemporain…*, p. 171.

26 S. Bouiffror, D.K. Nanopoulos, *Droit constitutionnel. Méthodologie*, Paris 2006, p. 38.

27 *Cf.* D. Chagnollaud, *Droit constitutionnel contemporain…*, p. 171–172.

28 *Cf.* D. Mineur, *Archéologie de la représentation…*, p. 214.

the great majority of instances under the juridical approach to representation), but to highlighting that the latter acts as a representative, i.e. he formulates the will on behalf of those whom he represents. The specific method via which the represented has been authorised to act on behalf of the representative is of no importance here. What matters is that in his actions he is the representative, which means that his actions always carry effects for third parties and, what's more, he encounters no competition in those actions. It may be worth noting that this way of comprehending the constitutional principle of representation is extremely benign to the concept of the free (representative) mandate. Here, the representative matures unto the beneficiary of full independence (*bénéficient d'une indépendance absolue*),[29] who expresses the will of the represented unrivalled and regardless of the form in which he has acquired the mandate and, more importantly, also regardless of its specific content (which under the concept of the free mandate boils down to the general, if not sketchy, idea of representation of the will of the nation-sovereign).

Yet another aspect of a purely juridical interpretation of the constitutional principle of political representation suggests that the rudimentary sense of this principle actually comes down to the downright conclusion that elections are the primary (in the classical sense) or core (for all the later concepts) mechanism of political participation of citizens; whereupon the representatives who later pursue the affairs of the *polis* on behalf of the voters are elected. This perspective on the principle of representation does not focus on the aspect that, for instance, representatives act on the account of the represented or that elections are a certain kind of distribution of competencies, or that when receiving the mandate, the representatives are granted the full right to speak on behalf of the constituents, but on the fact that the principle of representation creates an indirect mechanism for civil participation (of the nation-sovereign) in the exercise of power, *ergo* in the exercise of their sovereignty.[30] Therefore it is thought that such understanding of the principle of representation is a kind of furtherance of the principle of sovereignty, its concretization and, even more, some kind of variation or refinement, thanks to which the generalist political idea of sovereignty takes on a specific, i.e. legal form.[31] Such a way to tackle the issue makes sovereignty of a nation merely a political project, a general idea which is as much capacious as general, comprising above all intentions and slogans, while political

29 J.-C. Zarka, *Introduction au droit constitutionnel*, Paris 2006, p. 71.

30 M.-A. Cohendet, *Droit constitutionnel*, Paris 2008, p. 436.

31 *Cf.* D. Baranger, *Le droit constitutionnel*, Paris 2009, p. 34 *et seq.*

representation is the legal expression of this idea that gives a concrete shape to such an idea. The principle of representation thus gives the *pouvoir electoral* to the sovereign to be used at the time of the elections.[32] It is in a way of secondary importance who or what is actually transferred via this *pouvoir électoral*, or what further consequences ensue as a result. The crux of representation in its most typical variant here is that it introduces an indirect method of exercising sovereign powers by excluding or at least significantly restricting all types of direct democracy institutions. The principle of representation or otherwise the 'regime of representation' (which, by the way, is to validate the legal and not just the political nature of representation in general) is thus in this case merely an equivalent of the concept of indirect democracy in pursuance of the thesis that 'indirect or otherwise representative democracy is a system whereby the people exercise power through their representatives'.[33]

Along these lines it is therefore concluded that the constitutional principle of political representation means nothing but imposing the general principle of democratic governance in its indirect, i.e. representative formula at the level of fundamental law. It is to suggest two significant, strictly legal consequences. Firstly, that the system of the state is to fit in with the democratic concepts of state organisation, thus opposing all kinds of authoritarian or otherwise undemocratic trends.[34] Secondly, in turn, that the asserted democracy is not (and cannot be) put into effect in a simple, that is direct, way and that its only possible manifestation is indirect democracy that involves elections of representatives who then act on behalf of the subject endowed with an attribute of sovereignty. Consequently, the assumed structure provides for the so-called 'representative democracy' according to which 'power is an attribute of the people (nation), but it is exercised by their representatives who act on their behalf'.[35]

The presented view of the legal nature of representation as a constitutional principle is often criticized on account of potential deformation of the very essence of representation, that is, precisely the need to present the view of the

---

32 J. Barthélemy, P. Duez, *Traité de droit constitutionnel*, Paris 2004, p. 338.

33 M.-A. Cohendet, *Droit constitutionnel…*, p. 436.

34 Which in turn necessitates the existence of all these institutions and procedures that would facilitate free articulation and aggregation of views or, in other words, would be the methods (means) of attaining correlation, that is coherence of views of the represented and their representatives. *Cf.* P. Blachèr, *Droit constitutionnel*, Paris 2009, p. 53, 54.

35 *Lexique de science politique. Vie et institutions politiques*, (ed.) O. Nay, Paris 2008, p. 132.

subject that ultimately is to be represented. The objective of political representation, as it is highlighted, it to mirror the will of the represented subject at the level of the representative body rather than to ensure the mere existence of the representative, who will formulate a certain type of view, later on attributed to a subject which from a formal point of view is to be represented. By reason of the latter, at least hypothetically, we might have to deal with an instance where the representative will formulate a view quite contrary to the will of the represented, yet attributed, only formally, to the latter. In this perspective, therefore, only the idea of formal representation would come into play, regardless of how substantive representation would be concurrently implemented. Meanwhile, the etymology of the word 'representation' necessitates, as it seems, also a mandatory reference to the material substratum of representation. Therefore, it is spotlighted that the so-called sociological point of view, according to which representation is a reflection of the will of the subject that grants the mandate to be represented, is not so much in conflict or competition with the juridical exegesis of the constitutional principle of representation as it is its necessary, perhaps even indispensable, component.[36] After all, mapping the will of the subject, which – by law – is to be the represented is the fundamental as well as by all means juridical meaning of representation.[37] The aim of representation, particularly representation as a certain constitutional principle, is to enable the sovereign to exercise its will through the representatives. Hence, it is not and can never be the sense of activities of the latter to act in complete freedom, without any consideration for the sovereign's will, but in such a way that the activities are regarded as those of the sovereign not just as a certain legal fiction, but that they are genuinely and in reality activities of the sovereign. The volitional identity of the representative and the represented is thus not only a purely sociological understanding of representation, but clearly a legal imperative of how the constitutional principle of representation may and must be approached. In every type of representation it is essential that the subject who grants the proxy to someone else be properly represented by that representative, meaning that the representative actually expresses the view of the represented. The crux of representation is thus the so-called substantive representation, which means that the representative not only formally acts for and on behalf of the person he represents, but that

---

36 *Cf.* M. Duverger, *Institutions politiques et droit constitutionnel*, Paris 1966, p. 81.
37 *Cf.* J.-C. Acquaviva, *Droit constitutionnel…*, p. 39.

the said representation entails substantive compatibility between the actions by the representative and the expectations of the represented.[38]

The sociological convergence (correlation) of views of both the subjects (the representative and the represented) in a purely juridical aspect generates two major consequences. One of them collectively refers to the entire personal and political structure of the representative body (the parliament), and the other individually addresses a single deputy – the representative. The first imposes a requirement (or at least a postulate) of establishing a proportional representation, assumed to be better from the point of view of reflecting (transposing) the opinion of the electorate upon the personal substratum of the parliament.[39] This is one of the reasons why proportional representation is sometimes regarded as the proper or strict political representation in general, while departure from it is tantamount to deforming the will of the representatives, that is challenging or at least a considerably debilitating the idea of political representation.[40]

Various methods and techniques of proportional redistribution of parliamentary mandates are thus, clearly, regarded as a specific effect of the regime of political representation and even more – as a legal obligation implicitly arising from such representation.[41] Thus, following the same track, if representation does not faithfully mirror attitudes, views and the will of the electorate, then it is treated as lacking the component of coherence[42] between the wills of both the subjects, which is of key importance for representation. Thus, searching for perfect representation is nothing less than exploring such methods which, firstly, will ensure an authentic coherence between the wills of the representative and the represented, and secondly – in line with the sociological approach to representation – will make the representative a kind of 'reflection' of the represented. With regard to the parliament, a once popular slogan has been fostered that it is to be nothing short of a 'mirror image of society'. It was considered, otherwise rightly, that only then would the parliament as a body of political representation be capable of expressing the views of the represented. So, even if today the simple and rather

38 Which by the way makes the postulate of mimetic representation to be very often recognized as the basic directive arising under the constitutional principle of representation. *Cf.* D. Mineur, *Archéologie de la représentation…*, p. 154.

39 Particularly given quite a common view that it is the very proportional electoral formula that allows reflecting the mimetic form of representation.

40 *Cf.* M. Duverger, *Institutions politiques…*, p. 81, 82.

41 More on this topic: M. Gassner, *Représentations parlementaires: Méthodes mathématiques proportionnelles de répartition des sièges*, Paris 2000.

42 J.-M. Denquin, *Introduction à la science politique…*, p. 66.

banal statement that representation portends a parliamentary mirror that reflects the mood of the electorate is rejected, the postulate of proportional representation as an inherently better and more faithful form, remains valid. After all, proportional electoral systems are regarded as more compliant with the general idea of political representation precisely because they allow imitating the political preferences of electors in the structure of the parliament more or less in the same or at least similar scale in which they exist in reality.[43] In turn, the second consequence of the sociological approach, this time addressed to the individual representative, is associated with the requirement of introducing an imperative mandate as the only mandate compatible with the formula of representation according to which the representative has to 'reflect' the will of the representative in his actions.[44] If we were to assume that the essence of representation involves a mere conveyance[45] of views of one subject, that is the represented, by the other subject, that is its representative, it is logical that the representative does not express his own views, opinions and attitudes through his actions, but acts like a typical proxy of a person who entrusted him with the task (the mandate) of representation during the elections. Thus, despite the conformity of will of both the parties, i.e. the representative and the represented being at the heart of the sociological approach to of the principle of representation, one must admit that it introduces into this interpretation a relevant legal factor, namely the 'confidence'[46] vested by the represented in his representative.

Adoption of the existence of an elementary *confiance* between both the subjects of a relationship of representation is the most important legal consequence of the sociological interpretation of the constitutional principle of representation. Its detailed elaboration, sometimes perceived as yet another element of the *stricte* legal consequence of the sociological approach to representation, is the 'dialogue between the represented and his representative'.[47] Sometimes it is referred to as some kind of an obligation arising under the principle of representation, dressed in the form of an order to maintain 'the ties between a deputy

---

43 More on this topic: B. Owen, *Le système électoral et son effet sur la représentation parlementaire des partis*, Paris 2002.

44 *Cf.* Y. Déloye, *Mandat impératif*, [in:] *Dictionnaire du vote*, P. Perrineau, D. Reynié (eds.), Paris 2001, p. 611 *et seq.* More on this topic: P.-H. Zaidman, *Le mandat impératif. De la Révolution française à la Commune de Paris*, Paris 2008.

45 *Cf.* J.-C. Acquaviva, *Droit constitutionnel...*, p. 39.

46 J. Gicquel, J.-E. Gicquel, *Droit constitutionnel et institutions politiques*, Paris 2007, p. 111.

47 D. Baranger, *Le droit constitutionnel...*, p. 89.

and the voter'. Trust between the representative and the represented that can be fortified, amongst others, by the obligation to maintain ties between the delegate and the delegating person, ultimately generates probably the most important consequence of forcing the idea of sociological representation into a rigid corset of law. It is, of course, the principle of responsibility of the representative towards the represented,[48] whereas this principle can only have a political value (which is as much a general idea as it is abstract[49]), as well as juridical value if a sanction of losing the mandate is provided for, which – as we know – was typical for the structure of imperative mandate.[50] Today, the slogan of the representative's responsibility, incisively termed 'accountability',[51] departs from the traditional approach of the constitutional law theory according to which the only real sanction against the mandate holder can be the potential loss of the mandate. In the era of the universal and widespread formula of a free mandate, it would have indeed been a fiction. Hence, a whole set of other accountability procedures (for instance in the form of electoral responsibility) is formulated to keep up, at any price, the elementary confidence, without which representation could not function at all.

As can be seen from the foregoing, the sociological approach to the constitutional principle of representation does not devalue the juridical content of the relationship of representation. Sometimes it is even said that bestowment of legal consequences on the principle of representation is possible only when it is perceived as an at least partially sociological principle.[52] It is also highlighted, not without reason, that without the sociological connotation of the constitutional principle of representation, the most rudimentary, even ontological sense of representation as such is lost. Regardless of the different interpretations of the idea or principle of representation, the main target at all times remains mirroring, reflecting, replicating or reproducing views, opinions and attitudes in another place and by someone else, according to the epistemological understanding of representation as making the absent present.

The sociological approaches by no means eliminate the juridical (and hence the real) consequences of the constitutional principle of representation. This is perfectly evident, let's say, in the British theory of mandate, which, to be sure, is

48 *Cf.* J.-M. Denquin, *Introduction à la science politique*..., p. 65, 66.

49 *Cf.* D. Mineur, *Archéologie de la représentation*..., p. 256 *et seq.*

50 *Cf.* Y. Déloye, *Mandat impératif*..., p. 611 *et seq.*

51 More on this topic: P.F. Nardulli, *Popular Efficacy in the Democratic Era. A Reexamination of Electoral Accountability in the United States*, Princeton 2005, p. 180 *et seq.*

52 *Cf.* M. Duverger, *Institutions politiques*..., p. 81.

nothing less of an attempt to merge the juridical and sociological method of defining representation into some coherent and logical whole. Needless to say, the theory of mandate means that the deputy (representative) is bound by the content of the mandate, which also means that in his actions as a representative he cannot make decisions that were not promised in his 'electoral offer'. Thanks to this, the principle of the deputy's responsibility is being additionally put into service, which probably best corresponds with the basic understanding of representation as *le gouvernement du peuple, par le peuple et pour le peuple*. Even more so, given that the principle of responsibility (without going into details whether it is legal responsibility that is at stake or just political or even moral responsibility) is regarded as vital and typically legal consequence of putting the principle of representation in place. The British theory of mandate even more closely correlates the sociological, juridical and – last, but not least – political (not to be forgotten) approach to the principle of representation, if it is assigned a purely political party meaning.[53] It is then that the manifesto of the party being the central actor in the electoral game actually becomes equivalent to the mandate, thus sparking off two key issues. First of all, that the party must respect its electoral manifesto, which becomes nothing short of a contract executed between the party and the electors. Secondly, that an individual deputy (representative) must be fully loyal to his party for the simple reason that it is actually the party (and more specifically its manifesto) that is being elected by the represented. Quite obviously, this view is justified exactly by sociological and legal factors. Sociological, since the party manifesto chosen during elections is a manifesto for which the majority of the electorate has voted. Thanks to which the principle that representation must reflect the will of the represented (or, briefly speaking, the electorate) is fully respected. On the other hand, it confirms that the manifesto offered during elections is the proper (if accepted by the electorate) content of the mandate, meaning that it imposes upon the representative an obligation to faithfully act upon such a manifesto in line with the principle that people's choice determines people's democracy.[54] Failure to perform the party manifesto (formerly the election manifesto) will, after all, be seen as a failure to exercise the mandate, that is, going against the will of the represented.

The theory of the mandate in its British version shows not only that the sociological and juridical threads *can* be merged and, more specifically, that the sociological interpretation of representation can give rise to deeply juridical

53 *Cf.* A. Heywood, *Key Concepts in Politics*, New York 2000, p. 218, 219.
54 W.I. Jennings, *The British Constitution*, Cambridge 1966, p. 9.

consequences, but, beyond anything else, that the juridical interpretation of the constitutional principle of political representation alone cannot actually be demoted to a single factor only. Hence, it cannot be argued that the juridical interpretation of representation boils down to granting the investiture or that representation stands for merely the distribution of competences between subjects in a relationship of representation, or that representation is tantamount to a transfer to the representatives of the right to determine the general will, or perhaps even the 'transfer of popular sovereignty to the representatives'.[55] For obvious reasons, representation cannot be closed within the narrow confines of the elections and brought down to a mere 'election of representatives'[56] (*l'élection de représentants*), but also, clearly, the constitutional formula of political representation cannot be equated with a simple imperative that the representatives 'reflect' the will of the represented through a proportional electoral formula. The latter, incidentally, is a good example of a kind of synthesis of the sociological and juridical aspects of representation. Indeed, it is deemed that if in fact the constitutional principle of representation were to have at least its minimum sense, then it must result in the will of the represented being transferred (preferably as accurately as possible) onto the will of the representatives. In other words, representation is all about no less than expressing the genuine will of the represented by their representative and this requires similarity or some other analogy between the personal substratum of the representative body and the subject that appoints (elects) the said body.[57] This, as one would expect, is better accomplished by the proportional formula of allocating parliamentary seats. Therefore, the introduction of the constitutional principle of representation is sometimes taken in as a legal obligation to apply proportional representation (*représentation proportionnelle*) as a method of redistributing parliamentary mandates or at least introducing such an allocation mechanism so that – regardless of the arithmetic method of mandate allocation – the election result corresponds to the general idea of proportionality and, hence, representativeness. Nonetheless, it is the proportional electoral formula that is considered to be the formula that most faithfully embodies the idea of a truly representative electoral system. If, in accordance with the principle of political representation, the representative body is to be representative, then this representativeness is to be best achieved through an appropriate proportion between the features of the electorate and the

55 D. Chagnollaud, *Droit constitutionnel contemporain…*, p. 171.

56 F. Borella, *Élements de droit constitutionnel*, Paris 2008, p. 221.

57 More on this topic: A.-M. Le Pourhiet, B. Mathieu, F. Mélin-Soucramanien, D. Rousseau, *Représentation et représentativité*, Paris 2008.

features of the personal composition of the body, which the representatives are members of.[58] It is in fact obvious, if only we assume that representation requires a minimum of convergence. Convergence, or – in other words – assimilation or similarity of views between the representative and the represented also requires proper repetition of certain features (such as political and party features[59]) of the latter in the personal substratum of the body, which the representatives are members of. This, as it is commonly known, is better, that is more accurately, faithfully or simply in a more fair manner and in the right proportion reflected by the principle of proportional representation and its various application algorithms. Hence, it is sometimes deemed that *représentation proportionnelle* that expresses the sociological principle of representation as replication, is at the same time a deeply legal consequence of introducing the constitutional principle of representation.

However, the juridical consequences of introducing the constitutional principle of political representation cannot be brought to a common denominator. It is a certain political idea, but at the same time also a constitutional institution with the most strict and precise denotation. If we were to reduce political representation to a merely political idea, then this idea would be have been the generalist postulate of establishing a representative government.[60] Spreading accents in a somewhat different way, representation as an idea would envisage that power is exercised by persons (or governments remain in the hands of those) in whom the political confidence of the represented, i.e. all the people (nation), is vested.[61] Assuming, in turn, the most reductionist view, approach to representation as an idea would be tantamount to a simple statement that the power is never (or at least almost never) exercised by the people alone, but through their representatives. In this sense, the principle of representation is indistinguishable from the principle of indirect democracy.[62] If, however, the principle of representation is to be clad in a corset of a constitutional institution, it will be either a simple

---

58 *Cf.* H. Pitkin, *Representation*, [in:] *Political Innovation and Conceptual Change*, T. Ball, J. Farr, R.L. Hanson (eds.), Cambridge 1989, p. 132 *et seq.* More on this topic: N. Loenen, *Citizenship and Democracy. A Case for Proportional Representation*, Toronto 1997, p. 45 *et seq.*

59 What best corresponds with the concept of representation in sociological approach. *Cf.* M. Duverger, *Institutions politiques…*, p. 81.

60 *Cf.* B. Manin, *The Principles of Representative Government*, Cambridge 1997, p. 42 *et seq.*

61 *Cf. Lexique de science politique…*, p. 468.

62 M.-A. Cohendet, *Droit constitutionnel…*, p. 436.

transfer of power to representatives, thus delimiting competencies between the right of delegating and the right of speaking as a delegate, or the acceptance of elections as the principal form of implementing the rights of the sovereign in the form of the so-called *pouvoir électoral*, or imposing redistribution of electoral mandates through proportional elections (not necessarily in the mathematical sense, but always in the sense of their result), or transfer to the representative of an absolute freedom to mould the will of the represented, or imposing upon the representative a requirement to respect the will of the represented in line with a well-known concept of the imperative mandate.[63] The constitutional institution which can be derived from the principle of representation (or otherwise representative government or, else, indirect democracy) can also be trimmed down simply to the institution of a representative who represents the nation or the people, who by way of elections became the beneficiary of the right to form the will of the sovereign regardless of whether he has some flexibility while exercising this right or whether he is bound by an instruction contained in the imperative mandate.[64]

Regardless of what consequences are to be ultimately derived from the constitutional principle of political representation, the fact remains that it is acknowledged to be the fundamental principle of modern constitutional law. At the same time, this principle is perceived not only as a narrow legal (constitutional) institution, but also, and sometimes even above anything else, as a political idea, a certain project that cannot be properly understood without delving into political doctrines and various kinds of ideological and political ideas and concepts.

2. The Sense of the Constitutional Principle of Representation

Regardless of the potential interpretational nuances, political representation is quite clearly perceived as a principle according to which 'the sovereign power is directly exercised not by the people themselves, but by their representatives acting for and on behalf of the people' or – in simple terms – a principle whereby 'a sovereign nation exercises power through its elected representatives who thus act on behalf of the people'. Representation can also be understood as a principle whereupon the people can 'assign to their representatives the power to exercise state functions'. Alternatively, it can also be termed as 'the way of exercising power' by the subject to whom this power nominally belongs. Naturally, certain elements of this principle can be viewed from somewhat different angles by

63 *Cf.* J. Barthélemy, P. Duez, *Traité de droit…*, p. 91 *et seq.*
64 *Lexique de science politique…*, p. 467.

defining it, for example, as a 'legal legitimization of the exercise of state power on behalf of a collective bearer of sovereignty (the nation) by authorities of the state specified in the constitution' (meaning the parliament where the MPs are gathered) or as a principle according to which 'the people exercise sovereign power through their representatives appointed in free elections'. The principle of political representation can also be seen as a 'way of exercising power, where decisions are made on behalf of the sovereign by the elected representative body (the parliament)', or simply as the 'exercise of power by the people in the representative form', the latter being understood as the exercise of power by a sovereign nation 'through its elected representatives'. The aspect that the delegates are being elected is also highlighted in all the approaches that view the principle of representation as a principle whereby 'the people as the holder of all the attributes of power [...] can exercise it [...] by way of electing representatives'. This line of reasoning is shared by all the definitions of the principle of representation which identify it as a 'legally legitimized exercise of public power by persons acting for and on behalf of the people and elected by the people in a democratic way' or – to put it briefly – as a principle, according to which 'the people as a sovereign subject are to exercise their rights through their own, duly authorised, representatives'.

As we can see from the above, despite differences in details, the fundamental sense of the constitutional principle of representation remains quite clear. What's more, one can safely claim it has a pivotal core or – simply – a leitmotif. Firstly, it is a recognition of a collective subject (the people or the nation) endowed with the attribute of a sovereign power. Secondly, it is the recognition that the subject is not able to exercise its sovereignty on a daily basis, which in turn implies, thirdly, delegation of the right to exercise sovereignty to a smaller (other) subject thus endowed with the attributes of a representative and, therefore, a subject that never acts *sua sponte*, but for and on behalf of someone else. Fourthly, the subject to which we ascribe the qualities of a representative must be democratically legitimized, therefore – last but not least – the one and only lawfully acceptable form of its appointment are free (democratic) elections. As a result, somewhat reversing the order, it can be assumed that the basic sense of the principle of political representation boils down to the fact that the collective sovereign assigns the exercise of sovereign powers to someone else (the parliament) in democratic elections, the said powers being always exercised for and on behalf of the sovereign, which means that they cannot (and should not) be exercised in isolation from his will.

However, it is worth noting that, despite being broadly consistent, the above mentioned definitions or attempts at forming a definition or at least clarifying the concept accentuate different elements which, when combined together, define the sense of political representation. Certain definitions highlight that the bearer of sovereignty, i.e. the people or the nation, does not exercise power in person or directly under the model of representation. In other definitions, the collective nature of the said subject it emphasized above anything else, which in turn implies the need to revert to indirect methods of exercising power. Other definitions underscore that the key issue of representation is that the nation or the people are represented by their representatives. At times it is being stressed that the idea of agency in the exercise of sovereign powers lies at the heart of representation, which should be understood as meaning that representation embraces not only the representatives and the represented, but the most important factor that binds them, namely the exercise of powers nominally vested in the represented by the representatives, or – from a slightly different perspective – acting on their behalf, or – differently still – the pursuit by the representatives of the will of the represented rather than their own will. It is also mentioned that the most important element of representation is the process or the act of delegating the rights of the represented upon the representatives, that is – in short – the necessity of an electoral, that is democratic, legitimization of electing representatives. Sometimes, the issue is being simplified even more by saying that representation is all about a mere exercise of sovereign powers by way of electing representatives, which basically confines representation to the mere process of voting. Lastly – although it is certainly the widest (definitely far too wide) approach – it is highlighted that representation is tantamount to exercise of power, and more precisely speaking, exercise of sovereign powers.[65] Naturally, putting emphasis on diverse, not necessarily and not always the same, structural elements of the constitutional principle of political representation in no way alters the general image and the fact that the meaning of this principle is most often comprehended by merging all or nearly all of its components, that is recognizing the sovereign powers of the people (the nation); the inability or at least the difficulty of the direct or simple exercise of those powers; and the consequent need to elect the representatives who are elected in the process of elections and who will act for and on behalf of the sovereign. The perceptible definitional nuances and differently placed accents make the principle of representation often variously named, and it is often so that certain details in the name are to emphasize all that is considered to be the key elements of this principle. Accordingly, the principle of representation is also named the principle of political representation or the

65 *Cf.* M.-A. Cohendet, *Droit constitutionnel…*, p. 429 *et seq.*

principle of a representative form of government, or the principle of citizens' indirect participation in state government, or the principle of indirect exercise of the sovereign powers, or the principle of representative government, or simply the principle of indirect democracy, representative democracy or participatory democracy. Regardless of how this principle is eventually named and what verbal robe it is clothed in, its *rerum natura* is more or less clear, quite well-identified and invokes no serious dispute.

There is a shared view that such a structure of the principle of representation necessarily implies the existence of at least some institutional and procedural solutions, lacking which it cannot be implemented at all in practice and, even more, it cannot be provided for in the constitution. The first solution embodies the existence of a representative body, that is the parliament. Moreover, it is said that the parliament must not only function, but there can be no doubts as to its lawful nature. This in turn means that the body to which we ascribe, either explicitly or implicitly, the attributes of the parliament must jointly meet at least the two criteria. First, its representative attribute, that is, in other words, the fact that it is a body that houses the representation of the collective bearer of sovereignty must be undisputable. And, secondly, the next criterion implies that the said body must be empowered by the law to perform basic functions, conventionally attributed to the parliament, that is at least the legislative and control functions.[66] Unless it jointly fulfils both these conditions, there can be no saying that a parliament exists and, therefore, that the constitutional principle of political representation functions (or, more precisely, can be put into practice).

The second institutional and procedural solution, lacking which a real, genuine representation can hardly be imagined, is the institution of democratic elections.[67] Incidentally, it also predetermines the assignment of truly representative attributes to the parliament.[68] Nevertheless, uninhibited and free electoral procedure is today considered a necessary element of the principle of representation to function in practice, which is understandable inasmuch that, after all, some of the definitions of representation degrade the whole principle of representation

---

66 Although it must be remembered that these functions by no means exhaust the functions of the parliament. *Cf.*: D. Arter, *Parliaments*, [in:] *Understanding Democratic Politics. An Introduction*, R. Axtmann (ed.), London 2003, p. 125–127; A. Siaroff, *Comparing Political Regimes. A Thematic Introduction to Comparative Politics*, Toronto 2009, p. 145 *et seq.*; P. Norton, *Parliaments. A Framework for Analysis*, 'West European Politics' 1990, no. 3, p. 3 *et seq.*

67 *Cf.* F. Borella, *Élements de droit…*, p. 222.

68 *Cf.* P. Laundy, *Les parlements dans le monde contemporain*, Lausanne 1989, p. 28.

to elections alone, and even if they do not, elections of representatives are in fact regarded as an essential component of political representation. The famous *pouvoir délégué*,[69] or *pouvoir électoral*,[70] is in fact for many the core of the principle of representation, and at least the precondition of its existence.

Finally, the last, i.e. the third substratum of the institutional constitutional principle of political representation, lacking which – especially today – the existence of political representation would have been impossible, are political parties. Nowadays political parties are an essential, if not the only means of correlation, i.e. the means though which the will of the representatives and the represented is converged, hence non-existence of parties would bring about a collapse of the whole regime of representation in practice. Whilst the thesis that parties are at most a practical component that in a sense modifies the process of political representation could have been endorsed some time ago, it no longer seems promotable today. Firstly, because parties clearly dominate the electoral process, which still remains – all things considered – an essential form of correlation. Secondly, because as a result of legal institutionalization political parties have these days become not only, as it was once thought, a kind of epiphenomenon of political practice that deforms or otherwise mutates this practice, but a constitutional institution in the fullest sense of this word.[71] The juridification of political parties, including their *expressis verbis* constitutionalization made them no longer merely a product of practice, significantly changing – as we know – the process of political representation, but has turned them into an *a priori* inherent element of this process, often having an advance monopoly position. Hence, the law does not ignore so the parties, as was the case in the past, but acknowledges them and – what's more – recognizes their significance offering them a relevant role in the political system. After all, political parties according to their definitions in the constitution are to *form*, *influence*, *create*, or only *co-create* the *politics* of the state or, at least in the minimalist version – to compete in rivalling elections. At the end of the day, they are to be merged into the process of political representation. Thus, they enjoy constitutional guarantees and are recognized a subjects which, even if not exclusively, then at least with a clear dominance, influence first the articulation and then the aggregation of the sovereign's will.[72] Therefore, today one can no longer claim that political representation takes place with the exclusion

69 P. Parini, *Régimes politiques…*, p. 73.

70 J. Barthélemy, P. Duez, *Traité de droit…*, p. 91.

71 *Cf.* F. Rouvillois, *Droit constitutionnel…*, p. 244, 245.

72 *Cf.* P. Leroy, *Les régimes politiques…*, p. 78, 79.

of political parties or by largely minimizing their role.[73] Nor can it be argued that even if such a role comes to light, is remains only in the realm of *praxis* and in no case does it translate into the theoretical model of representation. Today, after all, political parties comprise not only an element that rectifies the process of political correlation and – consequently – representation, but also an element without which it is difficult to actually talk about representation itself. Thus, one can safely claim that political parties are like a pendentive in the representation model. Although they were not envisaged at the very outset, not only did they come to exist with the passing of time and became firmly rooted, but have very soon grown into the element, lacking which it is impossible to imagine the existence of political representation these days.

In consequence, political parties, elections and the parliament are the crucial components of the principle of political representation. Non-existence of any of these components, their malfunction, improper institutional arrangement, or non-performance or only inadequate performance of their functions causes political representation to malfunction or, under extreme conditions, to be called into question, actually becoming a superfluous institution, devoid of a greater sense, being at most an attractive *decorum* in the structure of the state designed in the constitution. Hence, if this point of view is to be taken into account, then the first (in the chronological, but also logical sense) legal consequence of the constitutional principle of representation is the requirement to lay down in the constitution the position of the parliament, the democratic mechanism of elections and, last but not least, the role of political parties which today comprise much more than just an element of a generally understood civil society as they are *par excellence* constitutional institutions. Thus, one can reach yet one more method of defining the principle of political representation or, perhaps more accurately, derive from this principle a plainly legal consequence, which above all accentuates the praxeological effects of the regime of political representation. Since elections constitute a crucial element of representation (and it is so, since representatives do have to be in some way chosen by the represented); and since nowadays political parties play a fundamental role in the elections, and then in transforming and revealing the will of the electorate (and become essential, if not the only, means of correlation in the electoral process), and since elections are ultimately crowned by the formation of a parliament with 'copyright' on decision-making on state affairs (in which party fractions play a key role), it may be assumed that the constitutional principle of representation is defined as

73 *Cf.* N. Loenen, *Citizenship and Democracy…*, p. 85 *et seq.*

a political principle that recognizes as binding those laws and other decisions that are passed by the elected body of representatives in accordance with constitutional principles.

Plainly, the principle of representation can be viewed bottom up or top down. It will be viewed bottom up in all these instances, where one would begin with either the sovereign (the people or the nation), or the elections, or the appointment (delegating) the representatives by the represented (which will lay emphasis not on elections as such, but on the nomination itself, that is the *stricte* juridical grant of the investiture). On the other hand, it will be viewed top down when in the definition the emphasis is placed on the actions (decisions) of the representatives or the actions (decisions) of the entire representative body, or when the decisions of the parliament are pointed to as the decisions which, as a result of attribution, will be assigned to all the represented. It means that in fact there is no single or universal formula of political representation, repeatable at all times and in all the cases; likewise there is no standardized or homogeneous approach to its comprehending.

3. The Constitutional Expression of the Principle of Representation

The manner of expressing the principle of representative government (political representation, representative democracy, etc.) in the constitution has not been made uniform any way as well. Indeed, most often the principle of representation is derived from a single general or framework clause, but at the same time, in order to reflect its full constitutional embodiment, one usually has to relay on a few other, in some way substantively related phrases of the fundamental law. More often than not, it is not before at least several clauses are jointly taken into consideration than the overall constitutional depiction of the constitutional principle of political representation is revealed. Commonly the clauses that either explicitly or implicitly put in place the principle of indirect democracy are pointed to as crucial in this regard; further on, the provisions that explicitly define the sovereign, further on the clauses that describe the deputy and the nature of his mandate; further on the clauses at least roughly drafting the outlines of the electoral law; and, finally, the clauses that specify the role of political parties in the country and, thus, in the mechanism of representative democracy. Of course, this approach is very much detailed, which means that it recognizes essentially every constitutional norm as relating to the principle of representation as long as it has any connection with the general concept of representation. Read in such a way, the constitutional principle of representation reaches its fullest dimension as it points to the holder of the power (the principle of sovereignty), the mechanism of exercising power (the principle of representative government), the relationship between the representative and the represented (the principle of free mandate or, *a contrario,* imperative mandate), and finally the role of political parties as the basic and often in fact the only means in the process of political correlation (the principle of political pluralism).

Thus re-construed principle of political representation takes into account all the basic components thereof, although it must be noted that at times it is even additionally expanded to embrace these constitutional norms that relate to the rules of the electoral law, and that particularly classify the so-called electoral adjectives. It is assumed that determining the minimum rules of electoral law, including defining the *corps électoral*, is also an inherent part of the broadly understood principle of representation, all the more so since thanks to this it is indicated on whose behalf the sovereign power, transferred in the electoral process of selecting the representatives, who would then act on behalf of the principal of the mandate, is in fact exercised.[74] The group of electoral decisions, from which the principle of representation is at times derived, particularly if we correlate it with the requisite to mirror the views of the electorate at the level of the representative body, also embraces the mechanism of mandate allocation laid down in the constitution, especially when based on the principle of proportionality.[75] In such case, the constitutionally decreed proportional elections are perceived as a constituent part or at least a certain continuance of the general principle of representation and its obvious outcome.[76]

Clearly, when it comes to electoral elements of the constitutional principle of political representation, they are understood in two ways. Representation is either related to the manner of defining the whole electorate (it was chronologically the first method of linking electoral issues with the concept of representation) or associated with the arithmetic method of transferring the will of this body to the personal substratum of the representative body. In the first case, representation is predetermined by who belongs to the group of the represented[77] or, looking at the problem from another angle, how extensive the principle of

---

74 *Cf.* P. Rosanvallon, *Le Peuple introuvable…*, p. 20 *et seq.*

75 N. Loenen, *Citizenship and Democracy…*, p. 56 *et seq.*

76 *Cf.* M. Gassner, *Représentations parlementaires…*, p. 18 *et seq.*

77 Historically it did not even matter that much, since the concept of virtual representation was well-known in the constitutional law. According to this concept, one does not need to have voting rights to be represented in the constitutional sense. In the virtual sense, the representative expressed not only the will of those who elected him,

universal suffrage is, or – in yet other words – how large the circle of those who are actually represented is; in the latter case, it is not the quantitatively measured *corps électoral* that predetermines representation, but how and to what extent its will would be ultimately reflected (conveyed) through the personal and political structure of representative bodies. Consequently, a body will remain representative because it maximizes the group of people endowed with electoral franchise, and therefore the people who are actually being represented or, under a different assumption, because it faithfully, accurately and precisely reflects, following the rules of arithmetic, a certain type of attributes (properties) of the represented subject and this, quite clearly, corresponds with the sociological interpretation of representation. It is noteworthy that a discussion on which of the two above-mentioned ways of understanding political representation or, as it is sometimes referred to, the 'bringing about' representation is accurate, superior or just more in keeping with the concept of political representation as such, is one of the longest and practically still unresolved political debates.[78] It is at the same time obvious that the answer to the question of when exactly a representative body is truly representative is crucial from the point of view of the degree of implementing the constitutional principle of representation. If we were to accept the view that this principle may, by definition, be implemented somewhat differently, that is irregularly, then it turns out that the principle of political representation need not necessarily envision a single, universal pattern of its practical application. Consequently, one may say that in one case it is implemented to a greater, and in another to a lesser, extent. It seems that it reaches its peak when on the one hand, the electoral components of the concept of representation guarantee a universal, that is, as wide as possible group of people equipped with at least the right to vote, and on the other hand, when the proportional formula remains the dominant model of redistributing the representative mandates.[79] Regardless of the discussion around this subject, one needs to be aware that the electoral elements of the constitutional principle of representation can be at most supportive, but never decisive in terms of deciphering the content of this principle. They *never* determine the substantive shape of the constitutional principle of political representation. Furthermore, it should be kept in mind that the sheer placement of constitutional norms relating to electoral franchise into the catalogue of

---

since they had the right to do so (electoral franchise), but also of all others, all those deprived of voting rights.

78 *Cf.* P. Rosanvallon, *La Légitimité démocratique: Impartialité, réflexivité, proximité*, Paris 2010.

79 *Cf.* D. Mineur, *Archéologie de la représentation…*, p. 171 *et seq.*

constitutional determinants of the principle of representation may be disputable. It is so, since it may give rise to a fairly legitimate question as to what the content of this principle is, what is its elementary particle (in the sense of a component part as well as the most crucial element), and what constitutes merely an additional constituent or even an end-result? One may still take the view that the electoral structures of the fundamental law relating to the electoral system in a strict sense of the term and the indication of the size of the whole electorate are not at all a component of the principle of representation and play at best an accessory role vis-à-vis this principle or, potentially, are the upshot of the principle of political representation, its concretization of some kind, or its *sui generis* continuance. Therefore, the electoral norms of the constitution may be regarded a crucial (structural) element of the principle of representation only in all those cases where representation itself is identified with the electoral process, without adding any other content to it.

It is generally recognized that the necessary minimum of norms contained in the fundamental law from which the principle of representation can be derived embraces, first, the norm that constitutes the grounds for representative democracy (most often related in some way to the principle of sovereignty or even interlinked with it) and, secondly, the norm that establishes one of two alternative models of the parliamentary mandate (that is either imperative or free mandate). Even if only these two basic norms were incorporated in the fundamental law, the constitutional principle of political representation could be derived from them.

In the case of the first of these norms that creates indirect or representative democracy or a mechanism, no matter how called, of exercising power through delegating such power upon representatives, most frequently constitutions stipulate that 'popular sovereignty shall vest in the people, who shall exercise it through their representatives' (Article 3.1 of the Constitution of France), or that 'the nation shall exercise power through their representatives' (Article 4.2 *in principio* of the Constitution of the Republic of Poland dated 2 April 1997), or that 'the popular sovereignty shall reside within the […] people, that shall exercise it by means of their representative bodies' (Article 2.1 *in principio* of the Constitution of Romania). The emphases of this general norm may of course change slightly from time to time, but its meaning remains the same at all times and anyplace. It is the statement that the sovereign power (sovereignty, supremacy) belongs to the people (nation), while its exercise is vested in representatives of the people (nation). On the other hand, the second norm, the substance of which is rooted in the establishment of such a sort of a mandate that would bind the mandator and the mandatary, most often provides for a negative version, that is introduces an explicit ban on the existence of an imperative mandate or a mandate otherwise conflicting with the idea of a representative mandate. It is quite well illustrated in a clause, according to which 'each Member of Parliament represents the Nation and carries out his duties without a binding mandate' (Article 67 of the Constitution of Italy) or 'Deputies and Senators shall exercise their office in person [...] and in doing so they shall not be bound by any instructions' (Article 26 *in fine* of the Constitution of the Czech Republic), or simply that members of parliament 'shall not be bound by a compulsory mandate' (Article 67.2 of the Constitution of Spain) or, in yet slightly different version, that 'no other orders are binding on' the representative (Article 29.2 of the Constitution of Finland). The most concise and perhaps the most well-known is the famous French statement that 'no Member shall be elected with any binding mandate' (Article 27.1).

The principle of representation can easily be derived from the aforementioned two fundamental constitutional clauses. One of them decrees what is most important in the whole system of representation, that is that a subject endowed with attributes of superior power cannot exercise its power alone permanently and on a daily basis, and therefore appoints its representative to act in its name and on its behalf. The second, in turn, implies that the representative is not bound by any relationship of dependence, and therefore acts not only for and on behalf of the actual mandate principal (i.e. his 'personal' elector), but also on behalf of other voters who *ex hypothesi* make up the represented subject, regardless of whether this subject has voted for the representative or not.

Accordingly, it may be said that the constitutional principle of representation is a complex principle in the sense that it enfolds at least two other, lesser principles. The first one is the principle according to which the sovereign power, formally assigned to a sovereign, is exercised on its behalf by another subject, regarded as a representative or otherwise [a sort of] a proxy of the sovereign. The second principle defines the relationship between this representative and the subject on whose behalf it exercises its functions. This relationship, in accordance with the today dominant concept of free mandate envisages that a representative is not in any way treated as plenipotentiary of a person who delegates him. As it is known, this relationship may well have an opposite nature, that is assuming that the representative is legally bound by the will of the subject that has entrusted him with the mandate. Considering the foregoing, it may be said that the constitutional principle of representation is a principle which has its rudimentary and in no way sacrosanct form and a certainly modifiable content. The form of the principle of representation is built around a general assumption that a subject equipped with the attributes of sovereign power in the constitution cannot exercise sovereign rights, and hence there arises the need to assign the right to exercise the same power to someone else. On the other hand, the relationship (representative relationship) between the representative and the represented forms the content of the principle of representation, modifiable within certain boundaries along the lines *imperative mandate* versus *representative mandate.*

4. Methods of Construing the Principle of Representation: *Rei Dubiae*

Thus construed principle of representation, despite its clarity and brevity, does nonetheless subsume a few disputable issues. The first and foremost is: Who actually exercises power in the name of the represented? The question is whether it is a (single) representative or perhaps a representative body? Various definitions of representation do not offer a clear-cut and extrapolative answer to this question. At times they suggest that a particular person is a representative; at other times that only a collective body may perform the function of a representative. Yet other versions invoke the proverbial golden rule indicating that both individual representatives as well as representative bodies may act as the representative, which is to be underscored by all those constitutional clauses that point to individual deputies (members of parliament) as representatives of the people additionally vested with a certain type of a mandate (imperative or representative), whereas it is clear, notably, that these deputies always act within the frame of the constitutional body of the state, that is, the parliament, which in turn decides that representation cannot be identified with only one or the other subject, but it has to be considered conjointly, since representation embodies both one and the other rather than one or the other.

Looking at the principle of representation from the side of the representative or, in other words, 'from the top', it would be fitting to take the view that an individual deputy is a representative of the sovereign acting upon the sovereign's instructions and in the sovereign's name, which is further enhanced by the correlation between the function of the representative and acquiring the mandate in the process of elections.[80] It is thus not surprising that recognition of an individual deputy as the representative is a frequently encountered solution with strong historical roots. After all, the relationship of representation traditionally had an

80 *Cf.* F. Borella, *Élements de droit…*, p. 222.

'essentially personal character'.[81] Thus, according to the conception, it was an individual deputy, and earlier the candidate, who was bestowed trust by the voters, the said trust being in no way vested in another deputy nor any political organization, such as a party. From the very beginning representation has thus been construed around a 'personal and direct relationship'.[82] A constitutional expression of this view may be, for instance, the content of Article 4 of the Constitution of Lithuania, according to which a nation exercises sovereign power 'through its democratically elected representatives' or Article 2.2 of the Constitution of Albania, which proclaims that 'the people exercise sovereignty through their representatives'. The Slovak Constitution takes the same assumption stating that citizens exercise state power 'through their elected representatives' (Article 2.1). Furthermore, it should be kept in mind that the constitutional formula of describing the political role of a deputy most often boils down to determining that he is a representative of the nation (the people, the sovereign, etc.) and that he always acts upon their instruction.[83] Therefore, assessing the constitutional features of a deputy as the representative of the people (nation), all the while taking into account all these clauses in the fundamental law according to which the essence of indirect democracy involves representatives acting in the name of a collective bearer of sovereign powers, it would be fitting, at least *prima vista,* to share the view that representation has an individualistic nature and that the representative is a person, not a body.[84] However, viewing the principle of representation 'from the bottom', that is from the point of view of the represented person, one may get an impression that the representative is collective by nature and that it finds its embodiment in a representative body,[85] which is very clearly revealed in all expressions to the effect that 'the powers [...] are vested in the people, who are represented by the Parliament' (Article 2.1 of the Constitution of Finland) or that the parliament represents the citizens, the people, the nation or simply the sovereign (for instance Article 66.1 of the Constitution of Spain, Article 80 first sentence of the Constitution of Slovenia) or directly that the parliament is a representative body (Article 94 of the Constitution of Russia). The collegiate

81 B. Manin, *The Principles...*, p. 202, 203.

82 *Ibidem*, p. 203.

83 *Cf.* M. van der Hulst, *The Parliamentary Mandate. A Global Comparative Study*, Geneva 2000, p. 6, 7.

84 *Cf.* G. Vedel, *Manuel élémentaire de droit constitutionnel*, Paris 2002, p. 134.

85 In line with the principle that the parliament, rather than a member of parliament, voices the will of the people. *Cf.* C. Haguenau-Moizard, *Les systèmes politiques européens*, Paris 2009, p. 69.

nature of the representative subject is also suggested, at least implicitly, by all the norms of the fundamental law that bring in an indirect mechanism of the exercise of power by the sovereign. Most often it is concluded that this indirect mechanism of exercising sovereign powers boils down to appointment of a body upon which the sovereign transfers the right to exercise its powers. It is anyway articulated in the expressions that equate indirect (representative) democracy with parliamentary democracy (*démocratie parlementaire*).[86] No matter how one would name it, it is acknowledged that without a representative body, *ergo* without a collegiate subject having the attributes of a representative, the constitutional principle of representation cannot be fulfilled, especially if it is correlated with the sociological approach, where representation is understood as a reflection of the views of the whole electorate. For obvious reasons, such views may, after all, be most fully expressed, if voiced at all, by a collective body in which diverse views and approaches may be presented. Hence, it is assumed that representation, if it is to reflect its elementary meaning as reiteration of views and opinions of the represented at another level, simply necessitates the existence of a collegiate body, inasmuch as only such a body may incarnate heterogeneous opinions and views.[87] Likewise, also an essentially juridical approach to representation, according to which representation implies taking action on behalf of someone else, reveals – though not explicitly – that a representative is a collegiate subject. It is so since, from a formal point of view, actions which are subsequently viewed as the actions by the represented are at all times taken not by an individual and single representative, but by a body where individual representatives constitute a personal substratum only.[88] Representation understood as the competence to make certain decisions for and on behalf of another person clearly reveals that such decisions are made by the representative body *in corpore*, and not by its individual elements or otherwise defined specific components (such as individual members of parliament). On the margin, it is worth noting that representatives cannot themselves be subjects of representation, since individual representatives as such are not endowed with any competence. Given such an approach, Article 20 of the German Constitution, according to which state authority 'shall be exercised by the people [...] through [...] bodies' or somewhat differently expressed, yet equivalent in substance, Article 2.1 of the Constitution

86 J. Barthélemy, P. Duez, *Traité de droit...*, p. 80. This view was shared by Hans Kelsen, for whom the concepts of indirect democracy, representative democracy or simply parliamentary democracy were synonymous.

87 *Cf.* M. Duverger, *Institutions politiques...*, p. 82.

88 *Cf.* F. Rouvillois, *Droit constitutionnel...*, p. 210.

of Romania, according to which the people exercise their sovereignty 'by means of their representative bodies' seems cogent. The Constitution of Ukraine, which clearly states that 'the people shall exercise power [...] through the state authorities' (Article 5.2) as well as the Constitution of the Czech Republic, according to which the people exercise their sovereign powers 'through bodies' (Article 2.1) adopt a similar approach to the problem. In consequence, the concept of competence is of key importance for recognizing that only the representative body, and not the individual representative himself, is equipped with the constitutional attributes of a representative subject, since only a body has the competence to act for and on behalf of the represented.

The two outlined approaches clearly depict that the view whereby a representative subject is perceived not as an individual deputy, but as a body of which he is a member, definitely prevails. This interpretation is supported, first of all, by its collegiate composition that naturally permits communicating multifold views within the represented subject and, secondly, by adopting an assumption that the competences though which sovereign powers are executed are vested in a body rather than in its personal substratum. It seems, however, that it does not necessarily imply having to reject the 'mixed' concept, which somewhat differently combines both these *prima facie* contradictory views. It is not that both the individual representative and the body which the individual representative is a member of that are representative subjects – it is the body that is the representative subject because the individual representative is a member thereof. This approach, therefore, indeed requires linking the representative status with both a body and a person, but at the same time implies a certain mutual relationship to exist between both these subjects, assuming that representative means a single representative, who alone cannot do much and therefore acts within the frame of a body which performs the representative function precisely because it gathers representatives.[89] Thus a body is the representative, but is it so because it is made up of representatives.[90] This interpretation shows that the alternative that a representative subject may signify either an individual representative (deputy, member of parliament) or a body (the parliament) is fundamentally false. The representative nature of both the subjects originates from their natural complementarity. What's more, if we were to correlate the concept of a representative

89 *Cf.* P. Laundy, *Les parlements...*, p. 28.

90 In line with a simple principle whereby it is only 'individual representatives make up a legislative body that is a true representative' – A. Esmein, *Deux formes de gouvernement*, "Revue du Droit Public" 1894, no. 1, p. 15 (as cited in: F. Rouvillois, *Droit constitutionnel...*, p. 210).

subject with the right to impose a statutory norm as a verbalization of the *volonté générale*, then also the concept of mutually complementary representation (i.e. a body and its individual member) is most fitting and correct. Although a legislative act is adopted by the parliament (thus by a body), yet individual deputies are remarkable contributors to the legislative process, acting independently at least at some phases of this process and often endowed with major competences in the area of law-making (for instance, the right of legislative initiative).[91] Hence, if the general concept of competence, of key importance for pointing to who the representative subject is, were trimmed down to the competence of law-making,[92] then both are representative subjects and one is a representative subject because the other one is as well.

Incidentally, it is worth noting that the recognition of legislative activity being a sort of indicator of the representative subject is also associated with a quite a significant expansion of the circle of subjects that can be qualified as representative bodies, including almost all subjects involved in bringing the legislative process to a successful end, particularly constitutional courts (which corresponds with the concept of the so-called constitutional democracy as an attractive alternative to the existing parliamentary democracy). However, from this point of view, a representative will be any subject (both individual and collegiate) involved in the legislative process.[93] Such stance is supported by the belief that a legislative act remains the most vital manifestation of the sovereign's will, therefore, logically, every subject that at some stage is involved in the process of expressing this will, *ergo*, in the process of adopting a legislative act, will be a representative of that sovereign.[94]

The concept of constitutional democracy as an otherwise interesting alternative to the classical approach to political representation, regardless of whether we

91 More on this topic: S. Frantzich, *Who Makes Our Laws? The Legislative Effectiveness of Members of the U.S. Congress*, "Legislative Studies Quarterly" 1973, no. 3, p. 409 *et seq.*

92 Which is justified with regard to representation, since a legislative act is an expression of a general will, while representation itself is nothing less of an expression of this will.

93 It is worth noting that such a view in a way breaks open the classical concept of representation. Firstly, because it no longer absolutely binds representation with elections (a subject not elected in the elections but involved in a legislative process may be a representative). Secondly, because the parliament not need be the representative on an exclusivity basis but, alike the constitutional court, it could be any entity involved to a certain extent in a legislation process.

94 *Cf.* F. Hamon, M. Troper, *Droit constitutionnel*, Paris 2011, p. 189 *et seq.*

agree with it or not, reveals another debatable issue that comes up in in respect of the constitutional principle of political representation, namely what are the bodies (assuming that these are bodies) that ultimately have the status of a representative. Here, quite clearly, two opposing concepts come into play. In line with the first concept, only the parliament, which holds a monopoly in terms of representation may be such a body.[95] According to the second concept, representative bodies can in no case be limited to parliaments only, since other bodies are (or at least can be) representative as well. Inasmuch as the first view is strongly associated with the belief that only an elected body can be a body of political representation, according to the second approach it is not the mechanism of building the composition of the body that is the most important, but its functions and its specific, political quality of action. The most traditional approach, where representation is understood very literally as acting as a substitute for the sovereign recognizes that the parliament has exclusive attributes of a body of political representation. The underlying assumption here is a fairly simple premise that since the actual sovereign is in fact *corps électoral* and since the competence of that whole electorate lies in the election of deputies, who then act 'for the voters', then the rudimentary sense of representation boils down to electing deputies who constitute the representative body, that is the parliament.[96] This body, as it is well known, acts for and on behalf of voters, i.e. the represented, and therefore the sovereign. Such a relationship, developing into a coherent and logical whole, is sometimes confirmed in the constitution in those clauses that trim down the essence of representation or, in other words, indirect or representative democracy, to the functioning of the parliament, or narrowing it even more, to elections of deputies (representatives).[97] The latter solution is perhaps best illustrated by Article 1 third sentence of the Croatian Constitution, according to which 'the people shall exercise [...] power through the election of representatives'. Likewise, the Estonian Constitution also clearly associates representation with elections, explicitly laying down that power 'is vested in the people who, through citizens eligible to vote, exercise it in elections of the Riigikogu' (§ 56). On the other hand, according to the Slovenian Constitution, citizens exercise power particularly 'through elections' (Article 3 second sentence). However, as a rule, representation is correlated not with the electoral process itself, but with the representative body elected via this process, thus linking the status of the

95 *Cf.* Y. Mény, Y. Surel, *Politique comparée. Les démocraties*, Paris 2009, p. 232.
96 *Cf.* G. Vedel, *Manuel élémentaire...*, p. 134.
97 If '*démocratie représentative, lorsque justement, l'ensemble de la Nation ou du peuple participe à la désignation des représentants*' – *ibidem*, p. 133–134.

representative with the legislature. Article 2 first sentence of the Constitution of Finland can serve as an example of this approach, wherein it is *expressis verbis* declared that the parliament is the representative, or § 4, first sentence, of the Swedish Act of the Instrument of Government, according to which 'the Riksdag is the foremost representative of the people'. This viewpoint is also shared by Article 147 of the Constitution of Portugal, pursuant to which 'the Assembly of the Republic shall be the assembly that represents all […] citizens'.

A second, completely different assumption is that representative democracy cannot be limited to the parliament and – even more so – demoted to elections alone.[98] This approach is based on the belief that actions by all bodies of state authority, not just the parliament, constitute the essence of indirect mechanism through which the sovereign exercises power. Every so often thus understood representation correlates with the principle of separation of powers in keeping with the principle that there is but one and indivisible power that belongs to the nation-sovereign, although it is only 'exercised' by various bodies of the state that always (regardless of their structure, procedure of appointment and scope of operation) act on behalf of the sovereign.[99] Hence, while respecting this approach, the principle of representation should be associated with two other constitutional principles, namely the principle of sovereignty and the principle of separation of powers, whereas the principle of representation lingers as if 'in the middle' between the two other principles. Consequently, the first and initial principle is the principle of popular sovereignty and the second principle, operating as a certain concretization of the first principle thanks to which the first principle (till then merely a juridical expression of a certain idea) is rendered viable for practical application, is the principle of political representation. Further on, the consequence and at the same time an elaboration of the principle of representation is the principle of separation of powers, best known in its famous version of a tripartite separation of power.[100] *Explicite* such a view is laid down in the Constitution of the Czech Republic, pursuant to which people are the source of all power in the state and they 'exercise it through bodies of legislative, executive and judiciary powers' (Article 2.1). By the same token, though not without differences, the Slovenian Constitution stipulates that the citizens exercise power 'consistent with the principle of the separation of legislative, executive and judicial powers' (Article 3 second sentence *in fine*). Also the Constitution of Russia

---

98 *Cf.* S. Pierré-Caps, *Le constitutionnalisme et la nation*, [in:] *Le nouveau constitutionnalisme. Mélanges en l'honneur de Gérard Conac*, Paris 2001, p. 74 *et seq.*

99 *Cf.* F. Hamon, M. Troper, *Droit constitutionnel …*, p. 99 *et seq.*

100 *Cf.* P. Ardant, *Institutions politiques…*, p. 167.

respects the view that representation goes much beyond the parliament alone in its wording that the people exercise power 'through State government bodies and local self-government bodies' (Article 3.2). The Romanian Constitution follows along the same path stating that the people exercise their sovereignty 'by means of their representative bodies' (Article 2.1), thus making it is clear and explicit that there are several such bodies and not just the parliament alone.

Recognizing that it is not only the parliament that is a representative body, but that there may be other bodies having the representative status beside the parliament, is interpreted in two different ways. The first one is quite typical and refers to elections.[101] According to this first method, any body endowed with electoral legitimacy, is a representative body for the simple reason that it is the process of elections that carries the attributes of representativeness.[102] From this perspective, when an elected body (even via indirect or otherwise restricted elections) enjoys the status of a representative subject, regardless of whether that subject is a multi-member body or not (which means that even monocratic authorities, nonetheless appointed through elections are, or at least can be, regarded as representative bodies). The latter is of importance inasmuch as now and then it is believed (particularly when the attributes of representation are assigned not to an individual representative, but to a representative body) that only a multi-member body can be a true representative, since only then the diversity of opinions and views of the body members can come to light (and this guarantees genuine representation). Today, the discussion on this subject has gained in importance so much that its pivotal point is now the head of state, more often than now elected in general elections, and thus increasingly regarded (or not) as a representative. The second method can be termed functional; it basically implies that a body can be considered a representative body, if only in its actions it exercises the powers nominally entrusted to the sovereign, which powers the sovereign for obvious reasons cannot directly exercise itself. The grounds for the proxy (either elections or some other non-electoral mechanism) has no decisive value here. What is of importance here is that in its actions, the given body expresses the will of the people, acts for the people and for this very reason enjoys constitutional recognition as a representative body. According to this scheme, all the three powers singled out by Montesquieu are thus classified as authorities acting on behalf of a collegiate custodian of sovereign rights, that is the nation, hence it is reckoned that all the bodies exercising legislative, executive and judicial

101 *Cf.* J. Gicquel, J.-E. Gicquel, *Droit constitutionnel...*, p. 113 *et seq.*
102 *Cf.* G. Vedel, *Manuel élémentaire...*, p. 134.

powers are representative bodies.[103] Hence, under this approach, the principle of representation is nothing less of a way of elaboration and concretization of the principle of nation's sovereignty.[104] Without representation, and more precisely without representative bodies, sovereignty would be but a trifle political idea, a constitutional value suspended in a vacuum. This value gains real shape, presence and practical dimension through the principle of political representation that legitimizes the actions of state authorities precisely because it assigns to them the virtue of acting for and on behalf of the sovereign.[105] It is pointed out that judicial authorities are becoming increasingly important today, particularly the constitutional courts with their case law, and specifically their protective role towards the constitution, which shifts the centre of gravity of the entire political representation towards this third power, the objective of which is to mastermind the correlation of wills of the represented and their representatives.[106] Viewed from this perspective, constitutional democracy is thus a guarantee of popular sovereignty intended to safeguard the classical representative regime, that is *démocratie parlementaire*, against any conceivable pathologies, particularly against distorting the genuine, true will of the represented.[107] It is not only the bodies directly elected by it (the parliament) that act on behalf of the sovereign, but also other bodies which, though selected according to very different rules, serve one and the same purpose, namely protecting truly responsible governance that respects the *volonté du peuple*. After all, every model of indirect democracy, no matter how it is ultimately arranged, aims to attain the same objective, that is to faithfully respect the will of the nation-sovereign that can be voiced in very different ways and using various mechanisms.

5. Legal Effects of the Constitutional Principle of Political Representation

The method of reconstructing the constitutional principle of political representation (that is, determining what norms ultimately comprise the content of political representation regarded not only as a certain concept, but also as a formal

103 *Cf.* J. Gicquel, J.-E. Gicquel, *Droit constitutionnel...*, p. 115 *et seq.*

104 *Cf.* M.-A. Cohendet, *Droit constitutionnel...*, p. 427 *et seq.*

105 *Cf.* O. Camy, *Droit constitutionnel critique*, Paris 2007, p. 57 *et seq.*

106 *Cf.* F. Hamon, M. Troper, *Droit constitutionnel ...*, p. 70 *et seq.*

107 This has always been perceived to be the greatest weakness and danger of the system of parliamentary representation or simply representation in its classical version. *Cf.* P. Ardant, *Institutions politiques...*, p. 171.

legal institution) and the list of debatable issues that arise *à propos* the principle of representation do not exhaust all the aspects relative to appropriate understanding of the essence of representation dressed in a corset of a constitutional principle. Certainly there is one more important aspect, namely the question what, if any, consequences arise under political representation treated as a constitutional principle and, if any, the type of such consequences. In other words, whether the principle of representation (no matter how expressed in the fundamental law) gives rise to specific conclusions, responsibilities, orders or prohibitions, or perhaps this principle in the constitution is merely a crafty stylistic figure, a kind of 'constitutional rhetorical device'? The answer to this question is obvious. Normative content should be derived from every unit of text of the constitution, and so from the principle of political representation, thus setting legal consequences in the form of certain orders, prohibitions or sanctions. It seems that effects of the constitutional principle of political representation should be divided into no less than two types, that is axiological and praxeological effects. The former refer to the intrinsic philosophy of representative democracy, while the latter signify nothing other than obligations as to the proper placement of representative bodies in the state apparatus.

Amongst the first type of effects, namely axiological ones, the first effect to be mentioned is the fact that representative democracy is perceived as the embodiment of the idea of democratic government in general.[108] Under such an assumption, the principle of political representation is an equivalent form of establishing a democratic regime that prevents (and at the same time excludes) such constitutional arrangements that interfere with the general and thus capacious concept of a democratic system, although it should straight away be highlighted that not all are of the opinion that 'representation is the same as democracy'. Indeed, some propagate views that challenge this certain automatism of the 'democratic effect of representation', pointing out that although these ideas are close to each other, yet by no means equivalent, identical or one and the same. Thus, in fact it is most likely that democracy and representation go hand in hand, but then, as history often attests, there are circumstances in which these two ideas do not necessarily make a pair. So, if we were to opt for a relationship of result, this relationship ought to be reversed and it should be recognized that representation is always the effect of democracy, but not necessarily the other way round. Representation need not lead to democracy anytime or anyplace. Nonetheless, in democratic constitutionalism it is actually quite common to unanimously

108 *Cf.* G. Vedel, *Manuel élémentaire…*, p. 133.

recognize the principle of political representation as the principle which at least implicitly forms the democratic nature of the political regime and that representation (as a constitutional principle) is nothing but an indirect (complex) form of democracy.[109] Of course, such a statement seems to be extremely general, at least vague *prima facie* and lacking the minimum content. However, it might be rendered more precise by saying that the essence of political representation lies in ensuring at least minimum involvement of citizens in the exercise of power, while democratic elections of parliamentary representation constitute such minimum.[110] Democratically established parliament perceived as a forum at which the interests of the nation-sovereign are aggregated and articulated is, in line with this view, the fundamental standard of democracy expressed through the principle of representation in the constitution.[111] It does not, however, mean that it is the only standard. Hence, going forward in drawing axiological consequence of the principles of political representation, it is pointed out that another equally important consequence is the establishment of a mechanism of accountability of the governing towards the governed, namely the establishment of a responsible government for which the confidence of the parties to the relationship of representation is of key importance.[112] A necessary condition for confidence to exist, *ergo* another axiological consequence of the principle of representation, is a system of proper correlation of the attitudes of the represented and their representatives. To be explicit, this system necessitates adopting specific techniques of mandate distribution and establishing a whole mechanism that will not only invoke confidence, but will also keep up political correlation of attitudes and views between the representatives and the represented. Axiological implications of the principle of political representation include the general establishment of representative democracy as the fundamental (and in the classical writings on constitutional law as the one and only) form of citizens' participation in the conduct of the affairs in the *polis*. Today, the principle of political representation is indeed very often understood as a principle that establishes democracy in its most typical and widespread indirect version, which means that, as a rule, decisions are made by the representatives, although the effects of these decisions affect the represented.

As we know, indirect exercise of sovereign powers no longer enjoys its monopoly today. A variety of direct (participatory) democracy mechanisms which

109 *Cf.* M.-A. Cohendet, *Droit constitutionnel…*, p. 435.

110 *Cf.* D. Chagnollaud, *Droit constitutionnel contemporain…*, p. 166 *et seq.*

111 *Cf.* M. Verpeaux, *Manuel de droit…*, p. 206 *et seq.*

112 *Cf.* B. Manin, *The Principles…*, p. 202.

constitute an alternative to indirect (representative) methods of determining *volonté du peuple* are more and more frequently and willingly applied. Therefore, given the present-day coexistence of various forms of direct democracy, an axiological consequence of the constitutional principle of political representation is the existence of the so-called 'mixed democracy' where direct and indirect methods of political participation complement each other, although a certain priority is, after all, afforded to indirect methods.[113] Last but not least, the general idea of justifying the whole mechanism of exercising political power can be pointed to as one of the axiological effects of the constitutional principle of political representation. In line with this convention, representation is regarded (besides sovereignty) as the philosophical foundation of the entire political system, the source and at the same time the purpose of the functioning of the state in keeping with the well-known principle that it works for the people, for the people and by the people'.[114]

Praxeological consequences of the principle of representative government seem to be much more specific, yet this does not mean that there is a consensus as regards their exhaustive list. Like everywhere else, disputable issues arise also here, even in the form of the accepted principles of the electoral law and the fact whether these principles must, may or at least should respect the proportional formula or perhaps whether this formula has no connection whatsoever with the principle of representation. If we were to consider that representation means not only acting in the name of and for the benefit of the represented, but also at least a minimal 'likeness' of the representative as compared to the principal, then one should take the view that the praxeological result of the constitutional principle of representation involves a mandatory establishment of such an electoral system that guarantees such 'likeness' to the greatest extent possible.[115] This shows that the ultimate assessment will always be relative and conditioned by the acceptance of specific theoretical and axiological assumptions. This will also be the case of a multi-party system (political pluralism) that can be directly linked up with the principle of representation, thus necessitating its establishment so that representation can be deployed at all; or not linked up, thus considering it to be completely independent

---

113 At the same time, when referring to priority of indirect democracy what is meant is not that it is more important or paramount (no doubt direct democracy is) but that is has fundamental (most common) application. Thus, in a sense, it is 'everyday democracy' as opposed direct democracy being 'Christmas democracy'.

114 F. Hamon, M. Troper, *Droit constitutionnel ...*, p. 183 *et seq.*

115 *Cf.* M. Duverger, *Institutions politiques...*, p. 82.

of the political representation regime.[116] If we are of an opinion that political parties indeed constitute an indispensable component of political representation, then going a step further, we need to acknowledge that only party pluralism and, therefore, freedom to create parties and freedom of their operation as guaranteed by law is a true warrant and at the same time the consequence of representation, if only it is dressed in a corset of a principle of state system. Revering this view, one has to accept that a multi-party system (at least formally) is very much a praxeological effect of the political representation regime. Finally, the structure of a parliamentary mandate and whether it should go with the concept of imperative mandate, or perhaps preferably a free mandate, is a debatable issue. The very connection between a mandate and the principle of representation is not the subject of discussion here, yet disputes centre around the aspect of what the mandate should ultimately be like in order to better (more faithfully) implement the principle of representation, and whether the principle of representation alone engenders any directives as to the specific model of the mandate (in a positive sense, meaning that one of its structures must be adopted, or in a negative sense, meaning that any of the classical structures of the mandate must be excluded *a priori*). As it is well known, imperative mandate was strongly advocated in the past, while today free mandate is considered to much more adequately reflect the essence of representation,[117] yet the issue whether one or the other mandate is a 'natural' or 'certain' upshot of the constitutional principle of representation is still left open.

One must keep in mind that the structure of the mandate (imperative versus free) was not an entirely autonomous and independent issue. It also stemmed from the decision as to who was eventually considered to be the representative. In a historical variant of personalized representation addressed to an individual delegate endowed with personal confidence of his voter, imperative mandate was simply regarded to be more appropriate.[118] The deputy was, after all, treated as a delegate of the voter, which perfectly confirmed adaptation of a civilistic formula of a proxy. However, when a representative body such as the parliament was considered to be the representative, while the represented was no longer identified with a single voter, but with the whole electorate (the people, the nation), then a free mandate was correlated with all this, thus tearing apart the simple and personal relationship between the mandator and the mandatary and making it (the relationship between the mandator and the mandatary) much more

116 *Cf.* P. Leroy, *Les régimes politiques*..., p. 63, 64.
117 *Cf.* M. van der Hulst, *The Parliamentary Mandate*..., p. 8.
118 *Cf.* B. Manin, *The Principles*..., p. 203.

abstract. Today it is hardly possible to resolve right from the outset which of the model solutions is a better one and more aptly fitting the principle of political representation. There is simply no universal and always provable formula, while the type of the mandate is in fact the sum of a number of other factors that, only when combined, define the sense of the constitutional principle of representation. The fact remains, however, that defining the formula of the mandate (free or imperative) remains a praxeological, although (as it seems) *a priori* indeterminate (alike the electoral system itself)[119] effect of the constitutional principle of political representation.

The emerging debatable issues as to the praxeological consequences of the constitutional principle of political representation should not, however, push aside all those consequences that are regarded a necessary and evident standard. These consequences include, first of all, the existence of collegiate representative bodies (parliaments); secondly, endowment of these bodies with powers, primarily legislative and control powers; thirdly, the obligation of these bodies to represent in their work a genuine will of the represented subject; and fourthly the obligation of all the remaining bodies of the state to respect the will of the represented and the bodies that are either *explicite* or only *implicite* recognized as the bodies that express the will of the nation-sovereign. Yet another purely praxeological effect seems to follow from the principle of representative government (political representation). It is the recognition that although the forms of direct citizen participation may be arranged and applied in practice to a different degree, they will never replace the indirect method. Although it does not preclude the application of the so-called techniques of pure democracy, the representative form of governance by a bearer of sovereign rights nonetheless continues to prevail in the daily exercise of authority by the nation-sovereign.

This shows that the constitutional principle of political representation may seem obvious and uncomplicated only at the first glance. In reality, there is a number of nuances to it, starting with what ultimately comprises the said principle, followed by determining what constitutes its proper content, and ending with the consequences it generates. Regardless of the emergent problems, it is certainly non-contradictory and homogeneous in the sense that despite revealing

---

119 Unless, of course, we are of an opinion that representation requires the proportional formula. If we take the view that representation entails a requirement to apply the mechanism of proportional allocation of parliamentary mandates, then the incorporation of the principle of proportionality in the constitution will also mean, at least *implicite*, upgrading proportionality as a principle of electoral law to the rank of a constitutional solution.

differences in details, its elemental, universal and everlasting content can still be established. In each of its embodiments, the principle of political representation corresponds, after all, to the idea of democratic and responsible government, where the governments are (or at least should be) of the people, for the people and by the people.

Chapter V: Representation and Interests

1. Representation as Aggregation and Articulation of Interests

Invariably, or at least since representation lost its virtue of philosophical, and, consequently, also symbolic expression of certain timeless, universal and permanent principles, ideas and values, it has been associated with interests. It was only in the historical, today completely obsolete, model of monocratic representation (usually fulfilled by monarchs) that representation was free from the grassroots pressure of interests, judgements, opinions and all sorts of pressures of parochialisms.[1] At most, it expressed the interest of the state as such, which meant that it operated more in the sphere of axiology than within a true clash of interests of the most diverse kinds, often conflicting or even mutually exclusive ones. The traditional monocratic royal representation, based on the assumption of philosophical embodiment of a certain state of things and the values contributing to it (imponderables), was probably the only type of representation which was truly free from the pressure of interests which wanted representation to be an outlet and, at the same time, a certain kind of protection for themselves. The subsequent modifications, although some of them did still referred to the model of value representation, like for example in the traditional representation of groups, which was to express the existing social and political order,[2] slowly abandoned the assumption of completely pure, abstract, unadulterated representation, free from particular interests, pressures of demands and expectations focused on protecting the *status quo*. Because once a member of parliament was expected to openly identify group membership, it was clear that the identification would be based on conceptualizing the group interest, while the interest (though under various names and with various assessments) would be put at the heart of the representation process. Later still, when elections became a necessary element of representation, even though at the beginning they were very exclusive and limited, it was a commonplace practice to correlate the elected representative with the specifically located interests. People did not delegate 'their own representative' to act on the basis of the mythical everybody's will. He was, first of all, 'their own',

1 *Cf.* T. Debard, *Dictionnaire de droit constitutionnel*, Paris 2002, p. 269.

2 As it was the case of archaic parliamentary assemblies, which did not represent everybody, like today, but individual, separate component parts of the society, in various forms of e.g. socio-economic groups, i.e. nobility, clergy, burgesses, etc.

which directly suggested the direction of his activities; secondly, a 'representative', which – referring to the initially applicable civil law models of representation – left no doubt as to what was actually expected of the representative, either. So it was not by coincidence that the representative was called a 'delegate', 'proxy', 'ambassador', 'envoy' or simply 'deputy'.

Therefore, from a certain moment, representation became presentation or even more: an open clash of very specific interests and other kinds of demands, opinions and suggestions,[3] although it has to be admitted that sometimes attempts were made at 'veiling' those interests with the ideology of acting *pro publico bono* (like in the case of free mandate). In other cases it was already openly indicated that the gist was to promote specific ideas and conceptions, while the representative was more of a lobbyist than someone who, led by common sense, was trying to find the mythical general will and prosperity of all.[4] At one point it was most fully expressed by the principle of imperative mandate, which *a priori* treated the mandate holder as an exponent of clearly defined interests, obliged to strictly represent and, consequently, safeguard them. Then the role of an elector as a mandate promoter authorized by law was taken over, by the way rightly so, by political parties ant the mandate holders started to be perceived mainly as 'good party men'.[5] Nevertheless, even in the party representation model, at least declaratively, it was maintained that what was represented was the interest of all, that mythical *volonté générale*, all kinds of parochialisms being doomed to fail from the start. Additionally, what made it possible was adopting the legal construct of a free mandate, which meant that the mandate holder, irrespective of how he acquired it, was obliged to represent everybody, not only his electors or – in another convention – his constituency. Representation in its modern understanding defined the elected as more of a trustee than a delegate or proxy, especially in the civil law understanding, which took the form of imperative mandate in the realm of constitutional law.[6] Thus the pattern of political representation founded on free mandate still respected the belief that a representative acts for the sake of everybody's good and that his actions are guided in the positive sense by the search for common interest, whilst in the negative sense by the rejection of individual or particular interest.

---

3 *Cf.* L. Stoker, *Interest and Ethics in Politics*, "American Political Science Review" 1992, vol. 86, p. 369 *et seq.*

4 *Cf.* D. Mineur, *Archéologie de la représentation politique*, Paris 2010, p. 70 *et seq.*

5 W.I. Jennings, *The British Constitution*, Cambridge 1966, p. 82.

6 *Cf.* P.-H. Zaidman, *Le mandat impératif. De la Révolution française à la Commune de Paris*, Paris 2008, p. 9 *et seq.*

For a long time, this belief did not change despite the very evident 'partisanship' of the process of political representation. Sometimes it has even been stressed that the partisan profile of representation (subsequently criticized) gives a better picture of the will of all, because it organizes, and makes a selection of, the disorganized interests, thus aggregating the rather chaotic will of everybody (*volonté de tous*) and transforming it into the orderly general will (*volonté générale*),[7] which by its own nature found, as E. Burke put it, 'mature judgement' or 'supra-individual common opinion' that could not be reduced to a simple, arithmetical sum of everybody's opinions.[8] Hence representation of a partisan nature tried, at least in some sense, to keep a balance between the increasingly clear and increasingly frequent perception of representatives as exponents of specific, individual, highly atomized interests (party ones in this case) and cultivating the principle that they were acting on behalf of the general public, having the general welfare at the foreground.[9] Of course, the belief could not always be successfully maintained, because it was often openly declared or just suggested that the deputy had much tighter links with a party fraction than with the electors seen as a people, whose general will he, as a representative, was to express. Nevertheless, even in the cases when the representative felt to be a representative of the party rather than of the electors or simply the *corps electoral*, as a certain fiction it was maintained that he acted for the benefit of everybody and in no event did he champion individual or group interests. These circumstances were actually similar in all those cases when the mandate holder felt just an 'envoy' of his constituency, recognizing that, due to the legal form of mandate, he had an obligation to put the constituency's interests first and general interest second, and only when it did not conflict with the interest of his own constituency. Therefore free mandate, as a principally abstract construct of constitutional law, remained a certain postulate, in fact modified by the mandate holder's links with either a parliamentary (party) fraction or with a constituency, or with other groups or circles which considered themselves mandate promoters to a lesser or greater extent. Yet it was maintained, as a legal fiction, that the representative was to express the general interest and at least give it a priority over partial and particular interests, which anyway only heightened the impression of fictionality of representation as a whole from a certain moment, because it was thought to

---

7 *Cf.* C. Ysmal, *Les partis politiques et leur rôle*, [in:] *Institutions et vie politique*, J.-L. Parodi (ed.), Paris 2003, p. 94 *et seq.*

8 *Cf.* H.-Y. Lee, *Political Representation in the later Middle Ages*, New York 2008, p. 15 *et seq.*

9 *Cf.* G. Bouthoul, *Sociologie de la politique*, Paris 1977, p. 105 *et seq.*

be just a skilful rhetorical figure, from the beginning (i.e. the moment of defining the nation-sovereign) to the end (i.e. recognition of free mandate, rejecting representation of clearly defined interests). Representation, irrespectively of how it was eventually institutionalized and how it was legally and politically legitimized, was always seen as a forum for aggregating and articulating interests. The only thing that remained disputable and was left to be determined by practice (or law and theories which laced up practice in a bodice of doctrine) was how those interests would eventually be called and identified.

2. Political vs. Functional Representation

From the very beginning it was obvious that representation meant first and foremost presentation and protection of interests (in the broad sense). Even the seemingly highest and unequalled ideal of representation as the supra-individual and supra-group interest of everybody did use the category of interest as the central notion of representation. With the proviso, however, that when it referred to a specific one, this interest was seen as clearly pejorative, while in the second instance, when the interest was to cover 'all' or 'everybody', it was the good and legitimate interest, which required protection in the form of political representation. The way the latter functioned always showed that interests did clash, that representation was a real melting pot where the most diverse, often conflicting pressures, demands and expectations would fight one another. Thus the directive to act *pro publico bono*, which was addressed to the parliament and its members, was seen as unquestionably right and justified, but unachievable for pragmatic reasons. The postulate according to which political representatives rise, in their activities, above various particularisms and narrow interests stigmatized by localized groups remained just a postulate, a request akin to proposals of 'what the law should be'. The gap between it and the reality was actually seen as one of the manifestations of the crisis of representation, its practical inefficiency and façade character, which required and dynamized the search for some other, better solutions.

This is why, at a certain moment the idea emerged that apart from the classical political representation another parallel kind of representation should be established, this time openly aiming at presenting narrow group interests. It was believed to relieve the parliament from the duty to take care of particularisms and hence enable it to become an authentic platform where the general will would be cared for and sought, with individual and partial interests being protected by other representative bodies. All in all, the structures of the represented were always internally divided, branded by numerous, sometimes very deep, stigmas and interests and any representation forum, even the best one, could not minimize, much less eliminate all of them. If representation is to be efficient, it cannot 'bury its head in the sand' pretending that the ideal of general and common interest can be achieved, but it must be built in such a way as to skilfully combine what is inherently separate and individual with what is common and universal.[10] This way it was finally accepted that the complex, heterogeneous composition of the represented group was an objective state of affairs and, by definition, could not be changed or replaced with something that would promote artificial and apparent homogeneity. So if representation is always a form of aggregation and articulation of interests, which as a rule are not uniform or common, then it is necessary to build representation that will enable disclosing both the interest of the general public and various group interests. It is only such representation that becomes the authentic, true and actual kind, which is nothing else but an interaction of plural structures typical of the contemporary society.[11] Such interaction requires the existence of pluralist representation, which takes into account and externalizes the socio-political and economic complexity of the represented group.

So when representation gained a pluralist character,[12] with the consequence that in addition to the political representation body other bodies of the so-called functional representation[13] started appearing, the individual interests (in most cases ones with very strongly individualist character) were given an already open platform to present themselves. Nobody expected representatives of trade unions or e.g. employer organizations to rise above particular demands. Quite the contrary: the reason why various functional representation fora were created was to give an outlet for remarkably sectional judgements and opinions, which promoted partial interests. Consequently, representing all kinds of sectional interests became the standard in the current mainstream approach to representation as the so-called pluralist representation, i.e. representation assuming that many partial reasons are taken into account in the political decision-making process so that the resulting decision carries the general reason. Nevertheless it is not the case that representation of particular interests (those of e.g. employees, employers, professionals, social or professional groups or groups distinguished by

10 *Cf.* I.M. Young, *Deferring Group Representation*, [in:] *Ethnicity and Groups Rights*, I. Shapiro, W. Kymlicka (eds.), New York 1997, p. 249 *et seq.*

11 *Cf.* R. Dahl, *Polyarchy. Participation and Opposition*, New Haven 1971.

12 *Cf.* T. Debard, *Dictionnaire de droit…*, p. 270.

13 *Cf.* R. Mouriaux, *Syndicats, organisations professionnelles et groupes d'intérêt*, [in:] *Institutions et vie politique…*, p. 115 *et seq.*

territorial divides) dominates the process of political representation. Functional representation (sometimes referred to as professional or corporate representation) continues to be a complementary form of representation for the basic and still most important representation, that is, the political one,[14] which is sometimes also treated as territory-wide or society-wide representation.[15]

The parliament as a nationwide body of political representation is still perceived as the body which is to realize the general good and the will of all, while the bodies of socio-professional (or other) representation play a clearly secondary and, at best, supplementary role. This is the reason for the current two-pronged perception of representation. In the first case, it has the status of political representation, aggregated and articulated on the forum of the parliament and political parties within it. In the second case, it has the status of functional representation, firstly, located outside of the parliament and, secondly, realized via entities which are not political parties (e.g. trade unions, employer organizations, associations and other relevant groups and organizations).[16] In this 'dual representation system' the parliament (and political parties) occupies, notwithstanding all the changes and transformations, a special place and the remaining representation fora, branded as particularistic, are still perceived as a tool of representation which has an inherently complementary nature that supplements the image of representation, as the latter has to present various standpoints, judgements and assessments in order to be truly complete.

The pivotal role of the parliament and, accordingly, political representation is additionally legitimized by the constitutional principle of sovereignty of the people (nation), of which the principle of political representation is a consequence and logical continuation. Other forms of representation (e.g. social or professional), even if legitimized by the constitution (like for example the Economic, Social and Environmental Council of the Republic of France), are not treated as 'extensions of popular sovereignty' (as the parliament is often referred to) and they consequently 'give way' to political representation. This means that the parliament still has a monopolist position as a representative.[17] Moreover, despite the clear supremacy of political parties, it is still believed that what should be represented in the parliament is the supra-individual, common and universal interests. In this context it is quite rightly pointed out that the very idea of emergence

14 *Cf.* Y. Mény, Y. Surel, *Politique comparée. Les démocraties*, Paris 2009, p. 125 *et seq.*

15 *Cf.* C. Haguenau-Moizard, *Les systèmes politiques européens*, Paris 2009, p. 73.

16 More on this topic: B. Barber, *Strong Democracy: Participatory Politics for a New Age*, Berkley 1989.

17 *Cf.* M. Lascombe, *Le droit constitutionnel de la Ve République*, Paris 2010, p. 191 *et seq.*

of functional representation, as a complement, but also, to some extent, competition for the traditional political representation, has the aim of upholding the overall assumption that the parliament represented the *volonté générale.*[18] This is so because the so-called dual model of representation (i.e. political party representation in the parliament and socio-professional representation in other bodies) was to maintain, side by side, two basic forms of representation, i.e. common and general representation, housed in a national representative body, and separate and detailed representation, for which functional representation bodies were established.[19] It was correctly recognized that functional representation had an inherently supplementary nature and was by no means a replacement for general political representation. It emerged when it had turned out that socio-political divides were generated not only by the classical cleavages, for which the parliament, structured according to political and territorial principles, was an absolutely sufficient forum.[20] At a certain time it was observed that other elements of the divides acquired political relevance, especially the socio-economic ones, which had to be given an adequate kind of institutional outlet and, together with the existing body of political representation, this helped maintain overall political stability. Consequently what was considered the optimum model of representation was pluralist representation, assuming parallel existence of political and functional representation.[21] The pluralist character of representation did not, however, entail that both forms of representation were anywhere near equal. Therefore political representation (reflected in the parliament) remains the basic one, while formal representation has a derivative and secondary status.[22]

Moreover, the secondary nature of the bodies that can be classified as functional representation (and include mainly advisory and consultation bodies or directive bodies) results, firstly, from the fact that they are not treated as an

---

18 *Cf.* S. Piattoni, *Clientelism, Interests and Democratic Representation,* [in:] *Clientelism, Interests and Democratic Representation. The European Experiences in Historical and Comparative Perspective,* S. Piattoni (ed.), Cambridge 2001, 193 *et seq.*

19 The question whether representation should have a more global (universal) or particular (individual) character is one of the most important issues, sparking lively and relentless debates in constitutional law. More on this topic: M. Duverger, *Institutions politiques et droit constitutionnel,* Paris 1966, p. 83, 84.

20 *Cf.* J. Delaney, P. Schwochau, *Employee Representation Through the Political Process,* [in:] *Employee Representation. Alternatives and Future Directions,* B.E. Kaufman, M.M. Kleiner (eds.), University of Wisconsin 1993, p. 265 *et seq.*

21 *Cf.* T. Debard, *Dictionnaire de droit constitutionnel…,* p. 270.

22 *Cf.* C. Haguenau-Moizard, *Les systèmes politiques…,* p. 74.

'extension' or 'embodiment' of popular sovereignty (only the parliament being regarded as such), secondly, from the fact that the complex structures of functional (or socio-economic, to use a different terminology) representation bodies are not usually legitimized by the constitution. The status of functional representation is, consequently, rather limited from the start, the more so that at the level of constitutional regulations it is usually not envisaged at all. And wherever (like in France) some of its forms are envisaged, they are treated clearly as accessory ones. In addition, thirdly, the secondary nature of functional representation bodies, which is visible *prima facie*, naturally results from the multitude of such entities. If the counterweight to the nationwide (political) representative body comprises at least several, if not a dozen, bodies of socio-professional and economic representation, it is obvious that they have (setting aside the formal legal limitations) a weaker systemic position. This results also from the historical development of functional representation bodies, in which this kind of representation was treated as only a correction of the process of political representation,[23] once it was at a certain time recognized that political divides coexisted with other divides, which needed to be somehow marked and institutionalized.[24] Political representation as reflected in the parliament is still, in spite of everything, the basic representation, while functional representation is just the supplementary and corrective kind.[25] There is another obvious reason for that, namely the atomized character of functional representation. From the very beginning it was treated as one whose *telos* is determined by promoting and protecting individual interest. And the latter, even though at some time it was deemed to need a separate representation mechanism, has never preponderated (at least not in the theoretical sense) over the general interest, which has always been perceived as the fundamental and, in every respect, the most important one.

The parliament's dominant position in the process of aggregating and articulating interests is the reason why it is basically only with regard to the parliament that the problem of selecting the externalized interests appears along with the

23 *Cf.* J. Delaney, P. Schwochau, *Employee Representation...*, p. 270 *et seq.*

24 More on this topic: D. Mineur, *Archéologie de la représentation...*, p. 199 *et seq.*

25 The more so that it bears a sort of 'original sin': the emergence of various functional representation bodies (in the form of corporate chambers) on the tide of intensifying processes of creation and consolidation of authoritarian systems in the 1920s and 1930s (a good example of which is the Portuguese Corporate Chamber established in by virtue of the 1933 Constitution). So their origin was clearly anti-democratic and ant-parliamentary, which for a long time disavowed the project of functional (professional or corporate) representation.

related issue of ethical or unethical conduct. In other cases the centrally designed paradigm of representation of partial and non-general interests, combined with absence of constitutional legitimacy for acting, which is, after all, correlated with the principle of popular sovereignty, makes the issue of ethical behaviour of the representative a less fundamental one, although it does not take ethics out of the equation. The functional profile of representation requires, however, the representative to have a sort of imperative mandate, which requires that in his activities he should present and protect the interests of the promoter.[26] So from this point of view, unethical conduct will mean compromising those interests and supporting other, alternative judgements, opinions and suggestions, especially if they openly conflict with the interests and expectations of the principal. In view of the above, functional representation is much closer to the design of the delegate than proxy model.[27] In the functional representation model a representative is authorized in such a way as to promote and protect interests of the group he represents. In the end, this is why he has been appointed. Therefore, ethical actions, compatible with the sense of professional representation, will include representation focused on individual interest, whereas promoting interests which go against the group protected by the umbrella of functional representation will deserve a negative assessment as unethical and contrary to the very idea of representation. *A contrario*, in case of a representative selected according to the principles of political representation, the actions that are appropriate from the point of view of the assumed representation mechanism – naturally if accompanied by free mandate – are *pro publico bono* actions, that is, focus in the first place on promoting general, rather than individual, interest.[28] The best guarantee of that is, of course, the free mandate. As amply demonstrated by the historical process of development of political representation, free mandate was introduced after acknowledgment that political representation should become detached from particular groups' interests, because its rudimentary sense was to seek general good.[29] Thus free mandate was a way of formulating a

---

26 *Cf. Les forces syndicales françaises*, G. Bernard, J.-P. Deschodt (ed.), Paris 2010, p. 181 *et seq.*

27 *Cf.* A. Heywood, *Politics*, Houndmills-New York 2013, p. 199, 200.

28 *Cf.* J. Uhr, *Democracy and the Ethics of Representation*, [in:] *Ethics and Political Practice. Perspectives on Legislative Ethics*, N. Preston, Ch. Sampford, A.A. Bois (eds.), New York–London 2003, p. 11 *et seq.*

29 *Cf.* O. Rozenberg, M. Blomgren, *Bringing Parliamentary Roles back in*, [in:] *Parliamentary Roles in Modern Legislatures*, M. Blomgren, O. Rozenberg (eds.), New York 2012, p. 111–113.

completely new paradigm of representation. Since the time of its establishment it has been, after all, recognized that what matters in political representation is seeking what is common instead of separate and partial (in line with the call 'we are all French'[30]). Free mandate was, therefore, in the axiological sense, a determinant of an alternative vision of representation and replacement of the delegate model with the trustee model. In the pragmatic sense this kind of mandate was a form of security against the pressure of particular interests, which always, in any model of representation, turned out to be relatively strong and in the case of political representation were additionally maintained by the imperative mandate, in which the representative was to be treated as a plenipotentiary of the principal's interests. It continued to be additionally upheld by the electoral mechanism which, regardless of the specific mathematical technique of mandate allocation (proportional or majoritarian systems), links the mandate holder with a specific elector and not the whole electorate.[31]

However, the change in the representation paradigm (from separate, partial and particular into single, global, common and universal) confronted the mandate holder with the problem of permissible and impermissible behaviours, which are difficult to translate into the language of the law. The mandate holder, in addition to the letter of the law (which in free mandate directs him to be guided by the good of all), operates also in the complex area of politics, morality, ethics, accepted customs and habits, as well as simple decency. The latter elements, which may or even should additionally determine the conduct of the mandate holder, make the issue of judging the representative's behaviour considerably more nuanced. Broadly speaking, various sorts of nuances in the assessment of admissible and decent behaviours of a representative result from, firstly, the personal relationship between the deputy and the voters and, secondly, evolutionary transformation of the mandate formula, which does not retain the form of a classic free mandate all the time. Free mandate has undergone various changes and mutations, with the resulting current far-reaching partisan character of the representative mandate, according to the (party) mandate model of representation.[32] At the same time, at least as the law stands, the form of free mandate is still maintained, making the question of (desirable and approved or undesirable, reprehensive and unacceptable) conduct one of the most important issues in the

---

30 L. Jaume, *Hobbes et l'Etat représentatif moderne*, Paris 1986, p. 154.

31 *Cf.* K. Strøm, *Parliamentary Democracy and Delegation*, [in:] *Delegation and Accountability in Parliamentary Democracies*, K. Strøm, W.C. Müller, T. Bergman (eds.), Oxford 2003, p. 55 *et seq.*

32 *Cf.* A. Heywood, *Politics…*, p. 200, 201.

whole system of political representation.[33] So what comes to the fore in political representation is the issue of mandate holder's ethics.[34]

3. Ethics in the Conduct of a Representative as a Politician

Ethics is defined as a set of rules and norms of behaviour applicable in a given community. So in order for ethics to emerge, there must exist a norm as a regulator of certain kinds of behaviour and a group or other community within which the given norm will apply. At the same time it is clear that ethics understood in this way can be present in almost every social or professional group, assuming a certain particular, often endemic, form, which – importantly – need not even be positive (as is the case of the notorious ethics of thieves). This is one of the reasons why ethics as such does not necessarily carry a positive evaluative connotation, because it is simply axiologically neutral. It assumes that a certain norm, rule or principle applies in a certain group only if said norm, rule or principle is allowed and accepted by the group, thus becoming a norm applicable to, and applied by, that group (the so-called ethics in the normative sense). The norm or rule need not be positive at all, it may – from the point of view of people at large or from the point of view of another social group or community – be seen as negative or even have the status of anti-norm and anti-standard[35] and in any case be a behaviour or a way of acting which is clearly perceived as bad. A decisively positive assessment which is linked to ethics is typical of the so-called descriptive ethics (often incorrectly identified with ethics in general) understood as a set of standards and behaviours which are morally desirable and approved.

---

33 *Cf.* P. Pasquino, *Emmanuel Sieyes, Benjamin Constant et le «gouvernment des modernes». Contribution à l'histoire du concept de représentation politique*, "Revue Française de Science Politique" 1987, no. 2, p. 219 *et seq.*

34 More on this topic: M. Rush, P. Giddings, *Parliamentary Socialization. Learning the Ropes or Determining Behaviour?*, London 2011, p. 9 *et seq.*; H. Best, L. Vogel, *The Emergence and Transformation of Representative Role*, [in:] *Parliamentary Roles in Modern Legislatures…*, p. 37 *et seq.*; G. Tsebelis, *Veto Players and Law Production*, [in:] *Patterns of Parliamentary Behavior. Passage of Legislation across western Europe*, H. Döring, M. Hallerberg (eds.), London 2004, p. 169 *et seq.*

35 It will be so if it only turns out that a certain community, another enclave or social or professional group recognizes and accepts a certain behaviour, commonly perceived as reprehensible, immoral or simply bad, making that behaviour a substratum forming ethics, that is, a set of rules of behaviour respected by a certain group or community. A norm accepted and recognized in one group need not always be accepted and approved in all other groups.

It is easy to observe that if we put the matter this way, it obscures an important difference between such normative systems as ethics on the one hand and morality on the other.

Once any community can create its own ethics, that is, a system of assessments, judgements and values that are representative of it, then clearly among many such systems of ethics we can also distinguish the ethics of a representative or a parliamentarian, or even more broadly, parliamentary ethics as the kind typical of holders of parliamentary mandates. In addition, such ethics, i.e. ethics concerning members of legislative bodies, should be seen as a subset of a much broader and bigger category, namely the ethics of a politician, that is to say, a person who professionally engages in politics[36] as a specific area of human activity. A parliamentarian (representative) is just one among the many persons involved in politics[37], that is, without delving into definitions, shaping the power relationships in a macro scale. This actually makes it impossible to speak of the ethics of a parliamentarian without mentioning the ethics of a politician, which in turn means that ethics may have, or at least be perceived by the public as having, a different tone than what is commonly assumed, i.e. precisely a negative one. Although ethics as such may be assessed both positively and negatively (once it is defined as a set of judgements, assessments and values correspondent with the given community), in the widespread perception it is usually assumed to have a clearly positive axiological value, as if recognizing *a priori* that it promotes the undoubtedly positive and exemplary patterns of conduct. Meanwhile politics is invariably associated with particularism, with the rivalry between conflicting interests, with unethical, immoral behaviour, with foul play, demands, expectations and various claims whose focus is on the good of an individual or, at most, of a group, but never or almost never associated with *pro publico bono* actions. In this sense one may even venture a statement that politics is commonly perceived to negate ethics; it is pushing through particular ideas instead of the general welfare that politics is supposed to serve. It is also usually a foul play and, worse still, hidden behind the veil of not entirely clear, legible or transparent interests, the latter being almost by definition judged as bad, negative and worthy of criticism. Consequently, politics and ethics are seen as quasi-antonyms, because

36 In literature there is much emphasis on representation being a sort of practise of a profession (*politique comme profession*): P. Pasquino, *Emmanuel Sieyes…*, p. 223.

37 It is not accidentally that the parliament is precisely a breeding ground of politicians, thus playing an important function of recruiting political elite. More on this topic: *Members of Parliament in Western Europe. Roles and Behaviour*, W.C. Müller, T. Saalfeld (ed.), London–Portland 1997.

what is political cannot be ethical. Therefore, it is assumed that something is either political (thus unethical or otherwise blameworthy) or ethical, thus good and just, *ergo* non-political. Politics is commonly believed to be governed by its own rules, which are not always the same as the rules of ordinary, mundane life, whose rhythm is determined by completely different scales of values than those relating to life in the realm of *polis*, understood as the area of political activity of individuals. But what those different scales create is precisely the ethics of a politician[38] or – even more generally – the ethics of politics, with its typically different standards of demeanour, different axiological patterns and different mechanisms of assessment, perception and, in the end, conduct.

The ethics of a parliamentarian is therefore a certain category or subset of the broad group of politician's ethics, which ethics is in most cases, though obviously not always and not everywhere, evaluated as reprehensible or, in any way, pejorative.[39] The phenomenon is even more pronounced if parliamentarian's ethics is correlated with his fundamental function, that is, representation of interests. The latter are usually seen as something inescapably bad, reprehensible, conflicting with the generally adopted and approved scales of values. As a consequence, if a member of the parliament is given the task of representing certain interests (which has to be done, because representation does not exclusively or mainly mean a correlation of interests, but precisely their prior aggregation and articulation), then the parliamentarian is somewhat *a priori* presented in a negative light. In the model of free mandate, in which the general interest is realized, it is actually recognized that an MP essentially does not represent any interest, because everybody's interest all too often turns out to be nobody's interest or, quite the contrary, the interest of a very narrow and small group. On the other hand, under the model of imperative mandate, which envisages protecting group interests from the start, the representative is seen as a promoter of specific rationales, standpoints and opinions, which should rather give way to the pressure of universalism, as a matter of course realized by the nationwide representative body. *Nota bene*, the actual expectations pertaining to an MP-representative are the axis of all disputes concerning political representation and the concepts of mandate which embody it.[40]

But what distinguishes the ethics of a politician, understood as a system of principles and norms of conduct of a person involved in politics, from the ethics

38 *Cf.* L. Stoker, *Interest and Ethics in Politics…*, p. 369 *et seq.*

39 More on this topic: J.M. Parrish, *Paradoxes of Political Ethics. From Dirty to the Invisible Hand*, Cambridge 2008, p. 183 *et seq.*

40 *Cf.* P. Avril, J. Gicquel, *Droit parlementaire*, Paris 2004, p. 30 *et seq.*

of a parliamentarian is not only the definitively narrower group of persons it applies to, because for obvious reasons not all politicians are MPs, but also, perhaps even predominantly, the way all these values that ethics comprises are conceptualized. Because while the ethics of a politician in general is characterised by a certain voluntarism, i.e. the fact that as a rule it is shaped by the politician himself or rather the class of politicians, the ethics of a parliamentarian is already, at least *in principio*, subject to legal regulation; it is characterized by a certain legal regime, which determines the most important elements (substrata) of the system which constitutes ethics. Thus any assessments, rules, norms and values of the conduct of an MP (representative) are not fully discretionary (in the sense of being at most subjected to public judgement, like in the case of politician's ethics), but are regulated by the provisions of law, which assume certain rudiments of those assessments, rules, norms and values.[41] So a parliamentarian shapes his behaviour according to certain models which are subject to legal regulation, which in turn eliminates the freedom of forming such models, makes them more coherent and at the same time verifies them. This way the ethics of a parliamentarian becomes a *sui generis* qualified form of ethics of a politician, because it is determined, organized, tidied up, and – no less importantly – controlled by the law.

It seems that the legal framework of the parliamentarian's ethics may be viewed from at least four different, but mutually complementary, points of view. The first one is the constitutional law nature of the parliamentary mandate, which defines certain duties of a mandate holder, shaping the substance of his behaviour, which behaviour in turn may be assessed – by confrontation with the principles relating to the overall structure of the mandate – as ethical or unethical.[42] The second point of view, though directly related to the first one, is the relationship between the parliamentarian and the electors, who are understood here as the direct electors of the mandate holder (therefore those who voted for him or who live in the constituency where he was elected), but also as the electorate, not correlated with the place of acquisition of the mandate or, the more so, with any individual elector who put his trust in the mandate holder. We should also add straight away

41 Although we have to realize that in many cases such juridified principles of ethics of a parliamentarian are succinct and rather general, often making their proper enforcement in practice difficult. Models of conduct for parliamentarians are often imprecise and their descriptions use evaluative, thus disputable, expressions. *Cf.* E. May, *The Law, Privileges, Proceedings and Usage of Parliament*, London 1989, p. 46.

42 In addition this element may be understood much more broadly and apply to the entirety of a parliamentarian's relations with electors. More on this topic: *Parliaments and Citizens in Western Europe*, P. Norton (ed.), London – Portland 1999.

that it is this relationship that, from the perspective of the overall relationship of representation, is usually associated with precisely the sphere of the parliamentarian's ethics. The simple reason is that it is probably this relationship that causes the greatest number of doubts as to the so-called loyalty of the mandate holder and, consequently, ethical or unethical conduct (usually described in categories or keeping election promises or failing to do so). This is why the whole issue of deputies' ethics is all too often trimmed down to behaviour towards the elector and respecting (or not) the earlier election promises.[43] The third issue which is taken into account in the assessment of ethical standards of a person holding a parliamentary mandate involves the various links between the deputy and his political party or, more broadly, his whole political base. The relationship between a deputy-parliamentary and a fraction, or even further: the relationship between a deputy and the political party which backs the parliamentary wing of this party is particularly important for several reasons. Firstly, because the relationship may considerably modify the theoretical assumptions of the mandate; secondly, because it may be in conflict with the basic relationship, namely the one between the deputy and his electors; thirdly, because it is characterized by its own, peculiar ethical system, which may not only provide a natural and logical supplement for the theoretical assumptions of the mandate (or, more broadly, relationship of representation), but also, at least potentially, clash with those assumptions or, in any case, fail to fit in smoothly, consequently generating unethical or at least ethically unequivocal situations. For the above reasons, the links between the mandate holder and the political promoters of the mandate are by all means a necessary element for assessing everything that the notion of parliamentarian's ethics comprises. Finally, the fourth and last perspective on the legal regulation of the parliamentarian's ethics is the issue of the parliamentarian's links with other, extra-parliamentary, but also extra-party circles and groups, mainly lobbying ones, i.e. with all sorts of pressure groups, which influence the MPs and the parliament to a greater or lesser extent, consequently influencing the final decisions taken by the legislative assembly.

All of those four perspectives on the parliamentarian's ethics create specific subsystems of ethics that jointly make up the proper ethics of a parliamentarian, understood as the area of permissible, required or prohibited conduct of holders of representative mandates. Yet it should be emphasised from the start that they only concern the legal shape of this ethics, leaving out the so-called

43 *Cf.* W.G. Hayden, *Politics, Public Responsibility and the Ethical Imperative*, [in:] *Ethics and Political Practice…*, p. 52 *et seq.*

good manners or even a certain kind of parliamentary *savoir faire*, which is all in all an important indicator and component of parliamentary ethics that allows parliamentary behaviours to retain the character of ethics (notably a system of norms which are not necessarily codified) and not just legally regulated detailed precepts and prohibitions, which are already transferred from the level of ethics to that of the law in the strict sense. The field of permitted or accepted, as well as unacceptable, conduct of a parliamentarian embraces, contrary to appearances, not only stiff norms clad in the bodice of legal regulation (by-laws or codes),[44] but also the behaviours and the underlying rules, assessments and models which are not in any way codified, which leave a certain necessary leeway in application and which fall between the law in the strict sense and ethics, morality, good customs or simply political culture and, last but not least, the ordinary personal etiquette.

4. Legal Framework of a Representative's Ethics: Representative Mandate

Parliamentary mandate, today commonly treated as representative (free) mandate, is the most general clause of the parliamentarian's ethics, obliging him to consider, in his parliamentary activity, the interest of the whole nation, while refraining from any actions which would give priority to partial, group, regional, area-specific or, say, professional interests. Naturally, in his activities in the parliament an MP can push forward particular conceptions, ones which are clearly addressed to certain groups or circles, but the principle of representative mandate requires him to coordinate and confront these conceptions with the good of the whole nation, that is, the whole electorate, and in case of conflict to always opt for those that benefit everybody, i.e. all the electors. So, in the event of a potential clash between an individual interest and a collective one, a free mandate, based on the principle of not being bound by the will of the individual elector, urges him to opt for the collective one. This is so even though it is commonly recognized that a 'representative is free (*libre*) in his decisions'.[45] However, it is stressed that freedom does not in any case equal discretion, which in turn means that the conduct of a representative should always be guided by certain ethical and political precepts,[46] which are formulated or determined in the most general

44 Which are created more and more commonly. *Cf.* M. Burgmann, *Constructing Codes: Pitfalls and Challenges*, [in:] *Ethics and Political Practice*..., p. 118 *et seq.*

45 P. Ardant, *Institutions politiques & droit constitutionnel*, Paris 2004, p. 168.

46 *Cf.* W.G. Hayden, *Politics, Public Responsibility*..., p. 52 *et seq.*

form precisely by free mandate, which is an expression of the trust that electors have in the representative.[47] Consequently, it is the underlying principle of free mandate, namely the principle of trust which the nation-sovereign puts in the mandate holder through an election, which creates the obligation of respecting the sovereign's interest and not just 'whatever' interest, as may be suggested, at least *prima facie*, by the principle that the deputy is free in his decisions (*'libre de ses décisions'*).[48]

So free mandate introduces the principle of weighing the values that the parliamentarian wants to achieve in his activities, formulating the directive of supremacy of common (general) good over any good which is partial, sectional or otherwise different and separate from what was traditionally referred to as the *volonté générale*. This way, the principle of preponderance of collective interest was introduced as one of legal rules of parliamentary ethics. For every parliamentarian, collective interest is the ultimate and fundamental value, giving direction to each action and behaviour of the representative mandate holder according to the principles of free and unbound representative mandate. This principle has particularly strong safeguards, which do not allow formulating any legally binding instructions or orders or, the more so, recalling the parliamentarian in a hypothetical situation when a specific group of electors considers that he fails to act in their name or that he protects their interests badly or insufficiently. As we can see, all the negative clauses, from which the principle of free mandate is probably inferred most frequently (*vide* the example of France), aim to introduce express and 'firm' prohibitions of binding the mandate holder with any individual interests, hence also establishing various sanctions on this account.[49] Consequently, it is prohibited to formulate any guidelines, instructions, orders, opinions or suggestions which would bind the representative. The most the representative can do is take them into account, but they can never determine his actions. In view of the above, prohibition of imperative mandate and, consequently, establishing free mandate as the general norm is the broadest base, not only legal, but also axiological one, for assessing the representative's conduct as ethical or unethical. The value which is upheld by the legal framework is the imperative of doing what will be more conducive to searching the supra-individual will of all rather than the arithmetic will of everybody.

---

47 *Cf.* P. Ardant, *Institutions politiques…*, p. 168.

48 *Ibidem.*

49 *Cf.* P. Avril, J. Gicquel, *Droit parlementaire…*, p. 32.

In view of the above, the key directive in the parliamentarian's ethics, which results explicitly from the capacious principle of free mandate, is being always guided by the general good, which in turn means clear subordination of any group, territorial or area-specific interests to the interest of the whole sovereign, that is, briefly speaking, the nation. Obviously, proper exercise of a parliamentary mandate, even if only for pragmatic reasons, has to entail maintaining adequate relationships with specific groups of electors, including mainly one's own constituents.[50] Yet these relationships cannot, according to the principle of free mandate, acquire the status of dominant or, much less, central ones, because in the hierarchy they rank below the fundamental relationship with the sovereign: the nation being the totality of voters.

Although maintaining a link with one's own constituency, understood as the place of acquisition (origin) of the mandate, cannot gain priority over the idea of free mandate and the resulting principle of representing everybody, it is still a very important element of the ethics of a parliamentarian, who always has to remember about his local obligations and local authorization, which enabled him to acquire a mandate at all. Thus the local anchorage of a parliamentarian requires him to maintain direct contact with the constituency; this contact is expressed, among other things, by representing local problems, including also the ones which are by all means sectional, at the level of the nationwide representative body. But presentation of interests or problems of local or regional character (relating to affairs of the constituency where the deputy obtained his mandate) does not in itself equal conduct whose aim would be to protect such interests at all costs and, all the more so, taking initiatives which would put such interests ahead of the global, universal and general interest. Thus representing individual interests, understood as presenting individual matters relating to the constituency is not in itself excluded or upfront prohibited by free mandate. An MP, even if just taking into account pragmatic reasons, still maintains various kinds of local ties, whose result is presenting on the public forum matters involving various local and sectional problems, big and small. But this cannot dominate, or the more so, cancel the principle of free mandate, according to which the mandate holder, although elected on the basis of localism or territorialism, always expresses the *volonté générale*. This being so, ties and other kinds of local links are obvious and indisputable, moreover, they are embedded in the very logic of the relationship of representation, which, although built around a partial (local,

50 More on this topic: *Back from Westminster: British Members of Parliament and their Constituents*, P. Norton, D.M. Wood (eds.) Lexington 1993.

territorial or regional) backbone, in its entirety expresses the idea of universal, global representation, voicing the interest of the whole *corps électoral*. Therefore local ties are, naturally from the strictly legal point of view, clearly secondary to the key link with the global electorate, that is, electorate not in any way connected with a specific constituency.

Nevertheless the secondary character of the relationship with the home constituency is of a highly legal, strictly normative, nature. The ethics of a parliamentarian – and this is, incidentally, a manifestation of its obvious particularity and ontological status as ethics proper – comprises not only legal relationships, but also political and moral ones, not regulated in any legal provisions. And it is often the latter relationships that are of key importance for a parliamentarian, because in practice they link him to the constituency, making him a *sui generis* representative of his own constituency on the forum of the national representative body. This is why a parliamentarian, in his activities, should deftly correlate the directives formulated for him by the law, which means pursing the general good, with directives having *par excellence* political and moral origin, one of them being the need to maintain ties with his own constituency, which always entails certain, somewhat obvious, protection of localism, that is, partial, particular or otherwise described individual interest. Adroit weighting of both kinds of interests and consequently choosing what is better, more justified or fairer on a larger scale (thus the political scale) is precisely the area of ethics in which a parliamentarian is repeatedly forced to synchronize various, often conflicting, values, judgements and views, in order for the final decision to be simply good: the best decision in the relevant contextual conditions. The current model of free mandate is only a certain theoretical or hypothetical one, remaining this way a sort of ideal assumption of the doctrine, which in practical application does not fully correspond to the textbook criteria of free mandate (*nota bene*, like any other mandate model, it is by design a model, i.e. a significant simplification and generalization).

Yet the ethical or moral and, consequently, extra-legal dimension of the relationship between the representative and the represented cannot be reduced to just the relationship between the mandate holder and his constituency. Of course, a relationship of this kind is the primary one (at least in the sense of origin[51]), but the ethical conduct of a representative refers also to constituents in general. In this context the key notions are that of 'trust' and 'election promise'. A deputy,

51 *Cf.* A. Rehfeld, *The Concept of Constituency. Political Representation, Democratic Legitimacy and Institutional Design*, Cambridge 2008, p. 29 *et seq.*

before formally acquiring the mandate, makes various kinds of declarations and promises, which constitute his electoral platform. The electorate's final election is thus a sort of contract, in which the electors put their trust in their representative and the substance of this trust is the 'election promise', as best demonstrated by first-past-the-post systems.[52] But the problem of the 'election promise' may and indeed should be approached from a broader perspective and discussed in terms of a certain understanding of honesty or decency vis-à-vis the slogans and promises declared by the deputy. What happens in the election campaign is after all the candidate defining his stance on the key issues which animate the public discussion. This gives rise to natural expectations that the declarations made by the candidate during the election campaign, once the candidate successfully acquires the mandate, will be put into practice, while the deputy's conduct will not conflict with the statements made during the election campaign. It is generally believed that a reliable or simply honest, or precisely ethical, representative is one whose behaviour during the campaign and the exercise of the mandate is the same, meaning that there are no discrepancies between his 'election promises' and his actual actions as a representative. Yet this begs the question whether simple decency, as a basic element of ethics in the descriptive sense, is an equally important element of ethics with respect to a parliamentarian?

There appears a basic problem of a legal nature, because the free mandate is sometimes believed to permit the parliamentarian to exercise his mandate in accordance with his own conscience and convictions, regardless of the earlier election promises and the advocated programme. What becomes apparent here is the potential discrepancy in the understanding of a parliamentarian's ethics: whether it will be ethical for a representative to act 'in accordance with his own conscience, regardless of the electoral promises he made' or, perhaps, whether it will be ethical to act in such a way which is defined by 'keeping the promises made'?[53] If one is to be consistent and regard that ethics is an endemic set of values, rules and precepts of conduct, one can assume that it will indeed be more ethical to act in accordance with one's conscience rather than to keep promises made during the election (which may be additionally legitimized by free mandate, thus the need to take into account the good of everyone, which may be in conflict with the election promise). If we understand ethics as a model of behaviour in a given circle, this may indeed prompt us to accept the thesis that in the circle of parliamentarians it is ethical to act in accordance with one's

52 *Cf.* M. Charlot, *Le povoir politique en Grande-Bretagne*, Paris 1998, p. 139.
53 *Cf.* M. Charlot, *Le povoir politique…*, p. 138, 139 [author's own translation].

conscience and not the promises made to the voters (referring to the construct of representative mandate, such conduct will not only be by all means ethical, but also undoubtedly lawful). As was mentioned earlier, this conclusion may also be encouraged by the original construct of free mandate, which assumes that the parliamentarian is somewhat 'freed' from the pressure of demands of his constituents and anything that can be perceived as private, individual, narrow and area-specific interest. And, undeniably, it is particularly the classical or original understanding of free mandate that will foster the perception of ethics of an MP as acting 'in accordance with one's conscience' regardless of other circumstances. It was Jean Antoine Nicolas de Condorcet who said that 'the people sent me to expound my idea, not theirs'[54] and this is precisely why 'absolute independence of my opinions is my primary duty'.[55] This shows that free mandate has from the very beginning been seen as a sort of guarantee of autonomy, but also – and this was perceived as its danger – discretion or even impunity of the mandate holder's conduct. So the group-related, clearly endemic origin of ethics in combination with the classical understanding of free mandate, which assumed 'freeing the deputy in his decisions'[56], might indeed have suggested that what was ethical (or even more, what is lawful) was conduct determined solely by the mandate holder's 'conscience'.

However, one should ask oneself whether this way of approaching the issue is not too radical, because the free mandate does not exactly introduce the postulate of acting 'in accordance with one's conscience'. This view is definitively overly voluntarist and can be referred at most to a politician's ethics, but not necessarily to a parliamentarian's ethics.[57] Indeed, a politician applying the well-known method according to which the end justifies the means may act exclusively according to what his own conscience dictates to him regardless of what other people think about it;[58] however, is a similar conduct actually dictated by the principle of free mandate? One has to bear in mind that this principle is by no means a principle *per se*, but it points to another, much broader, principle, namely

54 G. Burdeau, *Droit constitutionnel et institutions politique*, Paris 1963, p. 129.

55 *Ibidem*.

56 P. Ardant, *Institutions politiques*…, p. 168.

57 By the way. once free mandate in its very first, original form appeared, not only was no distinction made between politicians and parliamentarians, but the terms (and 'professions' denoted by them) were seen as equivalents. So ethical standards of politicians were very easily transferred to, or identified with, ethical standards of representatives.

58 *Cf.* J.M. Parrish, *Paradoxes of Political Ethics*…, p. 27 *et seq.*

that of political representation. And representation requires a minimum of coherence between the views and assessments of the representative and those of the represented; in addition it also requires aggregation and then articulation of specific, express interests (regardless of how we finally define and term them).[59] So if we are to retain at least a rudimentary sense of representation (which means not treating it as just a certain legal fiction), then there has to be an assumption that it is necessary for the representative to express the view (interest) of the represented. Otherwise the very idea of representation will be just a meaningless political project, albeit put in the constitutional framework, which project, however, will produce none or hardly any consequences. Representation, regardless of the theoretical perspectives in which it is viewed, establishes each time a certain *minimum minimorum*, namely treating the representative as a person speaking on behalf and on account of the represented.[60] Thus we cannot accept as certainty the principle that free mandate establishes a rule of acting in accordance with one's own conscience and without regard to earlier election promises. In extreme cases such an understanding of a parliamentarian's ethics (or the different understanding of his honesty or decency) might lead to questioning the very foundations of political representation.[61] If a representative consistently maintained that he was acting in accordance with his own conscience only, he would no longer act in anybody's but his own name. So, hypothetically speaking, he would not represent anybody but, at most, himself. Meanwhile, free mandate assumes something different, i.e. not so much freeing the parliamentarian from the pressure of individual interest, but rather establishing the supremacy of the interest seen as identical with the will of all voters.[62] Therefore, what should be

59 *Cf.* C.R. Hayward, *Making Interest: On Representation and Democratic Legitimacy*, [in:] *Political Representation*, I. Shapiro, S.C. Stokes, E.J. Wood, A.S. Kirshner (eds.), Cambridge 2009, p. 111 *et seq.*

60 *Cf.* P. Pettit, *Varieties of Public Representation*, [in:] *Political Representation…*, p. 61 *et seq.*

61 Which was one of the justifications of the theory of mandate, which in the very beginning was not correlated with a party, but with an individual Member of the House of Commons. *Cf.* P. Magdwick, *A New Introduction to British Politics*, London 1984, p. 275.

62 In addition, one should remember that free mandate, when it appeared, was also seen as an antonym of imperative mandate. Consequently, the assumption that a parliamentarian holding a free mandate acts ethically if he acts in accordance with his own conscience was, at least in some sense, a result of two important circumstances. Firstly, the fact that free mandate was the opposite of the earlier imperative mandate. Secondly, the fact that a parliamentarian was identified with a politician, who was

the guiding principle for the parliamentarian's conduct is not acting on the 'as I like' principle (because my conscience tells me so), but 'as my constituents would like me to', while assuming that in the decision-making process it is not the will of individually designated electors that should be taken into account, but the will of the *corps électoral*.

As can be seen from the above, the problem of permissible, *ergo* ethical and unacceptable, *ergo* unethical behaviours of the mandate holder should be approached from a slightly different angle, adopting different, revised points of view. This is not about the essentially primitive voluntarism, which allows the representative to do what his conscience and common sense tell him to do, but about such actions which – precisely because of free mandate – will adroitly combine various expectations and interests and consequently, generate a position corresponding as fully as possible to the idea of general (public) good in the melting pot of various, often mutually contradictory, judgements, movements and views. Hence the relationship which exists between the elected and the elector (or the representative and the represented) cannot be completely marginalized by maintaining that, especially from the point of view of ethics, it is eclipsed by free mandate, which tears the mandate holder apart from his constituents. Thus the constituent has to remain in the background of the relationship of representation, not least because he is after all an integral element and, actually, the most important one.

It is even more necessary to take into account the plane of bilateral bonds between the representative and the represented subjects, if we introduce the category of ethics. What is treated as ethical, as morally and politically justified (especially in the eyes of constituents) is such behaviour of the deputy that corresponds to the earlier 'electoral promise'.[63] Thus the paradigm of ethical (decent or honest) conduct in the case of mandate holders obliges them to respect that 'promise' and, as a consequence, to maintain the 'trust' linking them with the electorate. At the same time, the very same trust requires keeping an appropriately lasting and strong bond with the constituents, which bond, even if it does not take the form of binding guidelines formulated for the deputy, anticipates the relevant dialogue[64] between both parties of the relationship of representation. Consequently, the deputy's ethical conduct will mean, firstly, maintaining

---

assumed to have full freedom of action. Hence the traditional idea assuming that free mandate meant complete freedom of action for parliamentarians, whose conscience was the sole determinant.

63 *Cf.* M. Charlot, *Le povoir politique…*, p. 139.

64 D. Baranger, *Le droit constitutionnel*, Paris 2009, p. 89.

some forms of contact with the electorate, secondly, taking into consideration 'election promises' in the parliamentary activity and doing so as consistently as possible. On the other hand, unethical conduct will mean complete separation of the elected person from the elector and decisions that not only fail to respect the 'promises' made, but even contradict them.

In this context it is worthwhile to remember that an evaluation of the representative's ethics made on the basis of whether he respects the 'election promise' and for this reason maintains the 'trust' that electors put in him is by no means a purely moral or political evaluation. This means that in spite of its moral or, precisely, ethical character, it does have a certain, however small, legal and especially doctrinal anchorage. Ultimately, representation, no matter how we approach it, in the end is always based on the generally accepted concepts of public opinion government and responsible government. And they create an inseparable link between the electors and the elected, maintaining that true representation lies in a correlation of wills of both entities.[65] Free mandate and the resulting postulate of not seeing the constituents' petitions, instructions, judgements and opinions as binding cannot in any case be treated as a permission to ignore the electorate's opinion.[66] If it really were so, representation would lose its primary and fundamental meaning.

5. Political Framework of a Representative's Ethics: Ties with Subgroup or Party

Another important issue in assessing a parliamentarian's ethics is his ties with his own political base, because it is obvious that a contemporary deputy is a sort of emissary of his party or otherwise formed representation having mainly political features. This is fostered by both proportional and majoritarian electoral systems in which, in the vast majority of cases, the electorate votes according to the party key. This is why we hardly find any independent or non-partisan members of today's parliaments. Even when they do exist, in most cases they have become non-partisan or independent during the parliament's term of office, e.g. due to a conflict with their own party or, as also happens, a rift within the party causing it to split into subgroups or even into new, previously unknown, parties. But at the time of the election, at the time of acquiring the mandate, most of these persons

65 *Cf.* B. Garsten, *Representative Government and Popular Sovereignty*, [in:] *Political Representation…*, p. 90 *et seq.*

66 *Cf.* B. Manin, *The Principles of Representative Government*, Cambridge 1997, p. 163 *et seq.*

had more or less formal links with a certain political party or another structure with clearly political features, which stood for election precisely as a party with a certain manifesto and candidates selected according to specific criteria. Consequently party membership (or, more broadly, political identification) is the main element on which election of the deputy depends. In extreme cases, as we know, this led to the formulation of 'strong' or 'hard' mandate theory, according to which it is the party's programme which constitutes the proper essence of the parliamentary mandate. From the level of trust or, subsequently, delegation, political representation shifted in consequence to the level of mandate representation, where individual features and merits of the candidate lose importance, while the political party and its election manifesto are put at the heart of the relationship of representation.

This changes the theoretical assumptions underlying the relationship of representation, because the representative is no longer treated as a free representative of the constituents and becomes a representative of a political party and only *via* the party is he a representative of the constituents proper. This introduces far-reaching modifications in the theoretical and legal assumptions of the representative mandate, because parliamentary representation becomes fictional for two reasons. Firstly, at the starting point it is fictional when the representative is deemed to express not his own will or the will of a specific, individual elector, but the will of a collective represented entity, that is, the nation (sovereign). Secondly, it is fictional because it turns out that the will is not the 'pure', 'unadulterated' or 'unspoilt' will of the nation, but the will of that nation's organized structures, namely political parties. So it comes to light that the classical theory of political representation somewhat disintegrated as a result of actions of political parties (previously seen as *malum necessarium*). This is so, because today it is usually candidates recommended by parties that are elected to parliaments; moreover, as the vast majority of deputies have certain loyalty bonds with the party (in the form of party discipline) and finally, because the basic, classical form of representation – which elections to representative bodies still remain – is currently dominated by parties, without which one can hardly imagine the functioning of indirect democracy.

The mandate theory in both its varieties, i.e. the 'soft' one and 'hard' one, proves extraordinarily useful. The relationship of representation, some time ago perceived as an undistorted relationship between the elector and the elected person, underwent a sweeping and irreversible change. Realistically speaking, one should admit that the nation cannot (anymore) influence the course of the state's affairs without parties. Nowadays, well-organized parties have a much greater influence on the deputy than the abstractly defined citizens or even individual electors linked to the MP as constituents. This is why the influence of parties on the political representation process is by no means unilateral or unidirectional. The combination of classical representation and the party machine makes the deputy the master of his constituents and, at the same time, a minion of the party leader. This is why, first of all, the representative represents the will of his own political party and only then, as if secondarily, the will of the authentic, primary sovereign: the nation.[67] However, in contemporary democracies this will is not manifested spontaneously and in a disorganized way, but precisely via the parties, whose standpoints, views and assessments are treated as those of the sovereign itself. After all, it is recognized that in the present system of political representation the political party stands between the representative and the represented subject and in addition it enjoys a dominant position in this system.[68] Consequently, the specific choices of the electorate are no longer what they used to be: free and authentic indications of personal preferences only, but they are based on the principle of candidates' party affiliation. Thus electors vote for the party and not for the individual candidate.[69] This in turn means that, as a rule, they choose the party's programme and not the programme advocated and endorsed by any single candidate. Therefore, in the feedback mechanism, it is expected that an MP chosen from a given party will be its loyal 'envoy' in the parliament and will present its programme of political measures, not his own original one. It is not exactly the case that the MP becomes the proverbial captive of the party or that, worse still, he ignores the will of the constituent, placing the will of party organizations first. In the representative system, the party's will is still linked with the will of the sovereign itself. It is, after all, recognized that the party does not replace the sovereign at all, but limits itself to organizing it, helping to articulate and aggregate its judgements, postulates and demands. This in turn provides the basis for the expectation that the deputy will respect the party's programme, because – referring to the timeworn and discredited communist slogan – 'the party's programme is the nation's programme'.

However, the way the fundamental law stands, it is still free mandate that applies, even as a strongly emphasised constitutional principle, and this introduces an important correction on the line of dependencies between the parliamentarian,

---

67 *Cf.* D. Searing, *The Role of the Good Constituency Member and the Practice of Representation in Great Britan*, "Journal of Politics" 1985, vol. 47, p. 348 *et seq.*

68 *Cf.* F. Borella, *Les partis politiques dans la France d'aujourd'hui*, Paris 1973, p. 50 *et seq.*

69 *Cf.* W.I. Jennings, *The British Constitution…*, p. 82–83.

the political party and the electors, because free mandate acquires, at least partially, *semi-* or *quasi*-imperative features. Thus free mandate becomes a certain fiction again, or in any case an intermediate institution, because it retains the 'free' status only via-a-vis the electorate, but not the organized parties or other political organizations (as best demonstrated by party discipline), which have monopolized both the electoral process and the parliament, now perceived as a sort of political parties' condominium.[70]

As a consequence, the deputy is still independent of the elector and has the duty to represent general interests, not particular ones, but he is no longer independent vis-à-vis his own political base, which means that he should present the views of said base,[71] as best confirmed by the mechanism of party discipline, which expressly ties the deputy to the party, sometimes even against the will of the electors or, indeed, the will of the given deputy.[72] The latter situation, namely when party discipline is in conflict with the deputy's beliefs, is yet another example of a possible conflict of norms originating from two different and separate normative systems, in this case from the system of ethics (that is, norms relevant for a certain social and professional group) and the system of morality (understood as a universal system of normative order, not relating exclusively to specific groups or communities). The issue of conflict between the directives of party discipline on the one hand and the precepts of one's own conscience on the other one shows, however, another clearly 'conflict-prone' field of a representative's ethics. An indeed fundamental question arises here, namely which imperative should a representative follow in the end. Should he, for example, vote in accordance with his conscience, following the advice of J.A.N. Condorcet who advocated expounding 'my own ideas', or should he perhaps follow the recommendations of the party, bearing in mind that it was its programme that the voters chose and that 'the party's programme is the nation's programme'? One can easily guess that it is a vain search for the ideal answer. Obviously, there is no general answer, one which would work at any time and place. But it seems that the most appropriate behaviour, that is, one that satisfies, firstly, the logic

70 *Cf.* J.A. Fairlie, *The Nature of Political Representation*, „The American Political Science Review" 1940, vol. 34, p. 236 *et seq.*

71 One can even say more, namely that being independent of electors is currently acquiring such great and abstract dimensions that it actually turns into actual irresponsibility, which is replaced with dependency on, thus responsibility to, the political formation (party) with which the parliamentarian is connected.

72 *Cf.* Ch.J. Kam, *Party Discipline and Parliamentary Politics*, Cambridge 2009, p. 38 *et seq.*

of the relationship of representation, secondly, the institution of free mandate and, thirdly and finally, decomposition of representation as a result of political parties entering the representative system is such behaviour of the deputy which respects the will of the party in matters it discussed in its election manifesto and is guided by the directive of seeking the *volonté générale* in all other matters.

Yet party discipline is not, save for certain exceptions, in any way legally regulated, being a product of parliamentary practice, which, however, does not mean at all that it is rarely applied. Although not codified, it is an institution applied increasingly more frequently and commonly. In the vast majority of parliaments it is such an important element of eliciting the desirable, from a certain point of view, conduct of parliamentarians that in fact it becomes an element of a parliamentarian's ethics. This is, however, a special kind of ethics, because it is in clear conflict with the constitutional principle of free mandate and the moral convictions of the given deputy, for whom the command of party discipline may simply cause an internal conflict. But we cannot, at least not *a priori*, formulate any assessments to discredit the mechanism of party discipline. While it is true that it appears to be potentially in conflict with both free mandate and the precepts of conduct resulting from the representative's conscience, it is at the same time consistent with the broader and more general processes of reconstruction or even, as some say, disintegration of the relationship of representation, where political parties previously did not exist at all and then for a long time they were simply ignored. But today the role of political parties in elections and in political representation is fully noticed and appreciated, to such an extent that the essence of the modified concept of political representation is the nation organized into political parties speaking via its representatives. Thus representatives no longer resemble 'free electrons', but are delegates of political parties which structure and organize the electorate, who without parties remain dispersed and atomized.

This is why the mechanism of party discipline is used more and more eagerly and, moreover, why it is also formalized in various ways (just like the majority of parliamentarians' behaviours). It is recognized by parliamentary fractions as a kind of natural 'extension' of the electoral role of political parties. Once party candidates dominate among all the representatives, once they identify with the programme of a given party and once voters vote mainly on the basis of party programmes and not the personal features of individual candidates, it becomes clear that party discipline is a practically indispensable element for the mechanism of representative government to function properly.

Party discipline is an obvious example of a typical ethical norm, that is, a norm characteristic for a certain community. It was shaped as a result of a long process of 'partifying' the system of political representation and now is treated as a sort of guarantee of that system, which simply cannot operate without parties. At the same time, somewhat paradoxically, it seems to be in a particularly strong conflict with the occupational ethics of parliamentarians.[73] This is so because a parliamentarian is to represent the good of all, to express the most general and universal ideas, thus, in other words, to be above divisions and particularisms, including particularisms based on the principle of party membership or, more broadly, on the principle of politicality. Having strong ties with the parent party or another clearly political formation, he should represent that party or formation, enabling it to follow, in the best possible way, the programme which constitutes a *sui generis* electoral legitimation of that party. It is exactly because of that programme that the party obtained public approval and the party's representative received the parliamentary mandate, which means that he is perceived as the party's emissary and not an independent envoy selected because of his own characteristics, merits or achievements. Consequently, a parliamentarian who respects the principles of party discipline follows, at least *prima facie*, the principle of faithful, exact or strict representation. He is, after all, obliged to act (behave) in a way consistent with the party's political line approved in the election. But at the same time it may be the case that the line is in conflict with the good of all, *ergo* with free mandate, which is, after all, the most rudimentary and the most general, whilst also the most important, directive for the deputy's behaviour. And it is precisely in this sense that sometimes the unethical dimension of party discipline is mentioned, when said discipline confronts the good of all and the good of one political party and gives clear priority to the latter.

In addition, party discipline may turn out to be unethical when its precepts are contrary to the deputy's outlook, being in conflict with his private (personal) moral, social or even religious beliefs.[74] It is probably here that the socio-professional (group, localized) dimension of ethics becomes the most apparent along with the evident contrast with the commands of conscience, morality or e.g. religion. The model of behaviour instigated by the requirements of party discipline may be in conflict with other systems of norms, moreover, it can even be perceived as negative precisely because it entails a specific behaviour, which is nigh on endemic for a certain group or socio-professional formation. An ethical norm, as a norm typical of a certain circle of people, is consequently not identical to other norms and furthermore it may even not overlap with them at all, or – in

73 *Cf.* P. Cowley, *Conscience and Parliament*, London–Portland 1998, p. 79 *et seq.*
74 *Cf.* P. Cowley, *Conscience and Parliament…*, p. 24 *et seq.*

certain cases – it may clearly contradict them. This is exactly why ethics, as a set of rules of conduct typical of a certain community, need not necessarily be perceived as positive, because to some extent it may assume standards of conduct which differ from the commonly assumed and accepted standards.

It follows that in the legal sense a mandate holder is bound by nobody's will, that is, neither the will of groups of electors nor the will of the political party on the authority of which he acquired a parliamentary mandate. So in a certain sense he continues, as recommended by J.A.N. Condorcet, to act in accordance with his own preferences, presenting his own point of view in the first place. This indeed reveals the essence of free mandate, which *de lege lata* distances the deputy from any party or sectional dependencies, ordering him just to conceptualize as fully and faithfully as possible the general good identified with the whole electorate, that is, simply the nation-sovereign. But actually, in the political sense, a parliamentarian is bound by the will of the political party, because it is only within the party's structure that he could have acquired the mandate and then can count on political and state sinecures in the form of positions, offices and public functions. Thus the model of a parliamentarian's conduct and ethics requires the deputy to respect the will of his own political base that in its direct political effect is even more important for the parliamentarian than the will of the collective bearer of sovereignty, i.e. the nation itself. This state of things is in some sense sanctioned by legal regulations, including also constitutional ones, which treat political parties as special entities. In line with the principle of political pluralism, they grant political parties the position of a fundamental mechanism of articulating the nation's interests. This way, *de lege lata*, it is precisely a political party that is the entity transforming the sovereign's will and by the same token participating in the exercise of state (public) authority. This has a significant effect for the standard of ethical conduct, because such an extensive legitimacy of political parties means that in contemporary democracy the will of the majority of parties at a given point in time is equated with the *volonté générale*.

But here, again, a major discord appears. If, in accordance with express constitutional precepts, political parties are particularly predestined to aggregate the sovereign's will and then articulate it in the parliament, any conflict between a parliamentarian and his own political formation, ended with the deputy's final exit from the parent fraction, is also, at least in some aspect, contrary to the parliamentarian's ethical conduct in the broad sense. The electoral legitimacy of a parliamentarian is directly connected with the given political party or coalition, especially in the model of proportional party-list voting. On the other hand, the elector's voting behaviour is also determined mainly by the political likings, which oftentimes prove much more important than strictly personal preferences (as amply demonstrated by the majoritarian systems). Consequently, the election of a specific parliamentarian is, in the overwhelming majority of cases (and both in proportional and majoritarian systems) a function of political and party inter-dependencies, i.e. on the one hand, the candidate's connection with a given party or another political formation (coalition or electoral committee), and on the other hand, the overtly political choices of the electorate. This is why a subsequent secession of a parliamentarian from a fraction and move to another fraction or setting up a new one, albeit consistent with the precepts of free mandate, is plainly contrary to the specific electoral contract, whose essence is invariably the convergence of political views of the deputy and his elector. Upon election, the deputy makes a commitment to represent the elector, but to represent him in a specific manner, based on the election manifesto of a given political party or another formation having mainly political features. Therefore negation of this particular contract, which takes place when a parliamentarian changes his fraction affiliation, may be seen as at least unethical, because it contests the will of the electorate, which will in the vast majority of cases is conceptualized on the basis of political and party criteria of electoral offers. Consequently, any change of club membership is, in this situation, a sign of conflict not only with the parent political party, but also with the electorate. All in all, the electorate was given some other political alternative which either failed to obtain extensive electoral support or was not even submitted for the electorate's judgement. Consequently, the sphere of a parliamentarian's ethical conduct is also within the area of particular conflicts which may occur, on the one hand, against the background of the deputy's political and party affiliations and, on the other one, just as strongly political and partisan preferences of the electorate.

6. Functional Framework of a Parliamentarian's Ethics: Representation vs. Lobbying

Finally, the last aspect of the discussion about a parliamentarian's ethics involves mutual relations between the parliamentarian and lobby groups.[75] Determining a clear dividing line between a parliamentarian and a lobbyist seems a matter of truly paramount importance here. Because if the dividing line between the role of a deputy and that of a lobbyist becomes obscured or is just unclear, this disrupts the whole representation process; moreover this questions the

75 More on this topic: *Parliaments and Pressure Groups in Western Europe*, P. Norton (ed.), London–Portland 1998.

constitutional and theoretical assumptions concerning representative mandate and the special, after all, bond between the parliamentarian and his own political party. Once a parliamentarian becomes a representative of completely area-specific interests, performing strictly lobbying activities, he breaks both the principle of representative mandate and that of party dependency with his own political base, with which periodical or even incidental or episodic lobbying may be in conflict. In addition, this also seems to infringe the constitutional principle of political pluralism, which principle assumes a special role of the party in aggregating and articulating the electorate's will and does not envisage other, non-partisan, organizational forms with the same legal legitimization as parties to assume a standpoint comparable with the *volonté générale*. From this point of view the roles of parliamentarians and lobbyists are different or even opposing. Whilst a parliamentarian is obliged to represent the interest of all, a lobbyist, *ex definitione*, represents a narrow and particular interest group. These two roles are irreconcilable.[76] Hence the need for their clear separation and the consequential creation of various legal mechanisms of including lobbyists in the legislative's decision-making process, but at the same time clearly distinguishing them from MPs.

The incompatibility of roles of parliamentarians and lobbyists results also from one more thing which seems important, notably the whole model or system of representation, which currently is clearly quite distant from the concentrated or centralized political representation. Today, as we know, representation has a pluralist character, while the basic idea of representation, that is, encapsulating all the possible cleavages,[77] results in the emergence of functional or socio-professional representation bodies in addition to political representation bodies. Accordingly, the representation system becomes professional and specialized, with the body of political representation (the parliament) on the one side and various bodies of corporate representation on the other side. As a consequence of this state of affairs, the range of represented standpoints undoubtedly broadens, but at the same time the roles of a political representative (whose task is to express the general interest) and a functional representative (who is obliged to act as a promoter of individual interests) are clearly separated. From this perspective, the ban on traditional parliamentarians stepping into lobbyists' shoes stems from the fact that political representation is simply not designed as representation of

76 *Cf.* B. Pym, *The Making of a Successful Pressure Group*, "The British Journal of Sociology" 1973, no. 4, p. 446 *et seq.*

77 *Cf.* A. Lijphart, *Democracy in Plural Societies. A Comparative Exploration*, New Haven–London 1977, p. 83.

social, professional or economic interests. The latter always aims at expressing particular interests, while the *telos* of political representation is determined by the pursuit of the general will. This is why an MP has a completely different socio-political role to play than a lobbyist or a representative of professional or economic interests. These two roles, by design different and diverse, have been emphasised particularly strongly since free mandate was recognized as the generally applicable solution. In the previous model, that is, imperative mandate, a representative was indeed a *sui generis* lobbyist, for instance of his own constituency or, looking more narrowly, his own voters. So his first and foremost task as an MP was to take care of those interests that he was ordered to protect in the election process. But when imperative mandate gave way to free mandate, the MP was legally obligated to depart, in his parliamentary activities, from lobbying for individual atomist interests and, for a change, to become an exponent of the common and general interest. The task of protecting all sorts of particularities and individual interests was assumed by a lobbyist and, later still, at the time when dual representation was established, by the representative and advocate of interests reflected in various fora of functional representation. Thus the current role of a representative in the political representation model is to express the collective interest, while the role of a representative in the functional representation model is to express a single, individual interest, which is by definition separate and different from the mythical general will or the will of all.

From the point of view of a parliamentarian's ethics it is at the intersection of these completely different roles that the relatively highest number of hazards related to the general and extremely capacious term of corruption appear. Lobbying or even quasi-lobbying activity creates, at least potentially, the biggest risk of various kinds of abuses, irregularities or pathologies, which may not only be dysfunctional, but can also distort the process of representation (which they invariably do in practice) and can finally turn out to be forms of activity *praeter legem*, while in extreme cases even *contra legem*. Consequently the need appears to create extensive codes of ethics and anti-corruption regulations which will appropriately immunize parliamentarians against pressures of narrow, sectional interests of particular professions or groups. This is especially desirable in the parliament, where there is an obvious conflict of various local, group and similar interests.

The decisions finally adopted – in every case *pro publico bono* – by the deputies should be a result of choosing priorities and setting their hierarchy on the scale of the whole country and, in case of any conflicts of particular interests with general ones, it is always the universal interest, expressing the good of all, that should prevail. This is why a lobbyist should only be a source of information for a parliamentarian, whom the multiplicity of sources helps make an optimum decision from the political, social or pragmatic point of view. Consequently, if a parliamentarian acts like a lobbyist, his conduct has to be assessed as unethical, failing in the basic duty of a deputy, namely acting in the best interest of the nation. This is why we may suggest that if a parliamentarian steps into the role of a lobbyist, this is contrary to the concept of free mandate, both in its idealist theoretical perception (an MP representing the abstractly understood will of all) and in the realistic perception of practice (an MP representing the parent political party). Being a lobbyist, the MP for obvious reasons represents neither the constituents nor even his own political party, which clearly means a conflict of interests which might be solved precisely by ethical behaviour models.

As it seems, these models should first of all clearly define and delimit the roles.[78] The problem does not lie in creating simple or simplifying hypotheses like 'a parliamentarian always expresses the good of all, while a lobbyist expresses particular interest'. The standards of a parliamentarian's ethical conduct must be formulated with the assumption that articulating and representing interests is the true and overarching goal of all parliamentarian's actions.[79] So the issue is not that a parliamentarian represents some interests, but that these interests should correspond to the greatest possible extent to the constitutionally defined deputy's role of expounding the will of the whole nation-sovereign. Thus the behaviour of a parliamentary mandate holder is ethical, just, expedient, approved or merely acceptable only when it is not so much selfless, but rather when it maximizes the interest of all, while minimizing the force of influence of partial or group interests. And this is obvious, because the parliament is a place where interests are articulated in a systemically legitimized way. The parliamentarian's ethics, understood as the sphere of norms and standards of conduct should mainly assume, instead of some abstract lack of articulation of interests and completely selfless actions, transparency of rules of representation and articulation, which means, firstly, a clear identification of interests, secondly, an open procedure of articulating them and, thirdly, a legal (i.e. legally regulated) procedure of influencing the decision-making process in the parliament. It is only when all those boxes are ticked that true conditions exist to enable an assessment of the parliamentarian's decision-making process from the point of view of whether his

78 *Cf.* S. Dovi, *The Good Representative*, London 2007, p. 6 *et seq.*

79 *Cf.* M. van der Hulst, *The Parliamentary Mandate. A Global Comparative Study*, Geneva 2000, p. 34.

conduct reflects the interest of the global electorate, in line with the concept of free mandate, or whether the conduct was somehow distorted by the influence of various particular interests. Lobbying, as an institutionalized form of disclosure of sectional interests, should therefore have its specific, legally defined, form, but at the same time it should be clearly separated from the activities of an MP, who, invoking the representative mandate and making choices, is obliged to make the optimum decision, i.e. one which realizes as far and as fully as possible the postulate of 'people's interest', or – looking from a slightly different angle – 'general good', always taking into account the specific determinants, the most important of them being the interest of the general public.

The aforementioned dimensions or aspects of the discussion on the parliamentarian's ethics, i.e. the dimension of free mandate, the dimension of relationship between an MP and the electorate, defined as both his constituency and the whole *corps électoral*, then the dimension of relationship between the representative and his political party base and, finally, the dimension of inter-dependency between parliamentary and lobbying activities,[80] show that the parliamentarian's ethics is prone to conflicts, which is assumed almost implicitly. On the one hand, in the strictly legal sense, the deputy represents the whole collectively understood sovereign, while on the other, in the political sense, the deputy has to express party interests, as best manifested by party discipline. In addition, a parliamentarian, even if just because he is elected in a clearly specified constituency by a specified groups of voters, represents also some groups, by definition particular ones, whose opinions and judgements he always has to reckon with, which in turn draws on the construct of at least semi-imperative mandate. So perhaps the most important manifestation of a parliamentarian's ethics as a representative is his legal independence and autonomy, combined with very strong political ties with, or even dependence on, his own political base and various groups displaying certain noticeable lobbyist features. It is only formally that a parliamentarian is free from ties, while actually he has both party ties (due to fraction affiliation)

80 In this context one should realize that these dimensions or aspects do not exhaust the issue of a parliamentarian's ethics in its entirety. They only indicate the most important elements in the description of such ethics in determining the desirable, thus ethical, models of conduct of a deputy. Referring much more broadly to the problems of ethics of a parliamentarian (or even parliamentary ethics), we should stress that there are other components (elements) which are decisive for the ethics of a holder of representative mandate. They include the conditions of obtaining the mandate, specific duties of the deputy or, finally, the broad range of powers enabling active and real exercise of the mandate.

and political ones (by virtue of being elected by strictly defined electorate in his constituency, but also more broadly, by virtue of being elected from the list of a given party, of which he was a candidate). As we have already mentioned, the precept of respecting the will of a political party, although *prima facie* contrary to the idea of free mandate, in reality is constitutionally legitimized by virtue of the definition of the special role of political parties, which monopolize the process of political representation. So in his best possible pursuit of the electorate's will, aggregated by the political party which obtained the electoral mandate, a parliamentarian should obey party orders (as required by party discipline), but also be guided in his activities by the general interest, for whose identification it is necessary to recognize and diagnose particular interests, which in turn are best revealed by lobbing.

Thus the postulate of ethical (or simply decent) behaviour requires the parliamentarian to behave in such a way so as to respect the constitutional construct of representative mandate, while synchronizing the interest of all with partial interests, including party and lobbyist ones, because only this behaviour can produce a decision negotiated by the national representative body, which is the optimum decision in the given socio-political conditions. Thus any MPs' decisions, by their nature entangled in a conflict of various interests, differently aggregated and articulated, should always be a result of choosing and hierarchizing priorities on the scale of the whole country and in case of any collision or even lack of synchronization between particular and group interests, it is the nation's interest that should always have the decisive importance, because, formally speaking, the nation is the only represented subject whose will is expressed by the national representative body, that is, *tout court* the parliament. This context probably shows best that the issue of a parliamentarian's ethics, or perhaps rather the issue of honesty in a parliamentarian's behaviour, cannot be evaluated in abstract from the process of articulating interests, both individual and collective ones. Consequently, there are no grounds – for instance by invoking to the concept of free mandate – to demand that ethical conduct of a mandate holder be selfless, meaning isolated from interests. This approach to the matter would abstract from perceiving the parliament's role as a place where *ex definitione* various concepts, views, value and finally interests are put together and confronted with one another. Moreover, in the parliament, inscribed in the democratic rule of socio-political pluralism, conflict of interests is not only a structural or indeed defining or rudimentary feature, but also one which is legally and politically legitimized. In this situation, the constitutional assumption according to which a deputy represents the whole nation and by virtue of that is not bound by any guidelines or instructions of voters must be analysed without losing sight of the otherwise obvious assumption that the nation's interest or – more broadly speaking – the general good (of all) is not an independent phenomenon, but a certain product of the interests which exist in the society. For this very reason, the postulate that a parliamentarian should be a representative of the nation does not mean that activities of a parliamentarian should be unrelated to individual, sectional, group or local interests, claims and expectations, but that they should be correlated in such a way as to combine the individual, separately formulated requests (expectations, assessments, interests and claims) with everybody's good in the best possible way.[81]

Thus the ethics of a parliamentarian's conduct is, so to say, in between, notably, between the particular claims and interests that at most bind the deputy in fact, and the general or global claims and interests that formulate the legal obligation of such behaviour whose result will be to reflect the sovereign's will. Therefore pursuing the general good should involve formulating general public interests through compromises arrived at by means of synthesis of various partial interests. In this situation, a parliamentarian faces a constant, even permanent, conflict, firstly, between the requests of all and the requests of a group; secondly, between the directives of law and those resulting from the actual dependencies with individual groups; and finally, between the precepts that follow from the formula of free mandate and those that result from the obvious fact of a parliamentarian's affiliation with a certain political party.

The inevitability of conflicts, which is part and parcel of the rudiments from which the legal determinants of ethics of a parliamentarian (representative) stem, seems to create a certain, particularly understood, area of free choice, between the law and politics, which enables us to delineate the sphere of authentic, real ethics of a member of parliament.[82] A parliamentarian who strives to conscientiously exercise free mandate, has to always make choices within the sphere delimited on the one end by the legal principles of free mandate and on the other by the political dependencies between his own constituency, the political party which he represents and, finally, organized interest groups, which one way or another influence the deputy trying to direct his decisions. This free choice zone seems to be the high point of ethics of a parliamentarian, who has to act in such a way as to conceptualize the general good well and as efficiently as possible, all while respecting the political norms, principles and values, which after all define the area of *polis*.

81 *Cf.* P. Avril, J. Gicquel, *Droit parlementaire*..., p. 31.
82 *Cf.* S. Dovi, *The Good Representative*..., p. 27 *et seq.*

Conclusion

Currently there seems to be no attractive, impressive or, above all, effective alternative to the representative form of government. While it is true that simple democracy is applied on a growing scale, all the same – even in Switzerland – it remains a clearly complementary, thus secondary, form of implementing the idea of democratic government. Contemporary democracies continue to function as representative democracies.[1] But this does not mean that political representation, in the shape created by modern constitutional law theory, does not change. Quite the contrary. The principle of political representation, especially when understood broadly, i.e. taking into account the principle of popular sovereignty, parliamentary mandate (free or imperative, as appropriate) and, finally, the technical problems of how to man the personal substratum of the authority vested with political representation, is subject to constant mutations and transformations, intended to give it its optimum form. Apart from being a specific institution of constitutional law, representation is also, perhaps in the first place, a certain political idea, a theoretical project and, at the same time, a desire to make the *polis* a structure which will, on the one hand, be truly efficient and, on the other hand, possess democratic legitimacy. This is the reason for the historical changes and transformations that the institution of representation underwent. All of them were intended to ensure better application of political representation treated as a certain ideal, an idea for organizing the public space. In this context it is clear that the fixes in the mechanism of representative government, i.e. various ways of transforming the general and capacious idea into an institution, differ considerably in terms of their substance and shape. They are usually looked at from the historical angle and the perspective of how concepts of political representation changed in both theory and practice.[2] Constitutional and political approaches to representation, as well as various variants of their more or less successful translations into political tangibles show that political representation is, in some sense, a multi-dimensional phenomenon, as indicated by the very fact that it comprises many smaller (but no less important) constitutional principles, rules and values.

1 More on this issue: H. Roussillon, *Le citoyen et le suffrage: le mythe de la démocratie directe. De la démocratie participative à la démocratie réactive*, Toulouse 2006.

2 *Cf.* M.B. Brown, *Science in Democracy. Expertise, Institutions and Representation*, Cambridge, USA, 2009, p. 107 *et seq*.

The mutations to which the principle of political representation was subjected make it a not only multi-variant phenomenon. Sometimes it is even hard to find what defines or determines it to the greatest extent or what the common denominator of the diverse approaches and conceptions is. When viewed from various angles, representation takes on very different looks and cannot be put in a single, universal model, a homogenous one that can be repeated anytime and anyplace. If we look at it from a 'technical' point of view, it will just be a specific system of searching for a method to select the few who will act instead of many. In this sense representation will be equated with an electoral system and such arrangements that will actually enable one to say that Lincoln's postulate of government of the people, by the people and for the people is put into practice. Stressing the 'technical' side of representation will mean that representation and its optimization will be perceived as a selection of a certain (possibly the best) methods of choosing members of representative bodies (parliaments). And representation will be a technique via which electors will delegate their representatives.[3] This means that the essence of the technical approach to representation will lie in building appropriate electoral mechanisms in such a way that, firstly, they should permit the biggest possible, in the quantitative sense, group of the represented subjects to select their representatives and, secondly, they should replicate (repeat, present or, indeed, represent) the composition of the represented group as faithfully and as fully as possible.[4] A separate, though not isolated, idea from this pool is also perceiving representation much more narrowly and considering that the ideal of representation and representativeness is only achieved by such systems of allocating parliamentary mandates which are proportional in their results, which, contrary to appearances, does not mean an absolute necessity to achieve mathematical proportions. It is rather about creating a mechanism for selecting members of the parliament whose final result reflects proportionality, that is, in other words, about the result of parliamentary elections being proportional regardless of the 'technical' method used to achieve such proportionality.

However, political representation may also be viewed from a strictly normative perspective. Then, representation will not be a quest for the best electoral system (which the technical meaning of representation boils down to), but a certain concept which enables reconciling the principle of popular sovereignty (according to which power is vested nominally in everybody) with the principle

3 *Cf.* E.-P. Guiselin, *Le droit de la vie politique*, Paris 2004, p. 38 *et seq*. More on this issue: *Women and Legislative Representation. Eletoral Systems, Political Parties and Sex Quotas*, M. Tremblay (ed.), New York 2012.

4 *Cf.* M.B. Brown, *Science in Democracy…*, p. 201 *et seq.*

of indirect government (i.e. few acting in the name and on the account of many). Therefore, in the normative sense, representation means constitutional legitimacy of the power vested in representatives. It is legitimized, first of all, by the fact that it is simply impossible for everybody to exercise such power day in day out and, secondly, by adopting the construction of attribution, according to which the representative's actions are perceived as those of the represented subject. We should admit straight away that it is precisely this approach to political representation that is the most accurate or faithful one, touching the essence of the problem (naturally from the constitutional point of view).

Nevertheless, political representation can also be viewed from the functional perspective, in which case it is indicated that the correct decision-making process in politics should comprise articulation and aggregation of various interests, though not only those segregated and arranged according to political criteria or, more precisely, political and party criteria. So in its functional sense representation is an appropriate rendition (on the institutional and decision-making levels) of various social, political, territorial, economic or professional cleavages that stigmatize contemporary societies to a growing extent.[5] The functional model of representation shows that political and party (or parliamentary) representation is nowadays just one of the possible planes or forms of representation, but the heterogeneity of contemporary political systems requires supplementing it with the so-called extra-parliamentary representation, which is best expressed by pressure groups. Nowadays, representation of interests by public, professional, local or even cultural bodies is seen as a must, mainly from the point of view of ensuring proper representativeness (hence efficiency) of the decision-making mechanism. Representation with functional features is also the most serious adjustment of the representation mechanism these days.[6]

The presented meanings of, or approaches to, representation have accompanied its historical evolution. The latter may be typified in various ways, but as a matter of fact most of the presented proposals identify three basic types or models of representation which have been present in contemporary political systems. The first of them comprises the model of parliamentary representation, where the national representative body is the basic, if not the sole, body expressing the

---

5 *Cf.* A. Lijphart, *Democracy in Plural Societies. A Comparative Exploration*, New Haven–London 1977, p. 83.

6 *Cf.* R. Mouriaux, *Syndicats, organisations professionnelles et groupes d'intérêt*, [w:] *Institutions et vie politique*, J.-L. Parodi (ed.), Paris 2003, p. 115 *et seq.*; P. Muller, G. Saez, *Néocorporatisme et crise de la représentation*, [in:] *La Représentation*, F. d'Arcy (ed.), Paris 1985, p. 121 *et seq.*

interests of all. The second model, still positioning representation in the parliament, is the model of party representation. This model aims to accentuate mainly the role of political parties, which did not exist in the early days of parliamentary representation and once they appeared, for a relatively long time they were treated as an epi-phenomenon, something important, but nonetheless transitional. But when it transpired that parties were a permanent fixture in the political system and it was no longer possible to imagine the functioning of political representation without parties, which became not only *de facto*, but also *de jure* (as a result of their juridification at various levels of sources of law) a 'conveyor belt' between the representative and the represented, representation acquired a predominantly partisan character. Even though the parliament remained their abode, the logic of operation of the parties on the arena of both electoral and parliamentary rivalry (and, further still, also cabinet rivalry) changed the mechanism of representation, shifting it actually to the level of parties, not the parliament. The role of the latter clearly diminished in the conception of partisanship of representation: it became a 'voting machine', one of the reasons being that the whole mechanism of aggregation and articulation of interests moved to the party plane. All this caused a crisis of representation (understood as purely parliamentary representation), which became even more fictional than the political idea had it.[7] Against this background, as one can guess, there appeared various ideas for improving representation or – depending on the diagnosis of the gravity of the crisis – building it anew. All of them assumed that the key to building the optimum mechanism of representation was recognizing that the essence of representation was, firstly, aggregating and articulating various interests; secondly, correlating the wills of the representative and the represented subjects; thirdly, assuming that a representative acts in the name and on the account of the represented; and fourthly, giving the representative a democratic accreditation. Naturally, there were many ways of looking for the perfect form of representation, but at a certain point it was acknowledged that perhaps the best one was corporate representation or otherwise representation built around an institutional arrangement of various kinds of groups and circles selected not only according to political and party criteria.[8] This way, finally, corporate representation appeared as the third basic model of representation, which ended the political parties' monopoly in expressing views, opinions and interests. This,

7 *Cf.* D. Ryden, *Representation in Crisis. The Constitution, Interest Groups and Political Parties*, New York 1996, p. 33 *et seq.*

8 *Cf.* I.M. Young, *Deferring Group Representation*, [in:] *Ethnicity and Groups Rights*, I. Shapiro, W. Kymlicka (eds.), New York 1997, p. 249 *et seq.*

however, deprived the parliament of its special status of a representative body. Naturally, it is still the main forum for expressing and externalizing political and party interests, but besides the parliament there appear other bodies which at least to some extent embody representation too, e.g. social, professional, territorial or other particular forms of representation. Consequently, the currently prevailing model of representation is the so-called pluralist representation, which is not accumulated in a single body (e.g. the parliament), but may be achieved also in other bodies, fora or similar groups.[9] Combined with other phenomena, this certainly undercuts the parliament's importance. The current parliament is clearly pale in comparison to its nineteenth century equivalent, for a plethora of reasons (including the growing importance of the executive branch, intensification of processes of integration and internationalization of politics in general, globalization, visible crisis of political parties and consequential changes within organizations, etc.), but pluralist representation, which became a keen competitor of the parliament, certainly made a major contribution.[10]

Nowadays, the parliament is perceived as a body which definitively departs from the model of proper representation in the form in which it was promoted under the traditional constitutional law theory. There are at least several reasons for this, but certainly in the first place we should mention precisely political parties, which in a way 'take over' political representation and whose actions result in disintegration of the classical theory of representation. This is manifested mainly in a major disturbance of the relationship between the elector and the elected, because the actual elector is replaced by political parties, which become the true promotors of the parliamentary mandate. (In our time, this provokes an even greater criticism, because political parties lost the character of mass parties a long time ago and became a sort of elite formations, subsequently evolving into a modern model of catch-all parties. By the way, the latter almost completely reverse the logic of representation, once it is the party that tries to fit in with the elector's views instead of the elector trying to fit in with the party's views, as in the classical approach.)

Consequently this mandate has gradually been losing the features of a free mandate and transmuting into an imperative mandate. The latter was never uniform and could comprise various elements, which, however, required perceiving the holder of the mandate as a person who did not act in the name and for the benefit

---

9 *Cf.* T. Debard, *Dictionnaire de droit constitutionnel*, Paris 2002, p. 270.

10 *Cf.* D. Beetham, *Do Parliaments have a Future?,* [in:] S. Alonso, J. Keane, W. Merkel, M. Fotou, *The Future of Representative Democracy,* Cambridge 2010, p. 125.

of everybody, but for the principal (who sometimes could use legal instruments for enforcing his will, e.g. in the form of the right to recall the mandate). In today's parliaments, this is best demonstrated by party discipline, which clearly ties the deputy with the fraction to which he belongs. Another manifestation of the partisan profiling of the mandate and consequently – in some sense – turning it into the imperative form (though without all the elements this form entails) are the proportional electoral systems. As we know, they require voting for lists, which in practice are usually compiled by political parties. But it is worthwhile to point out that it is somewhat a case of squaring the circle: on the one hand, proportional electoral systems clearly work for parties, which translates into increasingly deeper and stronger ties between parliamentarians and political parties and, on the other hand, as many observe, these systems make political representation much more representative than any other mandate redistribution system.

At this point, however, we arrive at the fundamental problem of representation, notably the adequate manner of defining it. Should it be just a juridical method according to which some people act for and on behalf of others or, perhaps – drawing on the theoretical foundations of political representation – rather a form of correlation of the wills of the representative and the represented? If we adopt the interpretation which requires not only acting on behalf of somebody else, but also the presence of at least minimum convergence (conformity) of opinions of the representative and the represented, it turns out that political representation cannot be perceived only in terms of a constitutional principle. Consequently, the strictly juridical aspect has to be supplemented with the sociological aspect, which calls for similarity of attitudes, judgements and opinions of the represented and their representatives.[11] In this way it realizes in the best, that is, most faithful and exact, way the idea of responsible government or, with accents distributed slightly differently, public opinion government, which ideas are the foundations of the contemporary substance of political representation.

But today the correlation, i.e. the search for a common denominator in ideas, judgements and beliefs of the representative and the represented, has assumed an additional and very important form. For a long time the most important, available and, no less importantly, efficient method of correlation were the elections, whose result was not only the grant of a proxy, that is, a mandate determining the substance (imperative or free) of the mandate holder's behaviour, but also achieving coherence of political views of the two entities in the relationship of representation (which was perceived in literature as a form of mutual link

---

11 *Cf.* M. Duverger, *Institutions politiques et droit constitutionnel*, Paris 1966, p. 81, 82.

between the juridical and sociological interpretations of representation). This aim was served by various so-called means of correlation, among which the first place was and still is occupied by political parties. Apart from parties, means of correlation include, for understandable reasons, trade unions, employer organizations, pressure groups, religious associations and, last but not least, the media. The correlation, as traditionally perceived by academics, requires joint application of, as we can see, various means, while observing the fundamental (which does not mean the sole[12]) form of correlation: the elections. Currently, this typical mechanism of political representation (which, when approached from this angle, can be called a process of search for a common will of the representative and the represented) underwent a significant change. In the regional (European) dimension it was changed by European integration and the creation of a supranational representation forum: the European Parliament. Whereas some time ago there still existed a real danger that due to its underspecified form it will reinstate imperative mandate (because of the clear link between an MEP and the Member State from which he was elected), currently representation at supranational level can significantly contribute to the renewal of free mandate (and it gradually does so). Political parties are major contributors in this process. Even though at the national level they gave the mandate distinct features of imperative mandate (according to the principle that an MP expounds the will of the political party), at the EU level, thanks to the formation of a supra-state organization, they can reverse this trend, consequently contributing to projecting an image of an MEP who expresses the opinions of the European *demos*, in no way stigmatized by national, country or state divisions. As a result, we may see a true restitution of free mandate, which at state level is falsified mainly, though not solely, by the representatives' party affiliations. Another element which clearly violates the assumptions of free mandate is the traditional belief of the electorate that they elect deputies to represent their interests or at best interests of their constituency. Looking from this angle, deputies' behaviours which conform to the postulate of free mandate, which oftentimes means a collision with particular interests, selected on the basis of a map of constituencies or groups of electors, are perceived as almost 'betrayal' of the constituents and the constituency amounting to the proverbial attack on popular sovereignty. Among the individual electors-represented there still persists a very strong conviction that the deputy is a civil

12 Nowadays supplemented with other forms, including especially direct activity of citizens, not only those involved in politics *via* mechanisms of simple democracy (e.g. referendum, civic legislative initiative), but also in un-organized and spontaneous (pickets, demonstrations, protests, etc.), with a major contribution of the Internet.

law proxy, obligated by the fact of being elected, to adhere to his electors' instructions faithfully and accurately. All these convictions, additionally correlated with a strongly partisan nature of the mandate, seem, at least partially, to undermine the acceptance of supranational representation, where an important role is played by party organizations construed more and more often across state borders. It is precisely for this reason that, even though some time ago political parties were mainly accused of falsifying the classical approach to representation, currently parties which are more and more willingly and frequently created above country and state divisions are perceived as a chance for restitution of free mandate in every sense of this word.[13]

This restitution, in the particular dimension of a country or state, is possible also thanks to constitutional courts. *Prima facie* they leave the process of political representation aside. But when we look at it more closely and recognize that its essence is precisely expression the will of the represented by an entity having the status of a representative, one gets the impression that it is exactly constitutional courts that seem to have the greatest influence on redefining representation. This is so because, at the point of departure, the ideal of constitutional courts envisages respect for the constitution, that is, the sovereign's will, of which the fundamental law is a legal expression. Failure to respect this will, as a result of e.g. actions of political parties and priority given to party interests, is finalized in the law-making activities of the nationwide representative body. Hence review of such activity by a constitutional court contributes to correcting the mechanism of representation in the sense of enabling it to follow the sovereign's will articulated at the level of the constitution. This is why constitutional courts restrain the fictionality of the representative attribution of the sovereign's will, which until now has been probably the weakest link in the classical approach to representation. In extreme conditions it recognized (as a result of attribution) a will which was completely different from the true and authentic will of the nation-sovereign if only it was expressed or otherwise formulated by its representatives in the forms prescribed by law. Thus the increasingly catchy slogan of crisis of representation, which was often identified precisely with the fictional character of the concept of attribution and with its 'natural effect' being (at least potentially) a complete mismatch between wills of the representatives and the represented. Thanks to constitutional courts, political representation and the underlying conformity of wills of the representative and the represented is 'upheld' on both sides. On the

13 More on this topic: D.-L. Seiler, *La vie politique des Européens. Introduction aux pratiques démocratiques dans les de l'Union européenne*, Paris 1998.

one side it is 'upheld' by the electoral process, whose *ratio legis* is nothing else but delegating representatives. On the other side, it is 'upheld' by the constitutional court, which does not allow representatives to adopt laws which would neglect the sovereign's will reflected in the provisions of the fundamental law.

Regardless of how political representation is eventually understood and what forms and means of correlation are applied to satisfy the postulate of representation and representativeness at the end of the day, the goal is always to achieve the ideal of 'government of the people, by the people and for the people', which is the quintessence of democracy as such,[14] whether it assumes the form of indirect or perhaps direct democracy.

Incidentally, this last division is more and more often recognized as mistaken. Political representation changes not only because it is contrasted increasingly frequently with various kinds of mechanisms of citizens' direct intervention in the matters of the *polis* (referendum, citizens' initiative or popular veto, to name but a few), but also because of the growing importance of forms of alternative involvement of the sovereign, which simply cannot be classified as simple democracy or democracy distorted or deformed by its indirect (representative) level.[15] These forms are exhibited, on the one hand, by the more and more visible electoral absence, often identified with citizens being dispirited by politics and politicians (thus, accordingly, also representatives) and, on the other hand, by the quantitative growth of forms of participation whose main motive is opposing the decisions made by representatives (street protests, pickets, strikes, acts of civil disobedience). In effect, the slogan of 'counter-democracy' is gaining attractiveness as an alternative to the classical form of representative democracy or – more precisely – electoral-and-representative democracy.[16] However, civic opposition against the classical forms of political participation, such as elections and the traditional concept of representation based on elections, is manifested not only in the growing strength and popularity of protests, but also in negative voting. Elections are observed to slowly lose their etymological sense. The point is no longer – as it should be – to distinguish and select candidates, but rather to eliminate them. Consequently, electors vote not because they want to elect someone and make him their representative, but rather because they do not want to elect someone else. This way politics becomes strongly negative. In the

14 *Cf.* J.-M. Denquin, *Introduction à la science politique*, Paris 2001, p. 62 *et seq.*

15 *Cf.* H. Roussillon, *Éloge de la «démocratie réactive»*, [in:] *Constitutions et pouvoirs. Mélanges en l'honneur de Jean Gicquel*, Paris 2008, p. 475 *et seq.*

16 More on this topic: P. Rosanvallon, *La contre-démocratie. La politique à l'âge de la défiance*, Paris 2006.

purest form, this can be seen in protests against specific measures, not accepted by certain social groups. In the softened, though still noticeable, form, this is visible precisely in choices resulting more and more often not from the intention to indicate a representative, but rather to eliminate his competitor. Understandably, this is also noticeable in employing forms of direct democracy, correctly perceived as 'counter-power' against representative forms of governing. Popular veto as the purest form, but also civic initiative, are usually applied when it is recognized that for some reasons the mechanism of representation failed, having led to a decision seen as adverse (popular veto) or not having led to the adoption of expected decision (civic legislative initiative). All these measures together are nothing else but a response to the known and well-diagnosed slogan of crisis of representation in its traditional version.[17]

But what remains an open question is whether they are indeed an efficient form, one that improves the qualitative, not just purely quantitative, features of democracy. It is not accidental that replacing the sovereignty of expressing will (which we saw in the classical model of political representation) with the sovereignty of expressing objections (typical of reactive democracy or 'counter-democracy') cannot be exactly an effective remedy for the flaws of the representative system, mainly due to its negative and inherently episodic character. Reactive democracy (as Henry Roussillon calls it) or 'counter-democracy' (in the approach proposed by Pierre Rosanvallon) are merely forms of defending the true or authentic 'positive' democracy and for this reason, in the foreseeable future, cannot become real competition for it. Other forms of political involvement which are gaining attractiveness are either a certain myth, especially if we perceive them as the potential target basic form of political participation (like the Internet, for example), or they are 'pseudo-democratic' from the start (like strikes, pickets or street protests). For understandable reasons, it is also impossible to resort to the archetype of direct democracy, because nowadays it is unthinkable that direct democracy as such should be applied as the single or even the basic form of political participation.[18] This is why, even though the slogan of crisis of representation is still repeated and even gains in attractiveness, political representation (probably) is and will remain for a long time an unmatched form through which contemporary democracies are manifested and realized. The known and well-rooted forms of democratic systems are based on elections and on political representation, to which a better alternative is yet to be invented.

---

17 *Cf.* D. Mineur, *Archéologie de la représentation…*, p. 228 *et seq.*

18 *Cf.* H. Roussillon, *Éloge de la «démocratie réactive»…*, p. 476 *et seq.*

Bibliography

Ackerman B., *The New Separation of Powers*, "Harvard Law Review" 2000, no. 3.

Acquaviva J.-C., *Droit constitutionnel et institutions politique*, Paris 2005.

Adonis A., *Parliament Today*, Manchester–New York 1990.

Aguilar P., Sánchez-Cuenca I., *Performance or Representation? The Determinants of Voting in Complex Political Contexts*, [in:] *Controlling Governments. Voters, Institutions and Accountability*, J.M. Maravall, I. Sánchez-Cuenca (eds.), Cambridge 2008.

Ankersmit F.R., *Political Representation*, Stanford 2002.

Ardant P., *Institutions politiques & droit constitutionnel*, Paris 2004.

Arter D., *Parliaments*, [in:] *Understanding Democratic Politics. An Introduction*, R. Axtmann (ed.), London 2003.

Avril P., *Les origines de la représentation parlementaire*, 'Commentaire' 1985, no. 30.

Avril P., *Note sur les origines de la représentation*, [in:] *La représentation*, F. d'Arcy (ed.), Paris 1985.

Avril P., Gicquel J., *Droit parlementaire*, Paris 2004.

Barthélemy J., Duez P., *Traité de droit constitutionnel*, Paris 2004.

Beetham D., *Do Parliaments have a Future?*, [in:] S. Alonso, J. Keane, W. Merkel, M. Fotou, *The Future of Representative Democracy*, Cambridge 2010.

Best H., *Cleavage Representation in European Parliamentary History*, [in:] *Democratic Representation in Europe. Diversity, Change and Convergence*, M. Cotta, H. Best (eds.), Oxford 2007.

Birch A.H., *Concepts and Theories of Modern Democracy*, New York 2007.

Blachèr P., *Droit constititionnel*, Paris 2009.

Bluche F., *Manuel d'histoire politique de la France contemporaine*, Paris 2008.

Borella F., *Élements de droit constitutionnel*, Paris 2008.

Borella F., *Les partis politiques dans la France d'aujourd'hui*, Paris 1973.

Borowiak C.T., *Accountability and Democracy. The Pitfalls and Promise of Popular Control*, Oxford 2011.

Boulad-Ayoub J., Vernes P.-M., *Aux fondements théoriques de la représentation politique*, Paris 2007.

Bouthoul G., *Sociologie de la politique*, Paris 1977.

Brennan G., Hamlin A., *On Political Representation*, „British Journal of Political Science“ 1999, vol. XXIX.

Burdeau G., *L'evolution des techniques d'expression de l'opinion publique dans la démocratie*, [in:] *L'Opinion publique*, Paris 1957.

Burdeau G., *Manuel de droit constitutionnel*, Paris 1952.

Burke E., *Parliament as Representative of National Interest 1774*, [in:] *Democracy in Britain. A Reader*, J. Lively, A. Lively (eds.), Oxford–Cambridge 1994.

Camy O., *Droit constitutionnel critique*, Paris 2007.

Chagnollaud D., *Droit constitutionnel contemporain. Théorie générale. Les grands régimes étrangers*, Paris 2005.

Chandhoke N., *What is Relationship Between Participation and Representation?*, [in:] *Rethinking Popular Representation*, O. Törnquist, N. Webster, K. Stokke (eds.), New York 2010.

Charlot M., *Le povoir politique en Grande-Bretagne*, Paris 1998.

Conniff J., *Burke, Bristol and the Concept of Representation*, "The Western Political Quarterly" 1977, no. 3.

Clavreul C., *Sieyès et la genèse de la représentation moderne*, 'Droits'1987, no. 6.

Dahl R., *Polyarchy. Participation and Opposition*, New Haven 1971.

Debard T., *Dictionnaire de droit constitutionnel*, Paris 2002.

Déotte J.-L., *Représentation et politique*, [in:] *Représentation et politique*, J.-F. Robic (ed.), Paris 2010.

Déloye Y., *Mandat impératif*, [in:] *Dictionnaire du vote*, P. Perrineau, D. Reynié (eds.), Paris 2001.

Denquin J.-M., *Introduction à la science politique*, Paris 2001.

Dicey A.V., *Introduction to the Study of the Law of the Constitution*, London 2012.

Dogan M., *L'origine sociale du personnel parlementaire français élu en 1951*, [in:] *Partis politiques et classe sociales en France*, M. Duverger (ed.), Paris 1955.

Dovi S., *The Good Representative*, London 2007.

Duverger M., *Institutions politiques et droit constitutionnel*, Paris 1966.

Duverger M., *Les partis politiques*, Paris 1967.

Duverger M. , *Méthodes de la science politique*, Paris 1959.

Eckrsley R., *Representing Nature*, [in:] *The Future of Representative Democracy*, S. Alonso, J. Keane, W. Merkel (eds.), Cambridge 2011.

Elliott M., *Parliamentary Sovereignty and the New Constitutional Order. Legislative Freedom, Political Reality and Convention*, 'Legal Studies' 2002, no. 3.

Eulau H., *Changing Views of Representation*, [in:] *Contemporary Political Science: Towards Empirical Theory*, I. de Sola Pool (ed.), New York 1967.

Fairlie J.A., *The Nature of Political Representation*, 'The American Political Science Review' 1940, vol. 34.

Fournier P., *Institutions et représentations du politique:totu Espagne, France, Italie, XVIIe–XXe siècles*, Paris 2006.

Garsten B., *Representative Government and Popular Sovereignty*, [in:] *Political Representation*, I. Shapiro, S.C. Stokes, E.J. Wood, A.S. Kirshner (eds.), Cambridge 2009.

Gasparini E., Gojosso E., *Introduction historique au droit et histoire des institutions*, Paris 2011.

Gassner M., *Représentations parlementaires: Méthodes mathématiques proportionnelles de répartition des sièges*, Paris 2000.

Gastil J., *By Popular Demand: Revitalizing Representative Democracy Through Deliberative Elections*, London 2000.

Gaxie D., *La démocratie représentative*, Paris 2003.

Gazzaniga J.L., *Mandat et représentation dans l'ancien droit*, "Droits" 1987, No. 5.

Gicquel J., Gicquel J.-E., *Droit constitutionnel et institutions politiques*, Paris 2007.

Goguel F., *Quelques remarques sur le problème des institutions politique de la France*, „Revue Française de Science Politique" 1964 no. 2.

Goldsworthy J., *The Sovereignty of Parliament. History and Philosophy*, Oxford 2001.

Grzybowski K., *Teoria reprezentacji w Polsce epoki Odrodzenia*, Warszawa 1959.

Hall M.P., *Facing the Future: A New Theory of Political Representation*, Whitefish 2007.

Hamon F., Troper M., *Droit constitutionnel*, Paris 2011.

Haguenau-Moizard C., *Les systèmes politiques européens*, Paris 2009.

Haouet A., *Le concept de souveraineté en droit constitutionnel français*, Paris 2003.

Hayward C.R., *Making Interest: On Representation and Democratic Legitimacy*, [in:] *Political Representation*, I. Shapiro, S.C. Stokes, E.J. Wood, A.S. Kirshner (eds.), Cambridge 2009.

Held D., *Models of Democracy*, Stanford 2006.

Heywood A., *Key Concepts in Politics*, New York 2000.

Heywood A., *Politics*, Houndmills-New York 2013.

Hogga M., *Souveraineté; concept et conflit en Occident. La quête infinie de la liberté*, Paris 2007.

Jaume L., *La représentation: une fiction malmenée*, 'Pouvoirs'2007, no. 120

Jennings I., *The British Constitution*, Cambridge 1966.

Kam Ch.J., *Party Discipline and Parliamentary Politics*, Cambridge 2009.

Kishlansky M., *Parliamentary Selection: Social and Political Choice in Early Modern England*, Cambridge 1986

Krynen J., *La représentation politique dans l'ancienne France*, "Droits" 1987, no. 5.

Lascombe M., *Le droit constitutionnel de la Ve République*, Paris 2010.

Laundy P., *Les parlements dans le monde contemporain*, Lausanne 1989.

Leca J., *Représentation*, [in:] *Dictionnaire constitutionnel*, red. O. Duhamel, Y. Mény, Paris 1992.

Lee H.-Y., *Political Representation in the later Middle Ages*, New York 2008.

Leroy P., *Les régimes politiques du monde contemporain. Introduction générale*, Grenoble 2001, vol. I.

Lijphart A., *Degrees of Proportionality of Proportional Representation Formulas*, [in:] *Electoral Laws and their Political Consequences*, B. Grofman, A. Lijphart (eds.), New York 2003.

Lijphart A., *Democracies. Patterns of Majoritarian and Consensus Government in Twenty-One Countries*, New Haven–London 1984.

Lijphart A., *Democracy in Plural Societies. A Comparative Exploration*, New Haven and London 1977.

Lijphart A., Crepaz M.M.L., *Corporatism and Consensus Democracy in Eighteen Countries: Conceptual and Empiricial Linkages*, 'British Journal of Political Science' 1991, vol. 21, no. 2.

Loenen N., *Citizenship and Democracy. A Case for Proportional Representation*, Toronto 1997.

Nardulli P.F., *Popular Efficacy in the Democratic Era. An Reexamination of Electoral Accountability in the United States*, Princeton 2005.

Nguyen-Duy I., *Souverainete du Parlement Britannique*, Paris 2011.

Magdwick P., *A New Introduction to British Politics*, London 1984.

Mair P., *Political Parties, Popular Legitimacy and Public Privilege*, [in:] *The Crisis of Representation in Europe*, J. Hayward (ed.), New York 2005.

Manin B., *On Legitimacy and Political Deliberation*, "Political Theory" 1987, no. 15.

Manin B., *The Principles of Representative Government*, Cambridge 1997.

Manin B., Przeworski A., Stokes S.C., *Elections and Representation*, [in:] *Democracy, Accountability and Representation*, B. Manin, A. Przeworski, S.C. Stokes (eds.), Cambridge 1999.

Mansbridge J., *Rethinking Representation*, "American Political Science Review" 2003, vol. 93.

Marxer W., Pállinger Z.T., *Stabilizing or Destabilizing? Direct-democratic Instruments in Different Political Systems*, [in:] *Referendums and Representative Democracy. Responsiveness, Accountability and Deliberation*, M. Satälä, T. Schiller (eds.), New York 2009.

Maulin E., *La théorie de l'État de Carré de Malberg*, Paris 2003.

Mény Y., Surel Y., *Politique comparée. Les démocraties*, Paris 2009.

Miller W.E., Stoke D.E., *Constituency Influence in Congress*, [in:] *Legislatures and Legislators*, P. Norton (ed.), Sydney 1998.

Mineur D., *Archéologie de la représentation politique*, Paris 2010.

Mulgan R., *Holding Power to Account: Accountability in Modern Democracies*, London 2003.

Odugbemi S., Lee T., *Taking Direct Accountability Seriously*, [in:] *Accountability through Public Opinion. From Inertia to Public Action*, S. Odugbemi, T. Lee (eds.), Washington 2010.

Oliver D., *The Parties and Parliament. Representative or Intra-party Democracy?*, [in:] *The Changing Constitution*, J. Jowell (ed.), D. Oliver, Oxford 1989.

Owen B., *Le système électoral et son effet sur la représentation parlementaire des partis*, Paris 2002.

Parini P., *Régimes politiques contemporains*, Paris 1991.

Parrish J.M., *Paradoxes of Political Ethics. From Dirty to the Invisible Hand*, Cambridge 2008.

Pasquin P., *Emmanuel Sieyes, Benjamin Constant et le «gouvernment des modernes». Contribution à l'histoire du concept de représentation politique*, „Revue Française de Science Politique" 1987, no. 2.

Pateman C., *Participation and Democratic Theory*, Cambridge 2000.

Pauvert B., *Élections et modes de scrutin*, Paris 2006.

Pettit P., *The Common Mind. An Essay on Psychology, Society and Politics*, Oxford 1996.

Pettit P., *Varieties of Public Representation*, [in:] *Political Representation*, I. Shapiro, S.C. Stokes, E.J. Wood, A.S. Kirshner (eds.), Cambridge 2009.

Piattoni S., *Clientelism, Interests and Democratic Representation*, [in:] *Clientelism, Interests and Democratic Representation. The European Experiences in Historical and Comparative Perspective*, S. Piattoni (ed.), Cambridge 2001.

Pierré-Caps S., *Le constitutionnalisme et la nation*, [in:] *Le nouveau constitutionnalisme. Mélanges en l'honneur de Gérard Conac*, Paris 2001.

Pitkin H., *Representation*, [in:] *Political Innovation and Conceptual Change*, T. Ball, J. Farr, R.L. Hanson (eds.), Cambridge 1989.

Pitkin H., *The Concept of Representation*, Berkley 1967.

Prélot M., *Institutions politiques et droit constitutionnel*, Paris 1957.

Pym B., *The Making of a Successful Pressure Group*, "The British Journal of Sociology" 1973, no. 4.

Radice L., Vallance E., Willis V., *Member of Parliament. The Job of a Backbencher*, London 1990.

Reid J.P., *The Concept of Representation in the Age of the American Revolution*, London 1989.

Rehfeld A., *The Concept of Constituency. Political Representation, Democratic Legitimacy and Institutional Design*, Cambridge 2005.

Robbe F., *Démocratie représentative et participation*, [in:] *La démocratie participative*, (ed.) F. Robbe, Paris 2007.

Rœsz G., *De la représentation au politique*, [in:] *Représentaion et politique*, J.-F. Robic (ed.), Paris 2010.

Rosanvallon P., *La contre-démocratie. La politique à l'âgne de la défiance*, Paris 2006.

Rosanvallon P., *La Légitimité démocratique: Impartialité, réflexivité, proximité*, Paris 2010.

Rosanvallon P., *Le Peuple introuvable: Histoire de la représentation démocratique en France*, Paris 2002.

Roussillon H., *Éloge de la «démocratie réactive»*, [in:] *Constitutions et pouvoirs. Mélanges en l'honneur de Jean Gicquel*, Paris 2008.

Roussillon H., *Le citoyen et le suffrage: le mythe de la démocratie directe. De la démocratie participative à la démocratie réactive*, Toulouse 2006.

Rouvillois F., *L'avenir du référendum*, Paris 2006.

Rouvillois F., *Droit constitutionnel. Fondements et pratiques*, Paris 2005.

Rozenberg O., Blomgren M., *Bringing Parliamentary Roles back in*, [in:] *Parliamentary Roles in Modern Legislatures*, M. Blomgren, O. Rozenberg (eds.), New York 2012.

Runciman D., *The Paradox of Political Representation*, „Journal of Political Philosophy" 2007, no. 1.

Runciman D., Brito Vieira M., *Representation*, Cambridge 2008.

Rush M., *The Role of the Members of Parliament since 1868. From Gentleman to Players*, Oxford 2001.

Ryden D., *Representation in Crisis. The Constitution, Interest Groups and Political Parties*, New York 1996.

Sadoun M., *Représentation*, [in:] *Dictionnaire du vote*, P. Perrineau, D. Reynié (eds.), Paris 2001.

Samons L.J. , *What's Wrong with Democracy? From Athenian Practice to American Worship*, London 2004.

Shapiro I., *John Locke's Democratic Theory*, [in:] *John Locke: Two Treatises of Government and A Letter Concerning Toleration*, I. Shapiro (ed.), New York 2003.

Siaroff A., *Comparing Political Regimes. A Thematic Introduction to Comparative Politics*, Toronto 2009.

Sobolewski M., *Reprezentacja w ustroju współczesnych demokracji burżuazyjnych*, Kraków 1962.

Soroka S.N., Wlezien Ch., *Degrees of Democracy. Politics, Public Opinion and Policy*, Oxford 2010.

Stimson J., Mackuen M., Erikson R., *Dynamic Representation*, „American Political Science Review“ 1995, no. 3.

Stoker L., *Interest and Ethics in Politics*, "American Political Science Review" 1992, vol. 86.

Stokke K., Selboe E., *Symbolic Representation as Political Practice*, [in:] *Rethinking Popular Representation*, O. Törnquist, N. Webster, K. Stokke (eds.), New York 2010.

Strøm K., *Parliamentary Democracy and Delegation*, [in:] *Delegation and Accountability in Parliamentary Democracies*, K. Strøm, W.C. Müller, T. Bergman (eds.), Oxford 2003.

Strøm K., Müller W.C., Bergman T., Nyblade B., *Dimensions of Citizens Control*, [in:] *Delegation and Accountability in Parliamentary Democracies*, K. Strøm, W.C. Müller, T. Bergman (eds.), Oxford 2003.

Törnquist O., *Introduction: The Problem is Representation! Towards an Analytical Framework*, [in:] *Rethinking Popular Representation*, O. Törnquist, N. Webster, K. Stokke (eds.), New York 2010.

Tsebelis G., *Veto Players and Law Production*, [in:] *Patterns of Parliamentary Behavior. Passage of Legislation across western Europe*, H. Döring, M. Hallerberg (eds.), London 2004.

Tsebelis G., *Veto Players. How Political Institutions Work*, Princeton 2002.

Türk P., *Théorie générale du droit constitutionnel*, Paris 2010.

Turpin D., *Démocratie représentative et démocratie participative*, [in:] *Constitutions et pouvoirs. Mélanges en l'honneur de Jean Gicguel*, Paris 2008.

Uhr J., *Democracy and the Ethics of Representation*, [in:] *Ethics and Political Practice. Perspectives on Legislative Ethics*, N. Preston, Ch. Sampford, A.A. Bois (eds.), New York–London 2003.

Urbinati N., *Representative Democracy and its Critics*, [in:] *The Future of Representative Democracy*, S. Alonso, J. Keane, W. Merkel (eds.), Cambridge 2011.

Urbinati N., *Representative Democracy. Principles and Genealogy*, Chicago 2008.

van der Hulst M., *The Parliamentary Mandate. A Global Comparative Study*, Geneva 2000.

Vedel G., *Manuel élémentaire de droit constitutionnel*, Paris 2002.

Vermeule A., *Mechanism of Democracy*, Oxford 2007.

Verpeaux M., *Manuel de droit constitutionnel*, Paris 2010.

Waśkiewicz A., *Paradoksy idei reprezentacji politycznej*, Warszawa 2012.

Wessels B., *Performance and Deficits of Present-day Representation*, [in:] *The Future of Representative Democracy*, S. Alonso, J. Keane, W. Merkel (eds.), Cambridge 2011.

Woodruff P., *First Democracy. The Challenge of an Ancient Idea*, Oxford 2005.

Wright A., *British Politics: A Very Short Introduction*, Oxford 2003.

Young I.M., *Deferring Group Representation*, [in:] *Ethnicity and Groups Rights*, I. Shapiro, W. Kymlicka (eds.), New York 1997.

Young I.M., *Inclusion and Democracy*, Oxford 2002.

Young I.M., *Justice and the Politics of Difference*, Princeton 1990.

Zaidman P.-H., *Le mandat impératif. De la Révolution française à la Commune de Paris*, Paris 2008.

Zakaras A., *John Stuart Mill: Individuality and Participatory Democracy*, [in:] *J.S. Mill's Political Thought. A Bicentennial Reassessment*, N. Urbinati, A. Zakaras (eds.), Oxford 2007.

Zarka J.-C., *Introduction au droit constitutionnel*, Paris 2006.

Studies in Politics, Security and Society

Edited by Stanisław Sulowski

Vol. 1 Robert Wiszniowski (ed.): Challenges to Representative Democracy. A European Perspective. 2015.

Vol. 2 Jarosław Szymanek: Theory of Political Representation. 2015.

www.peterlang.com

For the avoidance of doubt, input of the whole or any part of this publication into any generative artificial intelligence model, chatbot, program, software or technology is expressly prohibited without the prior written consent of the publisher.